Achieving

QTS

Teaching
Early Years
Foundation
Stage

Achieving QTS

Teaching Early Years Foundation Stage

Editors

Jo Basford and Elaine Hodson

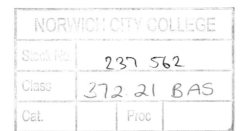

LearningMatters

First published in 2008 by Learning Matters Ltd.

British Library Cataloguing in Publication Data
A CIP record for this book is available from the British Library.

ISBN: 978 1 84445 175 3

The rights of Wendy Baker, Jo Basford, Rosemary Boys, Lynne Clarke, Teresa Curtis, Elaine Hodson, Val Melnyczuk, Tony Poulter, Elaine Spink and Wendy Whittaker to be identified as the Authors of this Work have been asserted by them in accordance with the Copyright, Designs and Patents Act 1988.

Cover design by Topics.
Text design by Code 5 Design Associates Ltd
Project management by Deer Park Productions, Tavistock
Typeset by PDQ Typesetting Ltd, Newcastle under Lyme
Printed and bound in Great Britain by Cromwell Press Ltd, Trowbridge, Wiltshire

Learning Matters Ltd
33 Southernhay East
Exeter EX1 1NX
Tel: 01392 215560
info@learningmatters.co.uk
www.learningmatters.co.uk

Contents

The Authors

Wendy Baker
Wendy Baker is currently a Senior Lecturer in Mathematics Education at Manchester Metropolitan University teaching on both undergraduate and postgraduate courses. She is enthusiastic about and dedicated to teaching in the Early Years.

Jo Basford
Jo Basford is a Senior Lecturer in Early Years and Childhood Studies at Manchester Metropolitan University. Her professional career has been within the Early Years sector where she has worked as a nursery teacher and for a local authority. Jo is a High/Scope Endorsed Trainer.

Rosemary Boys
Rosemary Boys is a Senior Lecturer in the Institute of Education at Manchester Metropolitan University where she teaches English, special educational needs and teaching studies. Rosemary qualified and taught for many years in Australia but has also gained extensive experience in England, working as a primary teacher and advisory teacher for English. She has been involved in consultancy work for several major publishers.

Lynne Clarke
Lynne Clarke is a Senior Lecturer in the Early Years and Childhood Studies Team at the Institute of Education at Manchester Metropolitan University and is Programme Leader for the full and long pathways of the Early Years Professional Status. Lynne has had a broad range of experiences in a range of Early Years settings. She has extensive experience of further education teaching on CACHE and PLA courses. She has worked as an assessor and verifier for the NVQ awards in Early Years. She has also worked for Cheshire Sure Start as an Early Years Consultant, supporting private, voluntary and independent Early Years settings in the development of the Foundation Stage curriculum.

Teresa Curtis
Teresa Curtis is Senior Lecturer in Childhood Studies at Manchester Metropolitan University. She was formerly a health visitor, midwife and general nurse and has a particular interest in the health and well-being of children and families.

Elaine Hodson
Elaine Hodson is a Senior Lecturer at Manchester Metropolitan University where she works on Employment-Based Routes into teaching. She was formerly head teacher of a nursery school and then of a primary school.

Val Melnyczuk
Val Melnyczuk is a qualified Early Years teacher and has worked in both the maintained and non-maintained sectors. Having studied for her first degree and then her masters with the Open University, she is now employed part-time as an Associate Lecturer and Early Years Professional assessor for the Open University. Val is a pedagogue with the Cheshire Children and Families Early Years Foundation Stage team. She is also a freelance trainer.

Tony Poulter

Tony Poulter is Senior Lecturer in Primary ICT at the Institute of Education at the Manchester Metropolitan University. He worked for 20 years as a primary school teacher, was an advisory teacher for ICT in Staffordshire and has been employed as a consultant for Becta.

Elaine Spink

Elaine is a Senior Lecturer in Primary Education for Manchester Metropolitan University. Elaine was a primary teacher and teacher adviser for science before joining the university. She has worked in Indonesia and South Africa as a consultant for primary education and school business management, and has published in the fields of science education and adult learning. She writes and delivers courses for the Science Learning Centre in the North West.

Wendy Whittaker

Wendy Whittaker is a Senior Lecturer in Early Years at Manchester Metropolitan University. Prior to that she was a children's centre manager in Crewe and a Sure Start programme manager. She completed her MA, with distinction, in integrated provision for children and families at Leicester University, taught at Pen Green Research and Development Centre in 2007. With four children of her own, her interests lie in how young children learn, multidisciplinary issues in working with families and children, and 'quality' provision in Early Years.

Introduction

From September 2008, the Early Years Foundation Stage (EYFS) is recognised as a distinct and unique age phase, supported by its own statutory framework. It is as a result of consultation (and at the time of writing, contentious debate) with key stakeholders in the field concerning the determinants of effective, high-quality Early Years practice. Interestingly the term 'curriculum' is no longer evident in the framework and there is now a definite commitment to single, play-based framework for early learning and care. Whether those critics, who felt the guidance was introducing the formal elements of education to very young children too soon, will be appeased, remains to be seen. Previously, the Foundation Stage had been the phase of learning concerned with three to five year old children, and trainee teachers had been required to demonstrate knowledge and understanding of the curriculum guidance which was pertinent to this age phase. However, EYFS takes account of the care, learning and developmental needs of *all* children from birth to the end of the Reception Year. As an Early Years teacher, this has significant implications for the knowledge, skills and understanding you will be required to demonstrate to teach in the Early Years Foundation Stage. Although you may find yourself working mainly with the older children within this phase, those between 30 and 60 months, it is vital that you understand the way that young children learn and develop from birth and the fact that they develop at different rates, and in different ways. Young children do not fit neatly into 'developmental boxes!

The Early Years Foundation Stage is supported by a series of key principles which are underpinned by research into children's care, learning and developmental needs. The principles are split into four key themes, which each have four corresponding commitments.

A Unique Child – every child is a competent learner from birth who can be resilient, capable, confident and self-assured.

Positive Relationships – children learn to be strong and independent from a base of loving and secure relationships with parents and/or a key person.

Enabling Environment – the environment plays a key role in supporting and extending children's development and learning.

Learning and development – children develop and learn in different ways and at different rates and all areas of Learning and development are equally important and interconnected.

(DfES, 2007, Practice Guidance for the Early Years Foundation Stage)

Chapter 1 of this book outlines the historical context and development of Early Years practice and provides an overview of the range of settings which represent the Early Years Foundation Stage. It then explores the commitments concerned with each of the themes in further depth. This chapter is mainly concerned with standards Q1, Q3, Q14 and Q15.

By the end of the Early Years Foundation Stage, most children will be expected to reach a number of Early Learning Goals which are linked to six areas of learning and development.

- Personal, Social and Emotional Development
- Communicating, Language and Literacy
- Problem Solving, Reasoning and Numeracy
- Knowledge and Understanding of the World
- Physical Development
- Creative Development

By developing your knowledge and understanding of how the principles are translated into practice – you will be in a better position to ensure that all children reach their potential, and achieve their Early Learning Goals. The aim of this book is to support and guide you through your own professional journey to becoming a successful Early Years teacher.

In Chapter 2 we recognise the central importance of each child's personal, social and emotional development, and the significant impact this has on a child's care, learning and developmental needs. (Q18 and Q19). This includes the importance of acknowledging and celebrating each child's unique background.

The next five chapters focus specifically on the other areas of learning and development, and address: Communication, Language and Literacy; Problem Solving, Reasoning and Numeracy; Knowledge and Understanding of the World; Physical Development and Creative Development. These chapters relate specifically to Standards Q14, Q15, Q16 and Q17. The underlying principles, themes and commitments pertinent to each of the areas of learning and development are exemplified in each chapter.

We have dedicated Chapter 8 entirely to ICT. Some readers may feel this is contentious, and there are indeed opposing views regarding the appropriateness of using ICT with very young children. We live in a media and technologically driven society. Information and communications technologies are explicit in the everyday lives of our children. They provide a context and motivation for learning for many children, and this is our rationale for committing a whole chapter to this area.

In Chapter 9 we lead you through the practicalities of documenting children's learning through a consideration of observation, planning and assessment strategies which are a key aspect of your role in tracking children's learning journeys. (Q11, Q12, Q13)

The final two chapters of this book are concerned with partnerships and relationships. Chapter 10 explores the fundamental importance of establishing authentic relationships with a child's parent/carer and family. Chapter 11 looks beyond the relationships you build within your typical classroom, and looks at the issues, challenges and ultimately benefits of working in a wider context with other professionals to ensure every child achieves the five outcomes as outlined in Every Child Matters.

We hope that the structure of this book will help you to make connections between the theory of child development, effective pedagogy, and the reality of working in an Early Years context. A number of tasks and classroom stories have been included in each chapter to help you make these connections. We have also provided you with further reading and research which will help you learn more about this important phase of a child's learning and development.

Working with young children requires a high degree of passion, enthusiasm and a genuine interest in what young children are about. You may well find yourself at times working in an environment where standards and target setting compete with a principled belief that children are entitled to a play-based framework where active engagement lies at the heart of the way children learn, develop and reach their full potential. We hope that this book will be just the start of your journey.

Jo Basford
Elaine Hodson

Manchester Metropolitan University

June 2008

1
The Early Years Foundation Stage: principles into practice
Jo Basford

Chapter objectives

By the end of this chapter you should have:

- **a working knowledge of the structure and content of the Early Years Foundation Stage;**
- **an understanding of the underlying principles of the Early Years Foundation Stage;**
- **an understanding of the aspects and commitments of the framework and how they are integral to effective pedagogy in supporting children to achieve the Early Learning Goals.**

This chapter addresses the following Professional Standards for QTS:

Q3, Q18

Introduction

The establishment of the Foundation Stage by the DfEE (now the Department for Children, Schools and Families [DCSF]) in 1999 was a major landmark in the education of young children. For the first time, the education of children between the ages of three and five years of age was recognised as a distinct and very important stage of education. The general aim of the Foundation Stage was to make a positive contribution to children's early development and learning, by providing children with activities and experiences which would help them make progress and develop in all areas of learning.

As we move towards the end of the first decade in the twenty-first century, the government has continued to demonstrate its commitment to our youngest children through the expansion of policy and initiatives. In 2002, the government published the *Birth to Three Matters* framework – guidance for all practitioners responsible for the care and education of children from birth to three. In 2003, *Every Child Matters* was published. The five outcomes of *Every Child Matters* became law through the Children Act 2004, and promoted the idea that all children should have the opportunity to reach their full potential. For the first time in English history, there is an expectation that a set of commitments, the five outcomes, underpin the work of all professionals working with children and families.

The five outcomes of *Every Child Matters* are:

- be healthy;
- stay safe;
- enjoy and achieve;
- make a positive contribution;
- achieve economic well-being.

In 2003, the *National Standards for Under Eights Day Care and Childminding* were also published. These set out the welfare requirements for all children attending sessional daycare, and formed the basis for inspection by Ofsted.

Over the last decade, the groundswell of interest in the field of Early Years has continued to influence policy and practice. The Independent Review of the Teaching of Early Reading (Rose Review 2006) builds on research concerning the effective teaching of early reading. Research into effective early years practice, such as the Effective Provision of Preschool Education Project (EPPE) and Study of Pedagogical Effectiveness in Early Learning (SPEEL) both provide ethnographic evidence of the factors which contribute to quality teaching and learning experiences for children. Additionally, the growing interest in approaches to Early Years pedagogy beyond the British Isles, such as New Zealand's Early Years framework 'Te Whariki' and the Reggio Emilia approach in northern Italy, have played a key role in forming a new framework which takes account of the care, learning and development needs of children from birth to five years of age – the Early Years Foundation Stage (EYFS). The *Early Years Foundation Stage* (2007) builds on and has been developed from the *Curriculum Guidance for the Foundation Stage* (2000), *Birth to Three Matters* (2002) and the *National Standards for Under Eights Day Care and Childminding (2003)*. The general aim of the EYFS is to ensure a 'coherent and flexible approach to care and learning so that whatever setting parents choose, they can be confident that their child will receive a quality experience that supports their development and learning'.

The underlying principles of the EYFS will be explored later in this chapter. It is important, first, to have a good understanding of how the Early Years Foundation Stage is now defined. Although your training and practice opportunities will be mainly focused within the context of a school environment, working with children in the three to five age range, you will need to understand about children"s prior Early Years Foundation Stage experiences. This is especially important when you consider Standards Q5, Q18 and Q21 and the importance of understanding about the impact of children"s previous experiences on their learning when they enter your class.

The range of Early Years Foundation Stage settings

Today, a large number of children will have attended an early childhood setting, or been cared for by another adult, before they reach the statutory school age.

The type of setting or childcare a parent chooses can depend on a number of factors. Some families require some form of daycare provision if they are working or have other commitments. Other parents may choose to look for part-time or sessional provision in order to provide their child with the experience of being with other children, away from the home environment and as a way of 'getting them ready for school'. There is a wide variety of provision available for young children, each catering for the diverse needs of children and their parents. These include:

- playgroup;
- childminder;
- nanny;
- informal care by family members;
- day nursery;
- local authority maintained nursery;
- children's centre nursery.

The government provides nursery education grant funding for all children in the term after their third birthday. This entitles parents to 15 hours of childcare for 38 weeks of the year. If a child has not experienced any care outside the home, this is traditionally the time that a child begins to attend some form of Early Years setting. Most children will remain in their settings until they enter the Reception class. There is an expectation that, regardless of the nature of the provision, all children are entitled to high-quality Early Years provision. The standards for welfare and learning are outlined in the *Statutory Guidance* for the EYFS.

It is important, at this stage, to acknowledge the range of experiences children will have had before they come into your care. As an Early Years teacher, you must be very sensitive to the way in which those experiences may have differed. This can consequently affect the way in which each child may settle into your setting. Factors such as adult-to-child ratios, the organisation of the learning environment and the daily routine can all have a huge impact on a child's personal, social and emotional well-being. Further reference to this is made in Chapter 2.

CLASSROOM STORY

The following classroom story illustrates the range of settings one child encountered in the Early Years Foundation Stage. Try to identify the factors which may have contributed to the way in which he settled in each new provision.

Tom had attended playgroup group for two morning sessions per week from the age of two and a half. The playgroup was situated in the local village hall. There was usually a ratio of at least four children to one adult. These consisted of the employed playgroup staff and parents who helped out on a rota basis. During the session, the children were free to play with any of the toys which the adults had selected. The adults planned a specific practical activity each day. Groups of four children at a time were invited to join in with the activity, under the careful direction of the supervising adult.

At the age of three years and eight months, Tom was eligible for a place at the local authority Nursery, which was attached to the school he would later be attending. Tom was allocated five afternoon sessions. The Nursery was a purpose-built building, and had its own outside play area, which was shared with the Reception class. The staff consisted of a teacher in charge, and two fully qualified nursery practitioners, equating to a ratio of one adult to 12 children. The Nursery was organised using a specific daily routine. Time was allocated for separate adult-directed and child-initiated activities, where the children were engaged in a plan–do–review process in which they made decisions about what they wished to play with.

When Tom first joined the Nursery, staff were concerned that he seemed tired and somewhat tearful – especially near the end of the week. During the child-initiated activities, Tom also needed a lot of encouragement to select his own toys. Through sensitive intervention with his key worker, and regular opportunities to share information with his parents, Tom soon became an active member of the nursery class.

Tom joined the Reception class the following year. He remained happy and settled, and particularly enjoyed helping the new nursery children to find a bicycle to play on, during the outside play sessions. Tom's parents were delighted with the apparent ease of his transition from the nursery to the Reception class.

The principles for the Early Years Foundation Stage

The underlying principles of effective, high-quality practice have been debated, documented, amended and supplemented over the past 20 years by a number of authoritative people in the Early Years field (see Rumbold, 1990; Ball, 1994 and Bruce, 1997, for example). These principles look beyond the content of what children learn. They are concerned with the factors which contribute to a child's emotional, social, physical and of course cognitive development – in other words, children's 'holistic' development.

They are concerned with our beliefs and values about the way young children learn and the skills needed to be an effective teacher. These beliefs and values include a consideration of the uniqueness of each individual child; the central role of authentic relationships between adults and children; the importance of the environment; and the significance of the interactions which occur between the child and his environment.

PRACTICAL TASK PRACTICAL TASK **PRACTICAL TASK** PRACTICAL TASK **PRACTICAL TASK**

Look at the 'Principles for EYFS' (Figure 1.1).What examples of Early Years practice have you seen that illustrate any of these principles?

A unique child – every child is a competent learner from birth who can be resilient, capable, confident and self-assured.

Positive relationships – children learn to be strong and independent from a base of loving and secure relationships with parents and/or a key person.

Enabling environment – the environment plays a key role in supporting and extending children's development and learning.

Learning and development – children develop and learn in different ways and at different rates and all areas of learning and development are equally important and interconnected.

(DfES, 2007, *Practice Guidance for the Early Years Foundation Stage*)

Figure 1.1 Principles for EYFS

The principles which guide the work of all Early Years practitioners are grouped into four themes, and four interrelated commitments. Thinking about these principles in relation to your own beliefs and practice will help you develop your own philosophy of learning and teaching, or pedagogical beliefs. It is important that you begin to develop your own philosophy. This may change either subtly or dramatically as you gain more experience and develop your own understanding of teaching in the Foundation Stage. By the time you become a fully qualified teacher, your philosophy should be evident in everything you do.

By exploring these four themes in more depth, you will begin to see how they, and their associated commitments, support you in your work within the EYFS. It is important that you spend time familiarising yourself with all the documents contained in the EYFS framework. The principles-into-practice cards and the associated EYFS CD-ROM in particular will provide you with in-depth support, and outline further academic theory which will underpin your practice.

The remainder of this chapter will explore the four themes and commitments in more depth.

A unique child

Within this theme, your commitment will be concerned with appreciating that every child is unique and brings along his/her own unique experiences, interests, skills and knowledge. It is then your responsibility to provide for each child's well-being within a safe, secure and inclusive environment.

The four commitments are as follows.

1.1 Child development Babies and children develop in individual ways and at varying rates. Every area of development – physical, cognitive, linguistic, spiritual, social and emotional – is of equal importance.

1.2 Inclusive practice The diversity of individuals and of their communities is valued and respected. No child or family is discriminated against.

1.3 Keeping safe Young children are vulnerable. They develop resilience when their physical and psychological well-being is protected by adults.

1.4 Health and well-being Children's health is an integral part of their emotional, mental, social, and spiritual well-being.

Child Development

Exploring the commitments to this theme, you may find that they raise some important questions. Understanding that every area of development is equally important, and that children develop at different rates and in different ways, means that your practice needs to be developmentally appropriate. This is a term which is used frequently by Early Years practitioners – but what does it actually mean? It is useful to define development in terms of the way a child's brain, body, abilities and behaviours become more complex as s/he grows and matures (DfES, 2007).

The EYFS categorisation of children within six broad developmental stages is based on the notion that development usually follows a predictable pattern. The children you will be working with will normally fall within the final two stages, 30–50 months and 40–60 months +. However, when you are planning learning experiences for children you will need to refer to both earlier and later stages of learning to take into account the individual needs of all the children in your care. The EYFS guidance outlines a broad expectation of typical patterns of development. Therefore, before you begin to plan learning experiences for the children in your class, it is important that you understand their developmental needs. You may find it useful to consider a child's development in relation to four specific aspects, namely:

- physical and mental well-being;
- responses to experiences on offer;
- relationships with family members, practitioners and other children;
- communication skills.

A child who experiences difficulties in any of these aspects may not be best placed to meet their full learning potential, and may not necessarily be performing at the final two stages of development. For example, a child who regularly misses breakfast may well be feeling hungry by snack time. You could see dips in energy levels and concentration which then have an impact on how they may respond to the experiences planned for them. Likewise, if a child has experienced a change in family circumstances, then she may well seem preoccupied, unhappy and perhaps react more extremely to conflict situations. It is your responsibility to ensure individual children are supported appropriately and sensitively during difficult times. If you know each child well, and have an understanding of their 'personal story', then you will be in a much better place to intervene as early as possible in supporting their needs. It also is very important that you share your concerns with other staff with whom you work and with parents/carers,. In a busy classroom, it is easy to miss small, but significant things. Several sets of eyes and ears are always better than one.

Inclusive practice

The EYFS represents a child – and family – centred, egalitarian, anti-discriminatory and inclusive approach to meeting children's needs and interests that promotes their learning and development. Inclusion is important because it promotes a culture of equality of opportunity and high achievement for all children, by encouraging the development of more flexible attitudes, policies and every day practices. It also promotes community cohesion and integration through understanding of and respect for others.

(DfES, 2007)

It is a significant part of your role as an EYFS practitioner to act as an advocate for the rights of the child as set out above, by meeting their diverse needs, and ensuring that the best possible progress is made by each individual.

However, meeting the diverse needs of all children can sometimes pose challenges for teachers, for a variety of reasons. For example, you may feel you have very limited knowledge and understanding about Islam and don't know how to communicate with a parent who does not speak very much English. Similarly, you may not be aware of the strategies to employ in order to ensure a hearing impaired child is able to engage in role play. You may be aware that there is a very able child in your setting who has exceeded the Early Learning Goals, and you are not sure how to differentiate the activities you plan to meet his/her needs. These are just a few of the varied and sometimes complex situations you may encounter There will always be a number of outside agencies and specialist professionals who you will be able to contact for support (see Chapter 11). Your role is to think about the needs of all young children in your class, and reflect on the way you might begin to meet them.

REFLECTIVE TASK

Think about the most recent class you have worked with. Consider the following questions in relation to what happens on a daily basis in your classroom.

- When planning children's learning experiences, have I taken account of each child's rich and varied background?
- What range of teaching strategies can I use which are most suitable for children's learning needs?

- How can I ensure that all children will be motivated and involved in their learning, so that they can concentrate and learn effectively?
- How can I ensure that I am providing a safe and supportive learning environment, which is free from harassment, where all children are valued, and where all racial, religious, disability and gender stereotypes are challenged?
- How will I monitor each child's progress, identify any areas of concern and decide what action to take?

The following classroom story illustrates some of the areas of practice one particular teacher addressed in order to meet the individual needs of all the children in her class.

CLASSROOM STORY

Miss Cook was responsible for a class of 27 Reception-aged children. The children had previously attended a variety of pre-school settings. In order to help the children settle into the new class, a series of induction sessions had been arranged. These occurred each week, over the final half of the term before the children were admitted to school. The first session was a story time, which the children attended with their parents. Over the next six weeks, the sessions were gradually extended, culminating in the children staying in their new class all morning, and then going to the dining room for lunch. In addition to this, Miss Cook invited parents to an informal meeting to discuss their child's first year in school, and had visited the children in their own homes.

By the time the new term began, Miss Cook felt that she had already developed very positive relationships with both parents and her pupils. She felt that the information she had gathered during the home visits had provided her with valuable information regarding each child's individual experiences, interests and needs.

There were 15 boys and 12 girls in the class. One child had a hearing impairment, and was supported by a teacher of the deaf for ten hours per week. Miss Cook had contacted the Hearing Impaired Services to seek advice about the support she would need to give to the child. As a result of her discussion, and a visit to the nursery the child had previously attended, an individual education plan was devised. Miss Cook ensured the classroom was made acoustically sound by adding more soft furnishings. She discussed the structure of the day with the teacher of the deaf, to ensure that he visited her at the times in which she would benefit from his additional support. There were also twin boys in the class, whose home language was Polish. Their parents spoke English as an additional language. Miss Cook contacted the bilingual support team. They helped her devise an individual education plan for the boys, which was primarily concerned with providing them with opportunities to build on their experiences of their home language. A member of the team was also invited to join Miss Cook in all parent meetings to ensure the parents were fully informed of their children's progress. In addition to this, Miss Cook looked at the resources in her classroom, to ensure they positively reflected the diversity of languages and cultures of the children. This included purchasing a number of dual-language books.

Early assessments revealed that a large number of the children in the class had very poor speaking and listening skills. Miss Cook decided that her medium-term planning needed to be amended, so that there was a greater emphasis on developing these skills. More practical games and role-play activities were included in the structure of the day.

REFLECTIVE TASK

Now refer back to the questions in the previous reflective task to help you consider what strategies the teacher employed to support the individual needs of the children.

There will be some children who you teach, who have very specific individual learning requirements. Some children will have already been identified as having specific special educational needs and may already have an individual education plan in place. In other situations, the child's particular needs or disabilities may not have been identified until they join your class. You have a key role to play in working with parents (see Chapter 10) to identify a child's particular needs, and then to attempt to develop an effective intervention strategy. This will usually involve working with other agencies in devising an individual education plan (see Chapter 11) which includes specific targets, and an action plan which specifies the nature of support. The SEN Code of Practice (DfES, 2001) specifies the particular requirements for intervention in Early Years settings. This is discussed in greater detail in Chapter 11.

Many children in an Early Years setting will have a home language other than English. Some children will be multilingual from birth, as their families have communicated in more that one language. Some children will need to acquire English as an additional language. In order for this to be a relevant learning experience, there are a number of factors which need to be taken into consideration. As with any learning experience, it must take place in a context which is both relevant and meaningful. Children need opportunities to engage and interact with others. They also need time to merely listen and experience the new language, before they attempt to speak it. Other forms of communication are equally important, and contribute to the child's understanding. For example, gesture, sign, facial expression and visual support such as pictures and objects should all form part of the learning process.

The EYFS Practice Guidance states clearly that you should plan opportunities which will help children develop English, and provide support which will enable them to take part in other activities. Examples given include:

- building on children's experiences of language at home and in the wider community by providing a range of opportunities to use their home language(s), so that their developing use of English and other languages support one another;
- providing a range of opportunities for children to engage in speaking and listening activities in English with peers and adults;
- ensuring all children have opportunities to recognise and show respect for each child's home language;
- providing bilingual support, in particular to extend vocabulary and support children's developing understanding;
- using bilingual support to ensure accurate assessment of children's understanding and knowledge:
- as far as possible ensuring that bilingual support staff have an understanding of child development and are preferably Early Years practitioners;
- providing a variety of writing in the children's home languages as well as in English, including books, notices and labels;
- providing opportunities for children to hear home languages as well as English, for example through the use of audio and video materials.

It is always a good idea to contact the bilingual services team for guidance. In addition to providing you with support with teaching strategies, they can provide you with the necessary information and contacts to purchase relevant resources.

Keeping safe and Health and well-being

Childhood in England today reflects the priorities and culture of twenty-first century, Western civilisation. The influence of the media, technology and the ever-changing construct of families and community all mean that children are now exposed to a range of potentially very different experiences. Some children continue to experience extreme poverty. There are growing concerns about the rise in cases of obesity and the sedentary lifestyle children seem to be experiencing. Finally there is the ever-present, risk-averse culture.

All of these factors undoubtedly have an impact on children's health, safety and well-being.

So what is your role in ensuring that children stay safe, and their health and well-being are supported? Of course there are the usual steps that institutions such as schools take to ensure that policies such as child protection and health and safety are in place. It is your responsibility to know and understand those policies. Keeping children safe is also about providing clear and consistent boundaries in relation to children's physical, social and emotional development. It is your role to challenge expectations, and support children in taking 'safe risks'. If children do not have experience of climbing and balancing, or using scissors, how will they ever develop any sense of emotional resilience? It is your role as teacher to ensure that the environment you provide is safe, but at the same time allows for children to explore and play in a way that challenges them physically, emotionally and cognitively. For example, in your outside area, do you provide a full range of wheeled toys that cater for all children, from three-wheeled pedal and push-along bikes to two-wheeled bikes with stabilisers removed? In your messy area, do children have free access to scissors, glue, sticking tape and paint to enable experimentation and problem-solving? There will be an opportunity to return to both the environment and the crucial role of the adult in supporting children to problem-solve and experiment later in the chapter.

Positive relationships

Within this theme your commitments are concerned with securing strong relationships with children, with parents and with other professionals, ensuring the best outcomes for all children. Positive relationships underpin the whole ethos of the EYFS. Relationships are built upon respect for each other. Chapter 10 looks particularly at parent partnerships, and Chapter 11 looks particularly at professional partnerships. Chapter 2 looks more specifically at personal, social and emotional development.

The four commitments are as follows.

2.1 Respecting each other Every interaction is based on caring professional relationships and respectful acknowledgement of the feelings of children and their families.

2.2 Parents as partners Parents are children's first and most enduring educators. When parents and practitioners work together in Early Years settings, the results have a positive impact on children's development and learning.

2.3 Supporting learning Warm, trusting relationships with knowledgeable adults support children's learning more effectively than any amount of resources.

2.4 Key person A key person has special responsibilities for working with a small number of children, giving them reassurance so they feel safe and cared for, and building relationships with their parents.

As you become familiar with the themes and commitments of the EYFS, it should become apparent to you that it is difficult to compartmentalise the adult role into any one section of this book. The final two themes of the EYFS discuss your role in creating an enabling environment, and the different ways you may support children's learning in a variety of contexts.

Considering standard Q1 requires you to be aware of the way you develop positive relationships with children and with families. How does you own behaviour in the classroom model the positive, authentic, relationships you aspire to achieve?

To what extent do you do the following?

● Model socially acceptable language and courtesies, such as 'please', 'thank you', 'excuse me'.
● Show a genuine interest and empathy in children's stories about home life, family events and personal difficulties.
● Model positive relationships while engaging in children's play, for example sharing resources, suggesting solutions to problems, acknowledging feelings during conflict.
● Share stories about your own life and experiences, such as sharing a story about your pet dog escaping, or asking children for ideas about what you should cook for tea that night.

By building and establishing authentic relationships with children and their families, you are in a much better position to understand each child in your care and help them deal with difficult situations. Elfer (1996) suggests that when young children feel confident, their energy for curiosity and exploration is at its greatest. When they are anxious, because of a new situation, or an experience which is beyond their developmental stage, they need to return to their 'secure base'. In the context of a classroom, that secure base is either the class teacher or another member of staff with whom they have formed a close attachment. If the adult does not respond sensitively to a child's emotional reaction then their energy for exploration and curiosity could be reduced or even disappear. Children need opportunities to express their emotions. Then it is only through experience and with the support of a caring adult that a young child can learn how they may be regulated.

Enabling environments

Within this theme your commitments are concerned with the contribution the environment makes to a child's learning and development. Here the term 'environment' looks beyond the traditional 'learning environment' provided for children, to also take account of the routines, systems and ways of working which support children through their own learning journey. Chapter 9 looks particularly at Commitment 3.1, and Chapter 11 will look at the wider context of working with other professionals (Commitment 3.4). Therefore, this section will explore more generic issues linked to enabling environments, rather than looking at each commitment in turn.

The four commitments are as follows.

3.1 **Observation, assessment and planning** Babies and young children are, firstly, individuals, each with a unique profile of abilities. Schedules and routines should flow with the child's needs. All planning should start with observing children. It is vital that you understand and consider current interests, prior experiences, as well as stage of development and learning.

3.2 **Supporting every child** The enabling environment supports every child's learning by including planned experiences and activities that are challenging but achievable.

3.3 **The learning environment** A rich and varied environment extends children's learning and development. It promotes confidence to explore and learn in secure, safe, yet challenging, indoor and outdoor spaces.

3.4 **The wider context** Working in partnership with other settings, other professionals and with individuals and groups in the community, supports children's development and their progress towards the outcomes of *Every Child Matters*: being healthy, staying safe, enjoying and achieving, making a positive contribution and economic well-being.

Transition

Transition involves a process of change, either from one setting to another, or from one experience to another. It is important that you take into account the impact of any form of change for a young child. Below is a list of questions adapted from the EYFS guidance which will help you consider effective practice in relation to supporting children through transition.

- To what extent do you provide routine and rhythm to the day to help children feel secure in knowing what and when things happen?
- How can you develop children's autonomy in learning by organising resources so that they are easily accessible, and children can manage them independently?
- To what extent do you involve children in their learning to give them a sense of ownership, predictability and belonging?
- How do you ensure that displays and resources reflect children's home communities and the wider world, so that they feel secure in knowing they belong and have confidence to meet new challenges.
- When children move from one class/setting to another, what will they find the same and what will they find different?
- How do you learn from parents about their child's needs, interests and sensitivities?

If you teach a Reception class, you will also need to consider how you and your colleagues manage the transition for children from Foundation Stage to Key Stage 1. Research by Sanders et al. (2005) highlights the issues that present challenges for children, staff and parents during the transition to Year 1. Children in your care could be potentially moving from a play-based approach to a more 'structured' Key Stage 1 curriculum. Certain children will cope less well with the transition. This includes children who are younger or less mature; those who are less able to cope with the demands of a more formal curriculum; and those who have special educational needs, or speak English as an additional language.

PRACTICAL TASK PRACTICAL TASK **PRACTICAL TASK** PRACTICAL TASK **PRACTICAL TASK**

Refer back to the classroom story of Miss Cook. How would you support the children in the class in their transition to Reception, and also at the end of the Foundation Stage to Year 1?

The daily routine

It is important that children have a feeling of predictability and consistency within their daily routine. Not only does this provide a sense of security for a child moving into a new class, but it provides them with a feeling of ownership and confidence if they know what is coming next.

Think about how you could involve children in gaining an understanding and ownership of the daily routine. A pictorial display of the routine is a useful way of visualising it for young children. Individual pictures can then be physically handled by the children, and used in an interactive way to predict and remember what is happening next. Snack and lunchtimes are a significant part of a child's day, so make sure that these are included alongside the other types of activities which happen in your class.

There are generally three types of activities which will occur within your daily routine. The EYFS states that you will need to provide a range of activities which allow children to have experiences across all areas of learning and development. Some of those experiences will be directly planned by you, others will be led by the child.

Adult-led/directed activities usually involve the adult working with a child or group of children, for the duration of the activity. The adult uses this time to encourage or develop a particular aspect of learning.

Adult-initiated activities may be a subsidiary activity which an adult initiates in the first instance, by providing a starting point such as a material, new resource or a skill. You may have a specific learning objective in mind, but when left to their own devices, children's own interests may lead to a different learning outcome. In order for these activities to provide valuable learning experiences, it is important that the activity is relatively open-ended, and provides opportunities for exploration and dialogue. Your role is to act as a facilitator and guide by sharing knowledge and expertise, as well as acknowledging children's own discoveries and achievements.

Child-initiated activities are activities where it is not possible to define a learning objective, or outcome. The EYFS defines child-initiated learning as when a child 'engages in a self-chosen pursuit'. Children are able to take responsibility for their own learning and pursuing their own interests by selecting the resources and activities independently. They can learn at their own pace, and in their own way. Debate regarding whether only self-chosen activities can be defined as 'play' remains a contentious issue. This will be explored in the final section of this chapter.

Providing an enabling learning environment

In order for children to develop a sense of independence, and to be able to pursue their own interests, you need to establish a physical learning environment which will enable children to do this. When organising your learning environment, it is important to consider the provision you have outdoors as well as indoors. Traditionally outdoor provision has been concerned with opportunities for physical development, such as riding wheeled toys and playing with balls. Yet all the learning experiences children have indoors can legitimately occur outdoors too. In fact the sense of space and fresh air is actually beneficial to many young learners who can often feel restricted by being indoors. Further reading of the work by Bilton et al. (2005) will provide you with a deeper insight into outdoor provision (see Chapter 4 for further discussion).

When you are planning the learning experiences for children, you will need to consider how you can enhance your learning environment to support children's learning and help them make connections. Role-play, for instance, will help children understand about features of everyday life which are beyond their own experiences. This means that you will need to ensure that the resources you provide for the children are relevant and are of a good quality.

For example, you may wish to set up a 'Health Clinic' in your classroom. An initial visit to a health clinic would give the children first-hand experience and provide a meaningful context. The knowledge they have gained can then be transferred and built upon, through their own role-play.

If you want children to be independent learners, they need to be curious and interested in what your learning environment has to offer them. You need to ensure therefore that all the resources in your classroom are attractively displayed, and organised in such a way that children can find, use and return them independently.

Hohmann and Weikart (1995) provide some useful guidance based on the High/Scope approach regarding how to plan an effective learning environment. Listed below is a check-list, which you may find useful.

Arranging the space
Divide the space into well-defined interest areas which support different types of play.

Choose names for interest areas that children understand.

Establish visual boundaries between the interest areas.

Choosing materials
Choose materials that reflect children's interests.

Provide resources/materials that are suitably open-ended so that they can be used by children in a variety of different ways.

Ensure the materials reflect the experiences and cultures of the children in your class.

Storing materials
Store materials so that children can reach them.

Use see-through plastic containers to store materials.

Make sure materials are consistently stored in the same place.

Label shelves and containers so that children can find, use and return materials.

Learning and development

The final set of commitments is concerned with how children learn, the relationship between play and learning, and the six areas of learning and development.

4.1 Play and exploration Children's play reflects their wide-ranging and varied interests and preoccupations. In their play, children learn at their highest level. Play with peers is important for children's development.

4.2 Active learning Children learn best through physical and mental challenges. Active learning involves other people, objects ideas and events that engage and involve children for sustained periods.

4.3 **Creativity and critical thinking** when children have opportunities to play with ideas in different situations and with a variety of resources, they discover connections and come to new and better understandings and ways of doing things. Adult support in this process enhances their ability to think critically and ask questions.

4.4 **Areas of learning and development** The Early Years Foundation Stage is made up of six areas of learning and development. All areas of learning and development are connected to one another and are equally important. All areas of learning and development are underpinned by the principles of the EYFS.

Play, active learning and critical thinking

Anyone who has observed play for any length of time will recognise that, for young children, play is a tool for learning and practitioners who acknowledge and appreciate this can, through provision, interaction and intervention in children's play ensure progression, differentiation and relevance in the curriculum.

(Moyles, 1994, p6)

There is no question regarding the value of play in relation to children's learning and development. Yet many teachers are presented with the problem of how to ensure that children are engaged in meaningful and valued play experiences – when the teacher is frequently engaged in other adult-directed activities. Research by Bennett et al. (1997) suggests that many teachers believe children are learning a great deal during play activities, but in reality, without the support of and intervention from an adult, the benefits of the play activity are only of a very low level. Your role in the classroom is fundamental in ensuring that the play experiences children have are both meaningful and beneficial to their holistic development. When children are playing, they become active learners. By physically inter-acting with their environment, children are making sense of the world around them.

As they come across objects, situations, people and ideas, they adjust and structure their knowledge by trying to make sense of their experiences. They actively build their own meanings by applying, revising, and reapplying what they know.

(Effective practice: active learning, p1)

Research from the Effective Provision of Pre-School Education Project (EPPE) (Sylva et al., 2004) has endorsed the central importance of play in young children's learning. The project concluded that there needs to be a balance of adult-directed activities and children's self-chosen play. Most importantly, learning is best promoted through shared, sustained thinking and conversation. When these rich interactions occur, children have the best opportunities to develop their 'creativity and critical thinking' (see Chapter 3). This means that adults and children together are solving a problem, extending understanding or imagination.

There are a number of different roles you may adopt in any play situation. Most importantly, the quality of the interactions you have with children is fundamental to supporting children's learning. You may act as a guide – where you are perhaps modelling how to use a new piece of equipment, so that a child is able to use it independently the next time. On the other hand, you may wish to use the opportunity to find out what a child already knows, and then help them build on that knowledge through further dialogue. You may do this by acting as a 'play partner' and the child takes the lead in the direction and purpose of the play.

When children are playing spontaneously, it is very tempting to join in, presuming that you know what the children are thinking about. Have you ever joined a play situation with a sweeping statement or question, to find that the children greet you with a look of exasperation at the irrelevance of your statement? You then quickly find yourself alone, as the children have gone to play with something else. The most important thing to do before joining in any play activity, is to observe silently what is happening. You need to give yourself time to understand the nature and focus of the play. Once you have established this, you can then enter the game at the children's level. It is important that you try to use the same language as them, at least in the beginning – until the children are comfortable with your presence. When the children are engaged in their own play, do not be tempted to steer them towards your own agenda. Children gain a great deal from spontaneous play.

There will be times when children prefer to play on their own. Some children need these opportunities to gain confidence, before joining others. It is important that you monitor solitary play. If a child continues to play on his or her own, there may be a specific reason for this. It is important that you try to find out what the reason is, then you should be able to sensitively support him or her.

One final thought about play. Children need to know that you value their play. When planning for play opportunities, think about organising them so that you are not always engaged in an adult-planned activity. In order to really know and understand what interests a child, and how they think and learn, you need to spend some time just watching and learning about them as individuals. This will also provide you with vital information which will help you plan their future learning experiences and assess each child's progress

The themes and commitments which underpin the Early Years Foundation Stage are fundamental to effective practice. By taking into account the philosophy of this age phase, you should feel confident that you are well equipped to support children in achieving the Early Learning Goals at the end of the Foundation Stage.

A SUMMARY OF **KEY POINTS**

> **Every child is unique. Children's personal experiences and the relationships they build influence a child's learning and development.**
> **The themes and commitments are the underlying principles of the Early Years Foundation Stage.**
> **The physical and emotional environment plays a key role in supporting a child's learning and development.**
> **Play provides an exciting and challenging way for children to learn. The role of the adult in supporting play is fundamental to a child's learning and development.**

MOVING *ON* > > > > > > MOVING *ON* > > > > > > MOVING *ON*

Ensure that you are familiar with all of the themes and commitments within the Early Years Foundation Stage. Begin to think about what the themes and commitments mean to you as an Early Years practitioner, and frame your thinking into your own personal philosophy.

REFERENCES REFERENCES **REFERENCES** REFERENCES REFERENCES REFERENCES

Ball, C. (1994) *Start Right: the importance of early learning*. London: Royal Society of Arts.

Bennet, N., Wood, E. and Rogers, S. (1997) *Teaching through play: teachers' thinking and classroom practice*. Buckingham: Open University Press.

Bilton, H., James, K., Marsh, J., Wilson, A. and Woonton, M. (2005) *Learning outdoors: improving the quality of young children's play outdoors*. London: David Fulton.

Bruce, T. (1997) *Early childhood education* (2nd edition). London: Hodder and Stoughton.

DES (1990) (The Rumbold Report) *Starting with Quality; The Report of the Committee of Enquiry into the Quality of Educational Experience offered to 3–4 year olds*. London: HMSO.

DfEE/QCA (2000) *Curriculum Guidance for the Foundation Stage*. London: Qualifications and Curriculum Authority.

DfES (2001) *Special Educational Needs Code of Practice*. London: DfES.

DfES (2002) *Birth to Three Matters*. London: DfES.

DfES (2003) *Every Child Matters*. London: DfES.

DfES (2004) *The Effective Provision of Pre-school Education Project: Findings from Pre-school to End of Key Stage 1. Final Report*. London: DfES/Surestart.

DfES (2007) *The Early Years Foundation Stage*. London: DfES.

Her Majesty's Government (2004) *The Children Act 2004*. London: HMSO.

Her Majesty's Government/DfES/Department for Work and Pensions/Department of Trade and Industry (2004) *Choice for parents, the best start for children: a ten year strategy for childcare*. London: HMSO.

Elfer, P. (1996) Building intimacy in relationships with young children in nurseries. *Early Years*, 2, 30–34.

Hohmann, M. and Weikart, D.P. (1995) *Educating young children*. Michigan: High/Scope Press.

Moyles, J. (ed.) (1994) *The excellence of play*. Buckingham: Open University Press.

Moyles, J., Adams, S. and Musgrove, A. (2002) *SPEEL: Study of pedagogical effectiveness in early learning*. London: DfES.

Sanders, D., White, G., Burge, B., Sharp, C., Eames, A., McEune, R. and Grayson, H. (2005) *A study of the transition from the Foundation Stage to Key Stage 1*. Slough: National Foundation for Educational Research.

Sylva, K., Melhuish, E.C., Sammons, P., Siraj-Blatchford, I. and Taggart, B. (2004) *The Final Report: Effective Pre-School Education*. London: DfES, Institute of Education, University of London.

FURTHER READING FURTHER READING **FURTHER READING** FURTHER READING

Bilton, H., James, K., Marsh, J., Wilson, A. and Woonton, M. (2005) *Learning outdoors: improving the quality of young children's play outdoors*. London: David Fulton.

Moyles, J. (ed.) (2007) *Early years foundations. Meeting the challenge.* Maidenhead: Open University Press.

2
Personal, social and emotional development
Jo Basford

Chapter objectives

By the end of this chapter you should have:

- **a working knowledge of the aspects related to personal, social and emotional development;**
- **an understanding of the centrality of young children's personal, social and emotional development in relation to their holistic development.**

This chapter addresses the following Professional Standards for QTS:
Q2, Q18

Introduction

This area of learning and development is central to young children's care, learning and development. The early years of a child's life are regularly referred to as being the most formative and their earliest experiences shape the rest of their lives. These early experiences can have a huge impact on not only their 'readiness' to learn, but also their success in learning in later life. Firstly, it is useful to consider the conditions for learning – namely the child's basic needs which need to be fulfilled before he or she is in a position to learn. Many academics refer to Maslow's (1943) hierarchy of needs, as a starting point for considering the needs of a child (see Figure 2.1). The Every Child Matters (ECM) agenda, with a commitment to ensuring that all children achieve the five outcomes, should mean that no child should be living in conditions which do not fulfil the basic needs of food, water and nourishment. Nevertheless, you will encounter children who are not provided with a balanced diet, do not receive the right amount of rest or stimulation, or who do not live in consistently loving and caring homes. Some reference to this is made in Chapter 1, in the 'unique child' section. It is important to consider a child's home situation, and demonstrate great sensitivity towards this. If a child's basic needs are not being met, then this manifests itself in many areas of their development, and in turn impacts on the likelihood of their meeting their potential.

Over recent years there has been an increasing interest in research related to brain development and the 'nature–nurture' debate, with a consideration of how this is linked to children's emotional and cognitive development. Some reference to these issues is included in Chapter 3. It can be argued that due to the complexity of the construction of the brain, as well as the still relatively limited scientific knowledge concerning gene research, any claims related to the influence on practice need to be considered with caution.

This is a very current and pertinent topic which is worth exploring in more detail. You may find it useful to consider the book by Helen Penn (2005), which considers a range of issues and controversies which concern the Early Years practitioner.

Figure 2.1 Maslow's hierarchy of needs

CLASSROOM STORY

Sonia is nearly five years old. She will join the Reception class in January. Sonia lives with her father. Her mother left the family home last year, taking with her Sonia's older brother.

The class teacher visited Sonia in her home in December, as part of the transition arrangements the school has established. On visiting the family home, the teacher noted that it was very cold and smelt damp. Sonia was wearing a thin summer dress and cardigan. Her father explained that she was recovering from a chest infection, and that she had recently been diagnosed as having asthma. Sonia sat on her father's knee for the duration of the visit, but was happy to answer questions the teacher asked about what she liked to play with, her favourite food and her friends. Sonia's father explained that he did not let her play with other children on the estate, as they had teased her in the past about their home circumstances. They spent a lot of time together at the local park, and drawing and writing at home. Sonia also likes visiting the library. Sonia stated that she was looking forward to starting school, and that she was particularly excited about dressing up in the home corner, and staying for school dinners. A next-door neighbour had given Sonia her daughter's old school uniform; she was very excited about that also. Her father was hoping to buy some new school shoes for her next week.

- Now that you have an insight into Sonia's background, what would you need to do to support Sonia's transition into school?
- How could you utilise her love of books and visits to the park to ensure she has positive learning experiences in school?
- What factors would you need to be particularly aware of that may cause her difficulty in settling in?
- How may these factors have an impact on her personal, social and emotional development (PSED)?

Having discussed the impact a child's home experiences may have on a child's development, it is important now to consider the impact of the experiences children have in Early Years settings.

Most people, when asked about their first teacher, have some lasting memory of the experiences they had in their first class. Think back to your experiences in your first Nursery or Reception class. Were they positive or negative? Can you identify what factors contributed to the type of experience you had? You may find it easier to categorise these factors into two broad areas – relationships and environment.

The nature of the relationships you established with the teacher in your class and your peers will undoubtedly have contributed to the type of experiences you remembered. The environmental factors such as the design and layout of the classroom, the materials and resources which were on offer and also the routines and types of activities you experienced may well also have had an impact on your happiness. The EYFS themes related to positive relationships and enabling environments are fundamental in supporting children's personal, social and emotional development. As the aspects related to PSED are explored, these themes will be considered in more depth.

There are six aspects of learning and development concerned with PSED. These are:

- dispositions and attitudes;
- self-confidence and self-esteem;
- making relationships;
- behaviour and self control;
- self care;
- sense of community.

The remainder of this chapter will consider each of the six aspects of PSED. It is particularly important that you have a sound understanding of child development within this area of learning. Expectations you have of a child's personal, social and emotional development must match where a child lies within the developmental continuum. Environmental and experiential factors play a substantial role is this area, and reference will be made to these factors from a theoretical and practical perspective throughout this chapter.

Dispositions and attitudes

The EYFS framework defines dispositions and attitudes being 'about how children become interested, excited and motivated about their learning'. There is a fundamental difference between a child's attitude and disposition to learning (Katz, 1995). A child's attitude towards learning could be defined as their belief or view about learning. Some children have a naturally positive attitude towards learning. Although they may not yet be able to articulate the fact that they understand that learning is an important aspect which contributes towards success in life, children will demonstrate this belief through showing a sense of enjoyment and a desire to learn.

It is useful to consider Glaxton and Carr's (2004) broad definition of a child's disposition to learning as being 'ready, willing and able' to tackle new experiences. You cannot 'teach' a child to develop positive attitudes and therefore dispositions to learning, but clearly a key role you have as a teacher is to provide stimulating and interesting experiences for the children which will both engage and motivate them. Yet it is not just what you plan for children to do, it is also how these experiences are presented to them. The emotional environment in which children exist on a daily basis can actually have a far greater impact on a child's disposition to learning. If children do not feel valued and understood as individuals, then they will not be in the best position to learn.

> *Katz suggests that it is reasonable to assume that if young children are regularly exposed to experiences that are intrinsically interesting and that absorb their energies, this might support a future disposition to learning. By the same token, those young children who are exhorted to compete with others and to complete tasks in order to gain adult approval, are not likely to be so disposed to learning but rather to perform and succeed against others.*
>
> (Dowling, 2005, p89)

In section 3.2 ('Supporting every child') of the Enabling Environment Commitment of the EYFS, reference is made to a child's individual 'learning journey'. In order to foster and encourage positive dispositions and attitudes to learning, it is important that the environment you provide 'achieves a balance between providing enough of the familiar to reassure, while presenting enough of the new to stimulate and extend' (p2). The organisation of your daily routine should support a child's learning journey. By providing a balance of experiences planned by the adult and those initiated by the child, you will be able to provide some assurance that children are having those new and familiar experiences.

Experiences planned by the child are sometimes referred to as 'child-initiated' (see Chapter 1). By allowing children to have time and space to follow through their own plans, you are providing them with the opportunities either to try something new, or to revisit something which they are familiar with. It provides authentic opportunities for a child to persevere and sustain concentration for extended periods of time. How you organise these periods of child-initiated learning is very important. The following two scenarios illustrate very different ways of providing opportunities for child-initiated learning. Consider the questions which follow, and think particularly about the impact of the interactions with the teacher and the organisation of the routine on the development of Sophie's interests and motivation to learn.

CLASSROOM STORY

Scenario A

After playtime, the children in the Reception class meet in their groups for 'Plan-Do-Review'. Sophie wants to make a birthday card for her Grandma, as 'we are having a birthday party for her today'. She plans to go to the making table where there are materials stored for her to access and use independently. After Sophie has made her plan, she swiftly sets to work selecting pink card, pens and scissors. Ten minutes later the teacher joins Sophie's table. She sits quietly for a couple of minutes to watch the children to gain an understanding of what the children's intentions are. She notices that Sophie seems to be struggling to attach a flower she has cut out onto the front of her card. The teacher says, 'Sophie, you look like you have got a problem – can I help you?' Sophie explains her frustration in trying to make her flower 'stick out the front...like we did last week when we made our clown pictures'. Together they experiment with folded paper and sticking tape, until Sophie is happy with the outcome. Sophie then says that she needs to write in her card. 'I know how to write "Grandma", but I don't know how to write "Happy Birthday"' she said. The teacher suggests she look in the drawer which contains lots of used greetings cards, to see if she can find one with the words she needed. Sophie quickly finds a birthday card...'I'm ok now', she says. 'I know which words to copy.' Sophie completes her card, finds an envelope to fit her card and then puts the finished article in her drawer ready to take home. The teacher moves away from the table and goes over to the Dentist's, where she has been invited to come for her appointment.

Scenario B
The Reception class is organised into four groups. Sophie is in the red group. The teacher and nursery nurse are working with two groups on a literacy activity. The red group have been allowed to 'choose' either to play in the sand, complete a jigsaw, or do a drawing at the making table. Sophie is making a birthday card for her Grandma. The paper and felt pens have been placed in the middle of the table. Sophie wants to cut out a picture to put on the front of her card, bit she cannot find the scissors or glue. At that moment the teacher comes over to the table. Sophie begins to tell her about her dilemma. The teacher responds by saying, 'Never mind about that now, Sophie, the red group are going to come and play a word game with me now. Tidy up your table, and come and sit in the literacy corner.' Sophie looks at her incomplete card; on her way to the literacy corner, she screws up the card and puts it in the dustbin.

PRACTICAL TASK PRACTICAL TASK **PRACTICAL TASK** PRACTICAL TASK **PRACTICAL TASK**

- To what extent does Sophie feel the teacher values her independent learning?
- How can the teacher make a judgement about what interests and motivates Sophie?
- What do you know about Sophie's attitudes and dispositions to learning?
- What impact on Sophie's attitude and disposition to learning could the interaction with the teacher have on her?
- How does the organisation of learning experiences and resources support Sophie's attitude and disposition to learning?

Assessment of a child's attitude and disposition to learning relies heavily on observation. You may find it useful to research the work done by Laevers (1996). Further reference to this work is made in Chapters 3 and 9. Laevers refers to a set of characteristics or signals to show the level of involvement in a child's learning. His study highlighted the differences in behaviour, and therefore dispositions to learning, between a child who is deeply involved in his learning and the child who is merely occupied. The two different scenarios of Sophie's learning demonstrate a marked difference in her behaviour. By scrutinising more closely the range of characteristics she demonstrated, it is clear which experience encouraged more positive attitudes and dispositions to learning.

These characteristics, or 'signals' include:

- concentration;
- energy;
- creativity;
- facial expression and posture;
- persistence;

- precision;
- reaction time;
- language;
- satisfaction.

PRACTICAL TASK PRACTICAL TASK PRACTICAL TASK PRACTICAL TASK PRACTICAL TASK

Observe a child in a self-chosen activity, and look for the above 'signals'. The extent to which a child demonstrates involvement through these 'signals' could be used to determine the child's disposition to learning.

Your level of involvement with children during sustained periods of self-directed activity will vary depending on the need of each child. In Scenario A, Sophie was able to articulate quite clearly when she needed help, and when she was 'ok now'. For those children who are less able to articulate their needs, you need to be able to 'read' their other non-verbal signs, such as facial expressions and responses to your interactions. As you build positive relationships with both the child and their family, your knowledge of their characteristics and interests will grow.

> A key goal for those caring for and teaching young children is to create the optimum conditions for learning to occur and this depends on understanding what and how children learn best.

> (Effective Practice: Supporting learning, p2)

The SPEEL research (Moyles et al., 2002) refers to three key factors or 'ingredients' which teachers would demonstrate. These are observing, enabling and facilitating. Referring again to Scenario A, the teacher demonstrated all three of those ingredients during the activity. She consciously observed Sophie to gain a sense of the Sophie's intentions. The organisation of the learning environment where materials were already accessible to her meant that she was enabled to locate independently what she needed to fulfil her plan. When Sophie struggled with sticking her flower onto the front of the card, the teacher facilitated the development of a new skill by working alongside her to solve the problem. An important aspect of this whole interaction was that the teacher and Sophie shared control of the situation. The teacher offered her help when needed, but Sophie was confident to state when she no longer need any help. This is a key feature of the support you provide. In order for a child to continue to be excited and motivated to learn, they need to feel a sense of ownership and control. Children need to want to succeed for themselves, not to please the adults around them. It can be very tempting to show a child how to do something, or impose your ideas of the solution to a problem, as this is human nature. This may be an aspect of practice you find you need to develop when working alongside children. When you truly know the individual characteristics of each child in your class, you will know those who enjoy the challenge of working something out for themselves, as well as those children who you know will quickly become unmotivated if they struggle for too long.

Self-confidence and self-esteem

The EYFS guidance states that self-confidence and self-esteem are about 'children having a sense of their own value and understanding the need for sensitivity to significant events in their own and other people's lives'.

A young child's self-confidence is undoubtedly shaped by their personal experiences. The well-known phrase 'Children learn what they live' is relevant in both the home and the classroom contexts. Therefore how we respond to children in the classroom can have a significant effect on the development of their self-confidence and self-esteem. Conversely, the experiences children have at home may be very different from those a child experiences in school. Research by Judy Dunn (1987) provides an interesting insight into the way a child's emotional understanding and social development appear to be far more developed within the emotionally charged contexts of their own families.

Imagine how it must feel for Tom. He is a four-year-old child who is not necessarily expected to share toys, or take turns when at home. He is constantly rewarded for completing tasks such as eating all of his lunch, or tidying his toys away. When he comes to school, he finds that he is expected to sit quietly and listen to his peers during carpet time, and that he has to take turns to ride on the new digger when playing outside. He is not very keen to tidy away toys before lunch time, particularly as nobody is tempting him with a reward of a bag of sweets if he puts all the bricks away.

Tom has a lot to deal with; he may well feel unhappy or confused when he comes to school, as the expectation to conform is not something he has been particularly used to. On the other hand, the expectations that the teacher has of him, and the acknowledgement the teacher gives him for letting someone else have a ride on the digger (even though she knows he really, really wanted to stay on it for longer), help him to understand what it feels like to be 'kind'.

Confidence can be linked to three factors: becoming aware of oneself (self-concept); developing a view of oneself, either positive or negative (self-esteem) and getting to know about one's strengths and weaknesses (self-knowledge) A confident child is not necessarily an outgoing child (Dowling, 2005). A confident child may seem quiet or reserved. What characterises a confident child is one who is aware of themselves, and over time is able to understand what is unique about themselves – what gives them their own identity, and how other people see them.

A child's self-esteem is not a fixed state. The people surrounding a child, and the environment he or she is in can have either a positive or negative impact . Periods of transition are also known to have an impact on a child's self-esteem. Reference is made to transition from one setting to another in Chapter 1. Starting school is probably one of the most significant times in a child's life. A child is facing new experiences, expectations and having to get know new people. Think about the level of anxiety you may feel when you begin a new job. Through your life experiences, and your own developed sense of 'self', you probably find strategies to deal with the uncertainty. When you are four or five years old, your sense of self has not yet fully developed, and in fact the experience itself will undoubtedly have an impact on the further development of self-confidence and self-esteem.

Part of the process of developing a sense of self and sensitivity towards others is about providing opportunities for children to understand each other. It is important that young children develop an awareness of similarities and difference between themselves, and that they are helped to see that this is 'normal'. Siraj-Blatchford (2004) emphasises the importance of focusing on similarities as much as dealing with human differences. She refers to the rights of all children who are entitled to a childhood curriculum that supports and affirms their gender, cultural and linguistic identities and backgrounds. The way in which young children construct their identity and self-concept is influenced by the way others view them and respond to them and their family. Chapter 1 challenges you to consider your own values and attitudes, and how these have a direct impact on a child's own construct of his or herself. It is worthwhile reconsidering your own values and beliefs, and considering the extent to which you demonstrate patience, care, tolerance and understanding to all children in your class.

There is always a danger when exploring diversity in the classroom – especially in relation to race, culture and ethnicity – that children belonging to a minority group are portrayed in an exotic or tokenistic way. By having a genuine and authentic involvement with parents and families, you will go some way to understand the uniqueness of every child's life and background. The uniqueness and therefore 'special-ness' is something which needs to be both acknowledged and celebrated. You need not necessarily do this through celebrating specific festivals and events, but by giving time to share personal everyday experiences with each other. This provides a natural forum for children to begin to understand that in fact there are many aspects of our day-to-day lives which are very similar, as well as under-standing that there are aspects of our lives which are unique to us and our family.

Making relationships

The EYFS guidance states that making relationships is about 'the importance of children forming good relationships with others and working alongside others companionably'.

The ability to make friends is a complicated business; once a child has been accepted into a social group, it seems more likely that they will be in a better position to learn (Parker and Asher, 1987; Howes, 1987). It is the responsibility of the adults in a setting to support children in developing relationships with others, and to feel a sense of belonging. Some children will have had a wide experience of interacting and playing with other children through their pre-school experiences and family circumstances. Other children will have had more limited experiences of interacting and playing with others. There will always be some children who find it more difficult to make friends, and the way a child's social behaviour is perceived by peers can contribute to the extent to which they are 'accepted' into their community. Dowling (2005) makes reference to a useful study by Rubin (1983), who lists a number of social skills involved in making friends. These include the ability to gain entry to group activities; to be approving and supportive of one's peers; to manage conflicts appropriately; and the ability to exercise sensitivity and tact. The most popular children were those who were particularly accomplished in these skills.

The following checklist will help you to think about the opportunities you provide for children to form and develop relationships.

- An area in the classroom where children can sit and chat, such as a soft, 'cosy' area or a den.
- The outdoor area which provides an opportunity for children to 'meet and greet', such as a friendship stop or an inviting seated area.
- Time, space and materials which allow children to collaborate with one another in different ways.
- The role-play area resourced with materials which reflect children's family lives and communities.
- Activities provided for children which encourage turn-taking and sharing.
- Decisions regarding codes of behaviour which are discussed and agreed collectively by the class.
- Children involved in making decisions about their class, such as the design of the new vet's surgery in the role-play corner, or where to store the new blocks.

Behaviour and self-control

The EYFS guidance states that behaviour and self-control 'is about how children develop a growing understanding of what is right and wrong and why, together with learning about the impact of their words and actions on themselves and others'. By the end of the Foundation Stage, a child is expected to 'Understand what is right and wrong, and why' and 'Consider the consequences of their words and actions for themselves and others' (ELG for behaviour and self-control). There are some key theoretical perspectives regarding child development which are useful to consider, and will help you as a practitioner perhaps understand what are reasonable expectations for children's behaviour.

The High/Scope developmental framework describes some important characteristics of young children which should be taken into account in supporting children's behaviour and self-control. The areas addressed are particularly useful when considering how to support children in resolving conflicts. Conflicts regarding sharing and turn-taking are a regular occurrence in an Early Years classroom. As an Early Years practitioner, it is important to consider your role in resolving conflict. An Early Years classroom is always busy, and there can be a temptation to mediate conflict between children by imposing your own solutions to the situation. This 'quick fix' solution may alleviate the situation for the time being – but if we want children genuinely to understand the difference between right and wrong, they need to do so from their own motives. It is difficult for an egocentric three- or four-year-old to understand right from wrong – when your priority is to wear the one and only fairy costume in the role-play corner before anyone else gets to it. Your role in the Foundation Stage is to sow the seeds and provide a supportive environment which offers opportunities for children on a regular basis to begin to understand about cause and effect.

Some useful considerations regarding children's developmental behaviour are outlined below.

Egocentrism: Young children view the world from the standpoint of their own feelings and needs. Children have very little awareness of the viewpoints of others, and therefore, without the guidance of a supportive adult, they will find it very difficult to understand a situation from another child's perspective. Therefore, when we ask a child to consider how another child is feeling in a conflict situation, we have to consider whether that is actually a reasonable expectation. Instead, it is far more useful to describe how you think children may be feeling in a conflict situation, as this immediate acknowledgement of feelings helps to release the emotion which may be getting in the way of thinking beyond the immediate.

Concrete thinking: Young children are concrete thinkers – they base their understanding of the world on obvious physical characteristics. During conflict situations, general solutions to a problem such as 'share' or 'take turns' are too vague for a child to understand. Children need more definition to their solutions, so that they get a sense of what the solution will look like and feel to them. For example, when two children are arguing over the possession of a popular toy, it is more useful to help the children consider 'How can we share the toy?' than a blanket statement of 'You must both share and take it in turns'. Sometimes situations like this can be avoided in the first place by just thinking about the resources in your environment. If there are particular favourite toys which always seem to be the focus of a dispute – why not make sure there is more then one of the same thing?

Limited verbal skills: For some children, their ability to articulate their feelings and needs can still be limited, and this can be especially compounded by the emotional tension which is usually present in a conflict situation. The adult has a key role in articulating a child's feelings for him – such as, 'You're both feeling cross... because you both want to play on the trike'. Sometimes this also includes reframing children's harmful words into more appropriate feelings.

Physical expressiveness: Young children express most of what they feel with their bodies. Until their verbal skills are established, young children will show their frustration by such physical responses as hitting and grabbing. It is important that we discourage, not punish, physical responses, and encourage children to develop their problem-solving skills through the support of an understanding adult.

Striving for independence: Children's developing independence is central to their growth, and often provides motivation to learn new skills. Yet the combination of a desire to do things for themselves and their egocentrism can sometimes cause conflicts. It is important therefore that we do provide room for children to exercise their emerging skills, by allowing them to share control in the process of problem-solving.

'One thing at a time' thinking: Children can focus on only one or two attributes or ideas at a time. As a result, conflicts can sometimes be confusing, muddled experiences in which they feel overwhelmed by the rush of emotions and demands. A simple strategy for an adult to adopt is to acknowledge children's feelings and restate the essential details of the problem. When children feel their wants and needs have been completely understood, they are in a better position to begin to negotiate a solution to the problem.

(Adapted from Evans, 2002)

As a final note in this section, it is important to remember that children will display a range of behavioural characteristics, some of which will be more difficult to deal with than others. Reference to children's home background and prior experiences before entering your setting are made consistently throughout this book. One factor which can contribute to some children's more challenging behaviour may be low-quality parenting. Walker-Hall and Sylva (2004) categorise low-quality parenting as being inconsistent, authoritarian, lacking in warmth, uninvolved, physically punitive and not providing adequate care. Conversely, it is also important to acknowledge that poor parenting may in fact be a reaction to the way a child conducts himself in the first instance. As you can see, this is a complex and sensitive area, which illustrates the importance of building relationships with parents to ensure a collaborative approach to behaviour management. Chapters 10 and 11 provide more information and guidance.

Self-care

The EYFS guidance states that self-care is about 'how children gain a sense of self-respect and concern for their own personal hygiene and care and how they develop independence'. There are a number of aspects of PSED which cannot necessarily be planned for, and this aspect is particularly pertinent. Nevertheless, the daily routines and opportunities you provide for children will support children's understanding of the importance of personal hygiene and care. Educational institutions traditionally tend to have specific routines and systems in place which ensure that children maintain high standards of personal hygiene. Hand-washing routines after toileting and before eating or preparing food should be standard practice. Natural links with the 'Health and bodily awareness' aspect of physical development can also be made to help children understand the need for high standards of personal hygiene.

There are other aspects of classroom life which also require children to develop a sense of self-respect, care and independence. Ask any nursery or Reception teacher which aspect of their teaching provides them with the most challenge, and it is almost certainly going to be PE. It is not unusual for a 30-minute slot booked in the hall for PE to consist of children taking 15 minutes to undress, followed by a 10-minute PE lesson (where there is time only for the warm-up) and the remaining time spent frantically helping children to get dressed again into their school clothes, while searching for odd socks, pants, shoes and any other article of clothing which has been mislaid during the process. Changing in and out of clothes can be a stressful time for children (and adults), especially if they are required to tie shoelaces, fasten small buttons and turn shirts back the right way round. Many parents will not appreciate the challenges of helping 30 children change their clothes. It is important that you communicate with parents about the value of providing their child with clothing which they are more likely to be able to put on independently – such as footwear with Velcro fastening, and shirts which easily slip over the head. This is the sort of information which is useful to include in induction meetings, with a gentle request that it is really helpful for a child at home to be encouraged to dress independently. For any parents reading this chapter, you know only too well how stressful it can be to get a houseful of children dressed, fed and out of the house in time to get to school, and then get to work. Sometimes it is a lot easier to dress your youngest child yourself – so be realistic about the expectations you have for families at home. Likewise, you need to be realistic about the expectations you have on yourself as a teacher. Do children really need to change into a full PE kit ? Perhaps for the first half of term, children could just take shoes and socks off and their PE session involves games and activities which do not require excessive physical movement. Remember, the experience of having a PE lesson in a large hall can be daunting itself for young children, so a gentle and gradual build-up of expectations would suit everyone all round.

There will be some children in your care who you have identified will need particular support in becoming more independent in their self-care. Some children may have a particular medical condition which means they will need specific identified support. Other children may simply have had limited opportunities or role models at home to help them become independent. It is important that you establish small steps, and that you model your expectations. For example, just by showing a child that to place socks in shoes ensures that they can be located at the end of a PE session, or showing a child that it helps to hold onto the bottom of your coat whilst trying to fasten a zip are all strategies, which once modelled to a child, gives them a clear goal to work towards. Clearly sharing this information with parents, means that the same goals can be worked on at home also.

The second Early Learning Goal for this aspect of self-care states that children are required to 'select and use activities and resources independently'. This will be possible only if the learning environment you provide for children is organised in such a way to facilitate this. Imagine your frustration when you are looking for products in a supermarket which you can't access because they are out of your reach, or when you can't find a product which is not displayed in the aisle with the other seemingly similar products. This principle applies equally to young children when they are looking for resources to support their chosen activity. Further guidance regarding how to organise your environment which optimises opportunities for children to be independent, is given in the 'Enabling Environment' section of Chapter 1.

Sense of community

The final aspect of this area of learning and development is concerned with 'how children understand and respect their own needs, views, cultures and beliefs and those of others'. If you were to consider the questions outlined in the 'Making relationships' section of this chapter, it is hoped that you can appreciate the interrelatedness of both aspects. By employing strategies for children to make relationships, it could be argued that you are also providing genuine opportunities to develop a sense of community, and for children to develop a real understanding and recognition of their place in their immediate environment and the wider world.

The planned and unplanned opportunities which occur every day should provide opportunities for children to develop an interest in and respect for each other and the lives they live. It is important that you consider how you ensure that all children are given support to participate equally, and that their views are included and listened to.

REFLECTIVE TASK

Read the practice guidance section of PSED, and the 'Principles into practice' cards. Look particularly at the 'Making relationships' and 'Sense of community' sections. Consider the guidance and questions posed in the light of your own professional development and understanding.

A SUMMARY OF **KEY POINTS**

> All of the aspects of PSED are interconnected.

> The importance of understanding and knowing about each and every child in your care.

> In order for children to be able to make relationships, and consequently manage the situations they may find themselves in, such as sharing, turn-taking and managing conflict, they need to have a strong sense of who they are, and a belief in themselves.

> Your role is fundamental in providing the attachment and comfort which children need to develop self-confidence and self-esteem.

> The physical and emotional environment you provide for children should reflect the unique classroom community your children belong to, and should also enable children to be independent, confident learners who display positive attitudes and dispositions to learning.

MOVING *ON* > > > > > > MOVING *ON* > > > > > > MOVING *ON*

In your next placement, or employment, consider how you will find out the context in which you are teaching.

What are the unique characteristics of the community you will be working in?

How will you begin to build relationships with children and their families so that you have a sound knowledge and understanding of the needs of every child?

REFERENCES REFERENCES **REFERENCES** REFERENCES REFERENCES REFERENCES

Dowling, M. (2005) *Young children's personal, social and emotional development* (2nd edition). London: Paul Chapman.

Dunn, J. (1987) Understanding feelings; the early stages', in J. Bruner and H. Haste (eds), *Making sense: the child's construction of the world*. London: Methuen.

Evans, B. (2002) *You can't come to my birthday party! Conflict resolution with young children.* Yipsilanti, Michigan: High/Scope Press.

Glaxton, G. and Carr, M. (2004) A framework for teaching learning: the dynamics of disposition. *Early Years*, 24(1) March, 87–97.

Howes, C. (1987) Peer interaction of young children. *Monographs of the Society for Research in Child Development*, 217, 53:1.

Katz, L. (1995) *Talks with teachers of young children*. Norwood, NJ: Abbex.

Laevers, F. (ed.) (1996) *An exploration of the concept of involvement as an indicator of quality in early childhood education*. Dundee: Scottish Consultative Council on the Curriculum.

Maslow, A.H. (1943) A theory of human motivation. *Psychological Review*, 50, 370–96.

Moyles, J., Adams, S. and Musgrove, A. (2002) *SPEEL: Study of Pedagogical Effectiveness in Early Learning*. London: DfES.

Parker, J. and Asher, S. (1987) Peer relations and later personal adjustment; are low accepted children at risk? *Psychological Bulletin,* 102, 358–89.

Rubin, Z. (1983) The skills of friendship, in M. Donaldson (ed.), *Early childhood development and education*. Oxford: Blackwell.

Siraj-Blatchford, I. (2004) Diversity and learning in the early years in G. Pugh (ed.) *Contemporary issues in the early years*, (3rd edition). London: Sage.

Walker-Hall, J. and Sylva, K. (2004) What works for families of children with behaviour problems? Evidence from research, in G. Pugh (ed.) *Contemporary issues in the early years*, (3rd edition). London: Sage.

FURTHER READING FURTHER READING **FURTHER READING** FURTHER READING

Penn, H. (2005) *Understanding early childhood. Issues and controversies*. Buckingham: Open University.

Useful websites

www..cego.be/
www.highscope.uk.org

3
Creative development and critical thinking
Elaine Hodson

Chapter objectives

By the end of this chapter you should be able to understand and appreciate the importance of the following factors in extending children's creativity:

- **providing wide-ranging experiences and a stimulating environment;**
- **ensuring that children feel secure in order for them to be adventurous;**
- **demonstrating to children that their own ideas are valued;**
- **ensuring children have opportunities to work alongside creative adults;**
- **accommodating children's specific religious and cultural beliefs in creative activities;**
- **ensuring that children have time to plan, carry out and evaluate their ideas and to return to them to modify and develop them;**
- **providing children with opportunities to express their ideas through a wide range of types of representation.**

This chapter addresses the following Professional Standards for QTS:

Q1, Q3(a), Q10, Q14, Q15, Q25 (a), Q25 (b)

Introduction

The requirements in the Practice Guidance state that 'Children's creativity must be extended by the provision of support for their curiosity, exploration and play'.

This means that as their teacher, you will need to ensure that you provide plenty of opportunity for children to initiate their own learning. Chapter 1 discusses the themes and commitments of the EYFS in detail. However, it is important to begin this chapter by underlining the importance of play to this particular area of learning and development. Play is the context which will allow these young learners to take risks, become absorbed as they explore, give opportunities for making choices and encourage risk-taking. This chapter will go on to support you in achieving the standards for QTS by defining creativity and considering the way in which you might provide a learning environment conducive to children working as imaginative individuals able to make their own unique responses.

Defining creativity

As a trainee teacher, you will be hearing the word 'creativity' used extensively in discussions on education, and in those concerning early education in particular. You will also begin to notice that the word is used very generally and there is little consensus about its meaning. As a teacher of the youngest children you will, however, need to begin to gain some clarity. You will be aware that the EYFS provides guidance on creativity as one of the six areas of learning and development. It also places creativity and critical thinking as a commitment in the theme of learning and development. The aspect of creativity and critical thinking is dealt with in Chapter 1, while this chapter focuses on creativity as an area of learning and development, but there will inevitably, be strong links between the two sections.

Defining what is meant in curriculum terms by creativity is in itself a challenge. In the DfEE document *All our futures: creativity, culture, and education* (NACCCE, 1999), it is defined as: 'Imaginative activity fashioned so as to produce outcomes that are both original and of value'.

Working with the youngest children, it would easy for you to see a capacity to be inventive as self-evident. From birth, babies appear to be inspired to investigate and interact with their environment. Think of a young baby, Daniel, 10 months old, who is left alone to investigate a basket of toys. Patiently he takes each object from the basket on his right, and places it on the floor to his left. He has seen all the objects many times before. Various ones command his attention. One toy is simply viewed, twisted and turned and considered from different angles, a second goes into his mouth as he uses what is still the most sensitive part of his body, to consider taste, texture, and resistance. He goes on to attempt to relate objects to each other; for example, for a while he concentrates on balancing a teapot lid on the teddy's head, and then struggles to join two plastic curtain hooks together in the same way he has just joined two interlocking bricks. Even at such an early stage, Daniel is challenging himself, and struggling to make sense of his world by interacting in it. None of his actions is random or uneventful.

Most children become quickly involved in opportunities to engage their imagination. It is not surprising, therefore, that creativity has long been valued as a central aspect of Early Years education. As you will be aware already, many of the pioneers of early education placed creativity at the centre of their philosophies; for example, Froebel, Montessori and Steiner all speak of the inner life of the child. Froebel saw children taking knowledge into themselves from their experiences, transforming it, and then storing it in their imagination for future use. It would be easy to transfer the description of Daniel to this model, as he investigates, manipulates and then lays each object aside. Play, the imagination, and the ability of the mind, were seen by these early thinkers to be vital in making the 'inner outer', that is, in allowing opportunity for the outward expression of the unique nature of each individual. Froebel also believed that each individual child's knowledge could be communicated to others through the use of paint, clay, music, drama, the written word, conversation, mathematics and so forth. Both Steiner and Froebel held that through imagination the child strives to make links between new experiences and previous knowledge.

Building on this pioneering philosophy, teachers of young children have long talked about a curriculum 'based in play'. This concept has included beliefs such as children being active learners, and the need to place children in control of their own learning.

Alongside these historical influences, the philosophy of the Reggio Emilio district in northern Italy has done much to influence thinking in this country in the last 20 years. There thinkers such as Malaguzzi argue that children are 'rich in potential, strong powerful and competent', and sees education as a process entered into by adults and children as co-constructors of knowledge. Malaguzzi suggests that formal education may actually reduce the child's competency as a learner.

Each of these philosophical strands has influenced government policy, and now has a well-defined place in the EYFS. Chapter 1 includes further discussion about active learning and the role of play in the EYFS.

Developing imagination

Encouraging children to develop their imagination is then a fundamental part of developing their creativity. However, being imaginative also appears to have strong links with creating a positive self-image. Some developmental psychologists argue that the young child's desire to learn about and contribute to a culture, if not innate, is certainly present at a very early stage. Trevarthen (1995) argues, for example, that the joint interactions of carers and babies in songs and rhymes is identifiable in most cultures, and therefore seems to be a significant feature of human social interaction. This adult/child engagement appears to play a significant part in nurturing feelings of acceptance and belonging in the young child. At the same time, these joint involvement episodes (JIEs) between adults and children (Schaffer, 1996) are recognised as a central component of intellectual development, serving as a focus for adult modelling and language development.

The fact that learners respond so enthusiastically to creative opportunities has led to research which suggests that in these circumstances learners are operating at their most effective. Work by Csikszentmihalyi (1992) describes learners engaged in creative activity to be in a state of 'flow', suggesting that when they are freed from necessity and allowed to focus creatively on aspects of their own individual interest, learners experience their greatest joy and become most deeply engaged with their tasks. Laevers (2003) built on this work in his studies of young children learning. Interested in the reasons that some children in the Early Years classrooms he researched seemed unable to learn and develop, despite being provided with a stimulating environment and sensitive adult support, he identified evidence that these disengaged children usually scored low on measures of confidence and self-esteem. He argues that the quality of any educational setting is most effectively assessed by focusing on two elements: 'emotional well-being' and 'involvement'. His research suggests that only when children feel completely at ease and secure, are they able to become fully involved with their learning and move on in their thinking. He argues that the characteristics of this 'state of flow' are concentration, strong motivation and fascination. Once reaching this state, the learner becomes unaware of the passage of time, and is at his/her most sensitive to stimuli. He describes learners as feeling great satisfaction and physically experiencing a stream of positive energy. Unsurprisingly, Laevers argues that learners will actively seek out this highly rewarding state. Most significantly for you as an EYFS teacher, he asserts that young learners find this state of flow in play. These findings are unsurprising for adults experienced in working with very young learners, and you too will no doubt have already witnessed the high level of enthusiasm and the extended concentration evident when observing children immersed in stimulating activity. Laevers's work, therefore, suggests that more than being simply desirable for its own sake, allowing children to make a creative response to tasks is essential for 'deep level learning' to take place.

Other research has identified a link between the recognition of a learner's creativity and their level of achievement. Fisher and Williams (2004) refer to research by Robert Sternberg (1999) which shows that when students are assessed in ways that recognise and value their creative abilities, their academic performance improves. Thus, not only do learners engage better with their learning when they are invited to make a creative response, but they also learn more effectively. Since schools are expected to constantly strive towards government targets for improved results, developing the curriculum to encompass higher levels of creativity for learners must surely be of benefit to both you as their teacher, and for them as learners.

REFLECTIVE TASK

Spend some time thinking about the practice you have recently experienced in a Foundation Stage classroom. Think of a time when you have been impressed by the unexpected or impromptu learning that has taken place; for example, a time when a child found a new and different use for a piece of equipment, a time when a child made a connection to some earlier learning as they approached a fresh challenge.

● Try to pinpoint the circumstances the teacher has created to allow this to happen. Has s/he provided particular resources? Has s/he encouraged a new and different approach? How has s/he interacted with the children in a particular way?

● Now focus on your teaching. Think about how you might develop a similar learning opportunity which could incorporate the same or similar features.

So far this chapter has focused on the contribution that making a creative response makes to personal growth, to satisfaction and to standards. It is important that you are also aware of the needs of our society for creative individuals. In the rapidly changing, techno-charged context of the twenty-first century, there is a growing awareness that human beings are being required to constantly and continually change and develop their patterns of thinking. Humans now inhabit a world well beyond the understanding of earlier generations; for example, it is documented that if Neil Armstrong had been handed a pocket calculator as he landed on the Moon, he would have had no knowledge of its use. It seems certain that this rapid development will continue and increase. Barrett (2006) suggests that most of the children starting school in 2008 will be employed in jobs which do not currently exist. Changes in society are dependent on its members being able to think creatively, since without creative thinking only the same patterns of behaviour can be repeated. The young children you are currently teaching will need more than ever before to be capable of thinking creatively.

Fisher and Williams (2004) argue:

'The challenge for schools and social institutions is clear: the focus of education must be on creating people who are capable of thinking and doing new things, not simply repeating what past generations have done, but equipped for a world of challenge and change. Creativity is essential if new ways are to be found of solving problems.

As a result of the way in which economies in the industrialised world have changed, both national and personal economic well-being have become increasingly dependent on creative ability: 'The intellectual property sector' concerned with communication, information, entertainment, science and technology is the fastest growing area of the economy' (DfEE, 1999).

It is quite clear, therefore, that for the children in your class to ultimately achieve economic well-being (*Every Child Matters*, 2003) it will be important that in the EYFS you have extended their creativity.

Fostering a creative response

The EYFS requires that:

> *Children's development must be extended by the provision of support for their curiosity, exploration and play. They must be provided with opportunities to explore and share their thoughts, ideas and feelings, for example through a variety of art, music, movement, dance, imaginative and role play activities, mathematics and design technology.*

You will probably have already understood that in order to make an imaginative response, young children need a particular context in which to work and it is on your role in creating this context that, as a trainee teacher, you will need to focus. Returning to the NACCCE definition, it may be useful to examine each of these elements in the light of good Early Years practice.

Developing imaginative activity

If the children in your class are to be encouraged to use their imagination, they will need to be able to draw on a wealth of ideas and experiences. Some children will already have heard many stories and poems, seen and joined in role-play, responded to a range of music and sound, experimented with colour, texture, form and so forth. Other children may have had more limited experiences. As a teacher, before you invite children to respond imaginatively, you will need to assess the support they will require in order to do this. The opportunities you offer to children for imaginative play will present them with the chance to explore personal relationships, develop empathy, explore emotions, investigate causality and develop their ability to communicate. You will need to provide, among other things, a role-play area, the use of puppets, the provision of small world and construction equipment, as well as access to a natural environment with places to hide, climb and test their skills. Imaginative play can provide a meaningful context for learning; for example by incorporating literacy events such as consulting a telephone directory or television guide, taking note of an appointment, or presenting a mathematical problem as in the need to decide how best to fit packets of food onto the shelves in the shop.

CLASSROOM STORY

Miss Zaidi had set up a shop in her Nursery class. She had supplied the boxes and tins of food on shelves, shopping bags, a till and money as well as writing tools, paper, posters advertising produce, etc. During the weekly review, the staff were concerned that the children did not know how to behave in the shop. Children did not seem to know how to take turns, queue, or know how to ask for items, or act as the shopkeeper.

REFLECTIVE TASK

What would you say about the way this play experience connects to the children's own lives? What suggestions would you make, if you were working in this team, to make the experience more effective?

Another issue impacting on imaginative play can be that sometimes adults have a different agenda from that of the children they are working with. Consider the following situation.

CLASSROOM STORY

Mrs Hirst has decided to create a hairdresser's salon in the imaginative area of her classroom as a part of a theme on 'Ourselves'. The area is set out with a range of resources, hair dryers, rollers, an appointment book, a till, magazines. On the first day of the provision, groups of children move in and out of the salon, cutting, blow-drying, making appointments, serving tea to clients, and so forth. In the afternoon, Mrs Hirst is disturbed to find a group of three boys in the salon having taken a 'client' (a rag doll) with long hair, and begun kicking and passing it across the shop amidst shouts of, 'Goal, good pass, come on Rooney'. The actions are well created and their comments clearly reflect the football match the night before. Angry at the abuse of resources, the teacher stops the play in the salon and talks to the boys about appropriate behaviour in the imaginative area. The boys are embarrassed and apologetic and Mrs Hirst moves on, leaving the boys alone in the salon once more. Satisfied that the adult has moved on, the boys begin once more to reenact last night's Premier League game. The doll continues to be kicked across the space, but this time they bend low as they play, to be safe behind the partition from the gaze and subsequent criticism of passing adults.

Fortunately for all concerned, the scenario is witnessed by a second member of staff, Mrs Musso, a new teacher. She stops the recommenced match, ensures that the boys restore the salon to order, then opens up the previously closed outdoor area and supplies the boys with a football and some goal posts.

REFLECTIVE TASK

What would you say these boys have learnt about making an imaginative response?

What could you conclude about the reactions of the two teachers? What might that team of adults reflect on at their next planning meeting?

If teddies are always in the microwave, and shoes and handbags thrust in the tumble dryer, what message are the children sending about the role-play being made available to them? Do practitioners sometimes criticise children's behaviour before evaluating the provision they have made?

As a teacher, you will need to be aware of the different imaginative opportunities you make available to children. Sometimes they may need support and advice; for example, to find the elements to create an outfit for Robin Hood. They will want to do this immediately, not at some point in the future, so materials need to be easily available and readily adaptable. While some children seem to become easily and quickly absorbed in imaginative play, others may need a prompt, such as, 'Shall we see if we can make an obstacle course for the play people like the one you enjoyed playing on yesterday outside?' Since different children will have different interests, it is important for you as a teacher to observe emerging ideas and be prepared to facilitate them. You will need to provide opportunities for children to observe, listen, make choices, play alone and with others, to review their play and to consider ways to develop and adapt it. The children will need opportunities to combine materials, move between areas, and return to ideas. Most importantly, they will need to do this both indoors and out, as well as moving between the two. Your role as an adult will be to show that you value their responses, to provide well cared-for and well-organised resources that reflect a variety of cultures and stimulate new and different ways of thinking, and to encourage children to employ all their senses as they play. You will need to consider ways, for example, to include a child with a visual impairment by providing resources that are attractively tactile, or that make interesting sounds.

The EYFS states that 'children need to play with ideas in different situations'. What does this suggest about the resources you provide and the learning environment you create? Firstly you will need to be aware of the range and variety of materials available to the children. How can you be sure that children have, for example, access to a range of construction equipment? Is the equipment clean, attractive and complete, without missing pieces? Are the children able to find and recognise it in the storage you provide by the labelling? Are the children able to make choices about which equipment they will use? Are they able to combine sets? If so, how do you ensure that materials are correctly returned to their storage? Are the children encouraged to link different areas of learning; for example, do you provide pencils and paper to design a model, or card to make a label for the finished item? Might cassette/video recorders and digital cameras be available for children to record their work? (See Chapter 8 for more discussion on the use of ICT resources to record achievement.)

As well as thinking about physical resources, you will also need to think about time. As a trainee, you will probably have experienced being asked to go into groups, consider a problem and report back, only to find that, hardly has the conversation begun, than you are being asked to reach a conclusion. Imagine how much more frustrating this is for a young child who already has an underdeveloped understanding of the passage of time and very little power of protest.

CLASSROOM STORY

One child in the Reception classroom was heard to comment, 'You are allowed to get the orange construction set out when you want to, but I never choose it. You only just have time to sort the right pieces out, then Miss says "It's time to tidy up". Then you have to sort out the tools and the screws into their boxes, and sometimes you're late for snack time and get told off for being slow. So I don't choose it now'.

PRACTICAL TASK PRACTICAL TASK **PRACTICAL TASK** PRACTICAL TASK **PRACTICAL TASK**

On your next period in your setting, take some time to observe the structure of the children's day. Make notes on the imaginative play they are involved in. Consider its duration, frequency and quality. Make notes also of the adult interruptions. How many were unavoidable? Is the pattern of the day seamless, or do children and adults stop and start activities in order to accommodate milk time, play time, assembly, PE? Would it be possible for these disruptions to be minimised or eradicated? Do children have opportunities to plan and review their play as well as return to it in order to develop and extend it?

Transforming understanding

It is beginning to become clear in this discussion that adults provide a most important resource for the children in their imaginative play. The view has already been considered that making new connections transforms understanding. Adults can support children's play by entering into dialogue with them, and challenging their thinking. Indeed the research paper *Researching effective pedagogy in the early years* (DfES, 2002) points to the significant contribution made by shared dialogue to the co-construction of knowledge. The researchers argue that in the most effective settings, children benefited by participating in 'sustained shared thinking' with adults. This was discussed in more detail in Chapter 1.

You could support the children in your class by:

- helping them work through a task, making sure it is neither too easy nor too challenging;
- helping them to bring aspects of partial learning together, 'Do you mean that...?' 'I think you're saying you think that...?' 'Do you remember how we...?';
- helping them to work through a task logically;
- helping them to select appropriate materials;
- checking responses are appropriate;
- keeping them involved with the task;
- maintaining appropriate pace in the discussion, asking enough challenging questions and not too many;
- drawing together learning at the end of a session.

(adapted from Meadows and Cashdan, 1988)

Since much of the children's experience outside your classroom takes place in their homes, it is helpful if adults work together to support and develop these connections. You will need to think how you can best develop effective communication in order to support creative development and learning. You will need to establish effective communication between home and your setting, as well as between the setting and the local community. Think about how you might convey information to parents and carers in the form of newsletters, photograph displays, scrapbooks, open days and evenings. Are parents and carers able to spend time in the classroom at the beginning or end of the day and involve themselves in learning activities? Do practitioners use emails or home/ school books to convey information about individual children whose parents and carers have less opportunity to visit? Do staff make themselves available as receivers of information enabling them to find out about a child's interests at home? (See Chapter 10, 'Positive relationships'.) As most EYFS settings have a high ratio of adults to children, you also need to consider how information about children's learning is also shared between practitioners. (See Chapter 9 on observation and assessment and planning.)

Learning dispositions

The idea of learning dispositions is central to the current debate in early childhood education. You will be aware that much attention has been paid to identifying the learning environment which promotes the skills and abilities necessary for lifelong learning. Learning how to learn appears to be most effective when young children are supported in their learning by sensitive adults. The key characteristics of lifelong learners appear to be self-motivation, involvement, perseverance, determination, concentration, flexibility and risk-taking (Carr, 2001). If the young children in your care are to develop these dispositions, they will need to be presented with stimulating subject-content by adults who have strong subject knowledge, and are able to introduce them to different ways of knowing and responding and remain 'open to children's ideas, contributions questions and comments' (Aubrey, 1994). In this way adults move away from having stereotypical expectations of thinking and responding, and by their own openness are able to offer the sustained shared thinking which supports creative learning.

Encouraging originality

Any discussion about creativity includes the concept of originality. As a trainee teacher you can easily become sceptical about this notion. Surely few human beings are likely to produce ideas that make a unique contribution to an area? It may be helpful to you to consider the way Boden (1992) develops this debate, suggesting that there are two other measures of originality worthy of value: firstly, an individual's ability to respond in a way original to their own previous responses, and secondly, an individual's response may be original in terms of his/her peer group. The development of this concept is clearly dependent on an ability to make judgements and evaluate responses. If young children are to be encouraged in their creativity, they must also be encouraged to evaluate their work and to be supported in their use of critical language. They need to be encouraged to step back from their work and make decisions about how it might be continued. They need support to sustain their interest over a period of time in order to return to work, make modifications, solve technical or visual problems or develop an idea. This has clear implications for you as a practitioner.

REFLECTIVE TASK

Take some time to consider how you will organise the learning environment to ensure work can be safely preserved, that sufficient material is available to avoid deconstruction of other models, that children have sufficient time to return, without being rerouted into a new activity by an adult and provide time for children to reflect, evaluate and respond.

Responding

Not only will creative experience need to include making and experimenting, it will also need to encompass responding. If you are to support these young children, they will need to experience the way ideas change and grow, and that there is no single right answer. The children will need to experience a wide range of music, painting and sculpture, and will need the opportunity to talk about these and express an opinion. You might find Liptai (2004) useful for the suggestions she makes about the use of community of enquiry methods to help children begin to make creative responses to music and art. Children will also need encouragement in beginning to make evaluative responses both to their own work, and that of their peers. You will need to encourage them in their discussion, helping them develop appropriate technical vocabulary about form, texture, shape, movement and sound. Providing young children with the opportunity to work alongside artists and creative adults will enable them to see this evaluative process unfolding and to participate in the sustained shared thinking which may underpin it. As their teacher, you will be aware of the children who will require additional support in order to join in such discussion. Some children may need the additional support of a known adult to act as an interpreter; others may need to use picture cards to express preferences.

Children will need opportunities to respond to the work of other artists and designers, both adults and their peers, if they are to become familiar with a variety and range of creative responses.

Taking risks

If the children in your care are to be the risk-takers that this area of learning requires, they will need to feel secure and cared for and to have evidence that their own ideas are valued.

Compare the practice demonstrated in these two classroom stories.

CLASSROOM STORY 1

As part of a topic on transport the practitioner has set up a creative activity. She has set out on the table pre-cut bus shapes complete with cut-out windows, a supply of green paint (the buses in this area have green livery) and a selection of implements for printing in a variety of shapes, circle oblong, star, etc. The children are then invited to 'do some printing on a bus'. The adult then interacts with the children by questioning them on their preferred printing shape and on their experiences of travelling by bus with their families.

CLASSROOM STORY 2

As part of a topic on transport a practitioner has set up a painting table. The children are provided with a range of paints they have assisted in mixing, and a selection of brushes. Pencils and marker pens are also provided. The children are invited to select paper from a range of textures colours and sizes. Around the area there are displayed drawings and photographs of buses and some model buses. Included are some particular photographs taken on a recent visit to the local bus depot. As the children arrive at the table, the adult reminds them about the recent visit. They discuss what they saw in terms of size, shape, and colour. She reminds them as well of the slippery, shiny surface of the bodywork and of the smell of the engines. She talks to them about the photographs, paintings and models set out around the area.

Spend a few moments analysing which of these examples presents the child with the principles enshrined in *All our futures* (DfEE, 1999), which states that creative processes

- always involve behaving and thinking imaginatively;
- overall the imaginative activity is purposeful, directed towards achieving an objective;
- generate something original;
- the outcome must be of value in relation to the objective.

REFLECTIVE TASK

Roxanna has been in your class for a term now. Whenever she is invited to work on a creative activity she becomes tearful. Despite reassurance, her participation always produces an attempt to reproduce the work of another child engaged in the activity. Reflect on the ways you have demonstrated that you value her work for its own originality rather than being a reproduction of something else. Has she worked alongside adults in order to gain first-hand experience of other confident people making a creative response? Are you aware of any specific religious or cultural beliefs her family may hold that relate to particular forms of art? What might you do next to help her to gain confidence in the value of her own creativity?

Exploring media and materials

Children will often respond creatively simply by being stimulated by new materials, sounds and movements. Clearly this has implications for you as a teacher. You will need to be aware of the need to present your learners with the kind of learning environment which provides this type of stimulation. You will need to think about the way your room is organised.

- How do you incorporate new approaches to exploration?
- Does the physical environment appeal to learners; is it colourful, exciting, does it appeal to all the senses, auditory, kinaesthetic and olfactory as well as visual? Does it reflect the range of cultural backgrounds of all the children?
- Do you change the classroom areas regularly? Do you rotate resources regularly?

In order to maintain the children's willingness to respond creatively, you will need to be vigilant in your observation and be prepared to extend and develop the children's responses. As children become more interested in colours, for example, you will need to provide opportunities for colour mixing, while at the same time encouraging them to discuss their preferences, modelling the appropriate technical language: light, dark, pastel, bright, and so forth. Children will need opportunities to:

> *mix colours, join objects, discover new materials, explore skills, concepts and ideas, and have the opportunity to return to their work to enjoy, develop or to refer to. They will need to be able to explore colour, texture, shape, form and space in two and three dimensions.*

(EYFS Practice Guidance)

REFLECTIVE TASK

How will you ensure that the children gain the necessary technical skills and knowledge base? How will you ensure you are able to support individual learners as they make a range of responses to a given starting point?

Creating music and dance

You will need to plan opportunities for children to listen to and respond to music. They also need to have time to create their own music with the use of body sounds, everyday objects, purpose-made instruments and voices. They need to learn how music can be written down and returned to at a later time, and to experience both adult-led music sessions and periods when they are able to extend their understanding through self-initiated activities. Children need opportunities to develop such concepts as sound, rhythm, pitch, tempo, and to become familiar with a range of instruments.

Clearly dance and music will be closely associated. It is vital that you provide opportunities for children to investigate moving to music. They need to experience a wide variety of different music including that from a variety of cultures. They need opportunities to respond both to recorded music and to that which they produce themselves. Dance in the Early Years should explore rhythm, space, direction and height as well as the concepts of speed and duration. Once again children will need opportunities to be involved in adult-led activities as well as self-initiated, and to work individually as well as in large and small groups. (Chapter 8 gives some useful information about the way ICT applications may be used to support the development of creativity.)

A SUMMARY OF **KEY POINTS**

In order for you to extend the creativity of the children in your class, you will need to ensure that:

> **they** are offered a wide range of stimulating experiences based in play;

> **they** feel sufficiently secure and valued for them to take risks;

> **their** religious and cultural beliefs are appropriately accommodated;

> **they** experience working with creative adults;

> **they** have sufficient time to evaluate and revisit and their work.

MOVING *ON* > > > > > > MOVING *ON* > > > > > > MOVING *ON*

As these children move into Year 1, it will be important to them that opportunities to continue to learn creatively remain available. Good communication between all practitioners and between practitioners and parents will help to ensure that this transition between key stages is seamless. As they mature, children might be encouraged to become involved in creative activity outside the school day; for example, lunchtime and after-school clubs focusing on drama or dance.

REFERENCES REFERENCES **REFERENCES** REFERENCES REFERENCES REFERENCES

Aubrey, C. (1994) *The role of subject matter in the early years of schooling*. London: Falmer Press.

Barrett, N. (2006) Creative partnerships: Manchester and Salford: www.ioe.mmu.ac.uk/cue/seminars/BARRETT%20Urban%20seminar1.doc (accessed 10 June, 2007).

Boden, M. (1992) *The creative mind*. London: Abacus.

Carr, M. (2001) *Assessment in early childhood settings: learning stories*. London: Paul Chapman.

Csikszentmihalyi, M. (1992) *Flow: the psychology of happiness*. London: Rider.

DfES (2003) *Every Child Matters*. London: DfES.

DfES (2002) *Researching effective pedagogy in the early years*. London: DfES.

Fisher, R. and Williams, M. (eds) (2004) *Unlocking creativity*. London: David Fulton.

Laevers, F. (2003) *Experiential education: making care and education more effective through wellbeing and involvement*. Leuven: Leuven University/Centre for Research in Early Childhood and Primary Education.

Liptai, S. (2004) Creativity in music and art, in R. Fisher and M. Williams (eds) *Unlocking creativity: teaching across the curriculum*. London: David Fulton.

Meadows, C. and Cashdan, A. (1988) *Helping children learning*. London: David Fulton.

National Advisory Committee on Creative and Cultural Education (NACCCE) (1999) *All our futures: creativity, culture, and education*. London: DfEE.

Schaffer, H.R. (1996) *Social development: an introduction*. Oxford: Blackwell.

Siraj-Blatchford, I. and Sylva, K. (2004). Researching pedagogy in English pre-schools. *British Educational Research Journal*, 30 (5), 713-30.

Sternberg, R.J. (1999) *Handbook of creativity*. Cambridge: Cambridge University Press.

Trevarthen, C. (1995) The child's need to learn a culture. *Children in Society*, 9(1).

FURTHER READING FURTHER READING **FURTHER READING** FURTHER READING

Craft, A. (2002) *Creativity and early years education*. London: Continuum.

Fisher, R. (2003) *Teaching thinking*, (2nd edition). London: Continuum.

4
Physical development, health and well-being
Elaine Hodson and Val Melnyczuk

Chapter objectives

By the end of this chapter you will have an understanding of the importance of the following factors in supporting the physical development of young children:

- **opportunities to be active learners and learn through physical activity across all areas of learning and development;**
- **increasing in confidence;**
- **experiencing the benefits of being healthy and active;**
- **gaining a positive sense of well-being;**
- **building a secure foundation for health and well-being in future life.**

This chapter addresses the following Professional Standards for QTS:

Q14, Q15, Q25 (a), Q25 (b)

The EYFS requirements state (Practice Guidance, p 90):

> *The physical development of babies and young children must be encouraged through the provision of opportunities for them to be active and interactive and to improve their skills of coordination, control, manipulation and movement. They must be supported in using all of their senses to learn about the world around them and to make connections between new information and what they already know. They must be supported in developing an understanding of the importance of physical activity and making healthy choices in relation to food.*

Clear links are evident with the entitlement for children outlined in *Every Child Matters* (see Chapter 1 for detailed discussion) in terms of ensuring that children are being physically active and making healthy lifestyle choices. This makes a significant contribution to staying healthy, having the ability to enjoy life and to achieve, making a positive contribution to both families and communities and, eventually, to achieving economic well-being. Within the primary curriculum there are also clear links, since physical education is one of the foundation subjects of the National Curriculum and issues about establishing a healthy lifestyle are incorporated in the area of PHSE and in the programmes of study for science.

Introduction

By the time young children enter the EYFS they will have changed and developed physically in many ways since birth. Thinking in terms of the of the three strands of physical development covered in the Practice Guidance: movement and space, health and bodily awareness and using equipment and materials, the learners you will be working with will generally have already made significant progress. In terms of movement and space, they will probably be confident about moving in a variety of ways, slithering, sliding, hopping, skipping and so forth. They will probably be able to use movement to express feeling, and negotiate space with others, enabling them to race and chase as they becomes more adept at both changing speed and direction while avoiding obstacles. Balance will be continually improving and it will be becoming easier for them to maintain fixed positions. Operating mechanisms by pushing and pulling will now be easier. Negotiating pathways by running, walking or using a mobility aid is now less challenging, and stairs are beginning to be negotiated using alternate feet. They may be becoming better at negotiating openings, making confined spaces more easily accessible and better able to persevere with physical challenges and to collaborate with others to share physical tasks. In terms of health and bodily awareness, they may now be showing awareness of the physical need for sleep, food and so forth, and be aware of appropriate healthy practices, but will still need adult support to perform those practices and meet those needs. They will probably be developing the ability to reflect on the effects of physical activity on their body. Finally, in terms of using equipment and materials, as hand–eye co-ordination improves, so too does the use of one-handed tools and equip-ment. Understanding of the need for safety is probably developing. The ability to deal with clothing and fastenings may have improved, as may the use of climbing equipment, and the manipulation of small items such as bricks and mark-making tools.

Why is it important to plan for physical development?

Psychologists, building on the work of Piaget, argue that young children have an innate desire to investigate and make sense of their environment. It is this process, they believe, that builds the foundation for learning. In order to investigate the environment, young children need an increasing control over their physical skills. Consider, for example, the following reflective task.

CLASSROOM STORY

As a newly born baby, Grace's physical development is limited. However, as Grace's neck muscles develop and she learns to control her head and neck, she becomes able to direct her gaze more effectively at the objects around her. As she becomes able to support her spine, she can reach out for favourite toys placed close by. Once she crawls, she is no longer dependent on objects being brought to her, but is able to move towards them. Standing and walking, she gains the ability to move freely around her environment, investigating cupboards, chasing the cat, answering the telephone, and so forth, restricted only by the deliberate restrictions imposed by carers, such as stair gates and playpens, or by the natural limits which she has not yet gained sufficient confidence to challenge; for example, a flight of stairs. When she learns to ride a tricycle, Grace becomes able, as far as safety allows, to move beyond the confines of her own home and begin to familiarise herself with the immediate neighbourhood. In a relatively short space of time, physical development has changed: a totally dependent babe-in-arms into a dextrous young child about to become part of a neighbourhood community. Each stage in her physical development has increased her independence and extended her learning environment. As her access to new experiences develops, so her ability to learn is extended.

Now spend some time thinking about the children in your class. Have they all experienced similar opportunities for physical development as Grace, or do some of them still need to progress through earlier stages? (See Practice Guidance, Physical development, Development matters, p92.)

When she arrives in your Early Years setting, it becomes your responsibility to ensure that you continue to offer Grace learning experiences which will build on and extend her skills, regardless of her position on the developmental continuum. Experts differ in their view of the extent to which Grace's ability to learn physical skills is determined by her biological growth, but there is general agreement that all practitioners need to be careful observers in order to spot individuals as they become biologically ready to attain a new skill. It is unlikely, for example, that Grace will have a mature enough sense of balance to be able to hop on one leg much before her fourth birthday. However, if you as her teacher present her with an environment that motivates her, by providing attractive playground markings and an adult model, she will become much more likely to practise, experiment and refine the developing skills she will need to successfully hop on one leg. You will not be surprised, therefore, that opportunities to meet Grace's physical development needs will have a high priority in her early learning. This contrasts with the frequently more restricted position in the primary curriculum. In contrast, the Year 1 child may have her opportunities limited to a timetabled PE lesson and the teacher-free periods of playtime and lunchtime, while the 3–5 year old will have much greater opportunity for physical play, as the holistic nature of the EYFS with its absence of subject hierarchies should facilitate this.

REFLECTIVE TASK

How might the Reception class teacher need to support children at the point of transition as they move into Key Stage 1?

CLASSROOM STORY

As Grace in her first weeks in your Nursery class becomes proficient in climbing to the top of the climbing frame, she will not only improve her ability to balance and support her own weight, but she will also gain a new view of her surroundings which will add to her appreciation of spatial relationships, attach new meaning to language such as 'on top of' and 'beneath', as well as adding to her self-esteem as she succeeds at a new challenge. From Grace's viewpoint, learning is not compartmentalised. She may practise a new song or rhyme as she climbs, recognise part of the climbing frame as a red triangle, like the one she saw in the logic game last week, and finally negotiate with a friend her turn on the slide as she returns to ground level. At the same time, she will experience the sensation of the cold wind whipping her cheeks, and the exhilaration of strenuous effort. The excitement and success of her venture may subsequently become the subject she brings to a discussion in group time later in the day, so giving her further opportunity for learning as she refines her communication skills.

Aside from this philosophical justification, you will be aware that opportunities for large movement and boisterous play are often lacking in our modern society. Homes may have inadequate space and carers may be reluctant to allow young children to play in outdoor areas where supervision is more difficult. You will know already that young children need opportunities to 'let off steam' and to move spontaneously as and when energy bursts occur.

They then need to be free to withdraw and to rest. This is not a requirement which sits easily with a rigorously timetabled day, and needs careful thought. Finally, as an early years teacher, you will be planning to develop the vital positive attitude to physical activity and a healthy lifestyle that Grace will need in order to become a healthy and active adult.

RESEARCH SUMMARY RESEARCH SUMMARY **RESEARCH SUMMARY** RESEARCH SUMMARY

Reference has already been made to the Piagetian view that young children are active learners. This concept has been developed and refined by later psychologists such as Bruner, Schaffer and Wood, who have each carried out research attempting to more clearly establish this process. Equally important has been Vygotsky's view that while children are indeed active learners, they do not learn in isolation, but from the relationships they have with those around them. Although some theorists are concerned that this research was all based in the Northern/minority world, (Davies et al., 2003), and is culturally specific, it has certainly contributed to the thinking underlying the EYFS.

More recent research into brain development has lent further evidence to the notion of links between all areas of learning. In normally developing humans the body cannot be divorced from the developing brain.

> We are born with the ability to discover the secrets of the universe and of our own minds, and drive to explore and experiment until we do.

(Gopnik et al., 1999, p3)

Technological advances in the past 25 years have enabled scientists to study the way the brain develops in young children, and consequently, its impact on intellectual development. It is becoming increasingly clear that the 'nature/nurture' debate is becoming obsolete, and that the development of each individual is dependent on the interaction between biological and environmental factors. Barnet and Barnet (1998) speak of 'a lifelong dialogue between inherited tendencies and our life history'. Consequently, the level of physical activity experienced by each individual will have a clear relationship to the child's life experiences, and bring a strong impact to bear on their capacity for intellectual development. Therefore, the interlinking of all areas of development means it is important for you to appreciate the way in which this may be happening. While newborn babies are defenceless and highly dependent on care givers, they are born with a range of reflexes which form the bases of later physical abilities. Their hearing is sensitive, resulting in sound being a source of stimulus (even before birth). Sight is less acute and is best at about 20 to 25 centimetres. But a highly developed sense of smell allows the baby to identify their own mother's milk. Early movements of arms and legs, although appearing random, provide practice and strengthen muscles. The development of physical control, supporting the head, sitting, standing and walking, all contribute to brain wiring, and exploration allows the production of mental maps of their physical space. Physical activity in young children allows children to begin to see the world from different perspectives (Karmilloff-Smith, 1994).

REFLECTIVE TASK

Adnan is a child in your class with some mobility problems caused by the malformation of one leg. While he is able to move around the classroom, his progress is slow and laborious. He does, however, enjoy being outdoors. What might you do to ensure Adnan maximises his opportunities for physical development in your Reception class and that his all-round development is catered for to the same level as Grace's?

Physically, young children develop from head to toe (cephalo-caudal development), from inner to outer (proximo-distal development) and from simple to complex (Bruce et al., 2006).

This means that children's heads and upper bodies mature more quickly than their lower bodies, and their internal organs more quickly than their hands and feet. While children of four or five years of age may be able to control their body movements more than a toddler, they have much less control over their movements than a child in Key Stage 2. It is not, therefore, surprising that Robin, asked to stop, stand up straight in front of the PE equipment and listen to the next instruction, loses his balance suddenly and falls over sideways, nor that he is very embarrassed by his 'failure' to do as the teacher has just asked, and fights hard against making an impolite response to her.

Within this general pattern, girls and boys develop at differing rates, with girls being born physically more mature and tending to continue this pattern. As children develop from the simple actions through to the more complex, they learn to walk before they can run and stand before they can climb. Gross motor skills generally develop at an earlier stage than fine motor skills, so one can expect a child in the final year of the EYFS to walk, run, jump and climb reasonably well but his/her ability to hold a pencil or use scissors to cut paper remains less refined. Evidence that performing physical tasks requires young children to apply a great deal of concentration can be seen in their working with tongues sticking out, and their turning material around to cut it. Similarly, they may find it difficult to use their hands and fingers without moving their feet and legs. This often results in early writing activities being accompanied by banging feet and swaying chairs!

Clearly adult sensitivity is paramount in encouraging children as they face physical challenges. Support may be necessary to maintain motivation, or an opportunity extended for a child who becomes totally absorbed in an activity. Children need to be given opportunities to develop their skills by repeating their actions. This repetition allows the neurons in the brain to connect and strong pathways to be developed until, eventually, everyday actions such as brushing hair, or eating food, become automatic. When a child has mastered a skill they may become playful with it, as illustrated below.

CLASSROOM STORY

During a family den-building day at the local children's centre, Zobeda, aged four years and three months, was seen to struggle using the masking tape while trying to fix two poles together. A sensitive family support worker helped her to achieve her goal by holding the poles together and encouraging Zobeda to tear the tape and entwine it around the poles. Pleased with her efforts, Zobeda repeated the process over and over until she and the family support worker made a very proficient team at constructing the structures for the material to be draped over to make dens. At school the next week, her class teacher observed Zobeda using masking tape to wrap around the railings in the playground connecting the poles together and making 'ladders'; she was playfully extending her learning using the new physical skills she had mastered by tearing and wrapping masking tape around poles.

As discussed earlier, the physical area of learning and development in the Practice Guidance for EYFS is divided into three aspects: movement and space, health and bodily awareness, and using equipment and materials. You will need to develop your understanding of the requirements in each of these areas in order to meet the standards for QTS. You will also need to understand the Early Learning Goals which are associated with this area, which state:

by the end of the Reception year most children should be able to:
- *move with confidence, imagination and safety;*
- *move with control and co-ordination;*
- *show an awareness of space, of themselves and of others;*
- *recognise the importance of keeping healthy and those things that contribute to this;*
- *recognise the changes that happen to their bodies when they are active;*
- *use a range of small and large equipment;*
- *travel around, under, over and through balancing and climbing equipment;*
- *handle tools, objects, construction and malleable materials safely and with increasing control.*

(QCA, 1999 p11)

Movement and space

The aspects of development theory outlined earlier demonstrate how important it is that you provide appropriate activities for the children in your care. The children you are planning for will need opportunities to develop their gross motor skills through making large movements. They will need large equipment which they can move co-operatively and use in an open-ended way, such as large blocks which will present opportunities to explore ways of moving on, off and across objects in an increasingly controlled manner. In order to meet the full range of abilities it will be important that you provide different levels of challenge such as equipment at different heights, and wheeled vehicles with two or three wheels and some without pedals. You will of course need to check all resources are safely erected and safely maintained. The children will need to learn the language which accompanies these activities, such as 'slide', 'slither', 'leap', 'follow' and 'lead', the vocabulary that expresses the associated emotions – excited, scared, happy – and also to name the body parts they are using and the actions they are performing, such as 'stretch', 'reach' and 'curl'. Incorporating action rhymes and songs will support this, as will introducing imaginative experiences based on stories such as *The Gingerbread Man* or *Three Billy Goats Gruff*. You will need to support them as they build movements into series and use movements to express feelings and ideas. They will also need help to understand the impact of their movements on others, the need for space and the recognition of safety considerations. You might plan games involving throwing, catching and using skills in different ways; for example, hopping, striding or moving sideways. Clearly, in order for some of this to happen you will need a large indoor or outdoor space, and allow sufficient time for children to become immersed in chosen activities. Here, as in any other teaching area, you will need to remain aware of the important principles of incorporating observation, balancing child-initiated learning with adult-focused activities, and offering individuals opportunities to plan, return to activities, repeat and review their ideas, to work alone and to work with others. You will also need to think carefully about how you will intervene and extend learning, employ additional adults, and provide differentiated experiences, not least for those children requiring modified equipment. The role of the adult during active play is discussed in Chapter 1. It is most important that you are generous with your encouragement, always approaching children sensitively and with appropriate offers of support.

The following is a list of suggested materials and equipment, which you might provide:

large construction equipment; drainage pipes for rolling balls down; streamers to run with and catch in the wind; bikes and scooters; dolls' buggies; push-along carts that allow children to transport objects or each other; natural materials; large paint brushes and buckets/containers with water to paint the walls or fence; large chalk boards with large chalks; whiteboards with chunky felt-tip pens; bean bags; climbing apparatus to climb, balance on or to hang from; cardboard boxes in a variety of sizes; rolls of wallpaper to spread along the ground or to pin to a wall for painting and other forms of mark-making; a large sandpit that children can climb into.

Health and bodily awareness

Good health in the early years helps to safeguard health and well-being throughout life.

(EYFS, 2007, p90)

It is important to make mealtimes and snack times social occasions where adults join children to eat and drink. A relaxed atmosphere encouraging conversation while eating and providing nutritious and healthy meals or snacks will promote good eating habits. Mealtimes that become anxious affairs where children feel pressurised can turn into a battle of wills and should be avoided. Younger children sitting with older children and/or an adult will often follow their lead. Young children may need help to manage their cutlery and may require assistance to cut their food, but at the same time they should be encouraged in their desire to be independent; therefore it is important that adults provide appropriate 'tools' for eating. Consider how difficult it is to eat jelly with a thick plastic spoon that neither cuts the jelly nor allows a child whose manipulative skills are still developing, to scoop the slippery jelly up and then manoeuvre the wobbly spoonful into their mouths – a child accomplishing this tricky feat deserves an accolade! You will also need to take careful account of family and cultural backgrounds when promoting independent eating. Encouraging children to choose their own plate, cutlery or cup, pour drinks and mop up any spillages themselves promotes independence, develops fine motor skills and gives children a real sense of achievement and social responsibility. Discussion with parents and carers may help you to provide sensitively for a child unused to manipulating a knife and fork.

Practitioners within schools may, quite justifiably, feel they have little control over food provided, as it is either cooked within the school kitchen, delivered to the school or brought from home. Positive relationships with parents, and kitchen staff, supported by senior leadership, are important if health issues are to be taken seriously and form an integral part of providing for children's learning and development.

However, even children who may have become very confident about managing their own eating and drinking needs when at nursery or pre-school, may find the challenge of eating in a large school hall very daunting. This may lead to a lack of confidence in their abilities and cause unnecessary stress. Primary schools with Nurseries and Reception classes need to think very carefully about the arrangements they make for their very young children during lunchtimes. The EYFS brings together care, education and welfare requirements for children up to the age of six years, and it may be these practical considerations that require the thought and adjustment to ensure children do not take a backward step in their development during the transition from their pre-school experience into school.

In addition to a healthy diet and vigorous exercise, young children need adequate rest. Vigorous activity, particularly outside in the fresh air, makes young children tired. You will need to ensure you provide a learning environment which can facilitate periods of rest and recuperation both indoors and out. All children will need access to fresh water, and some may need a chance to recover if they become breathless.

Using equipment and materials

An important part of developing physical control for humans has been an ability to manage their environment through the use of tools and equipment. As our youngest children begin to take their places within our culture, adults have an expectation that their mastery of tool use will improve. In our Northern/minority world, these young children grow up in a society heavily dependent on tools. In order to obtain a degree of independence, they will need to learn to manage their own clothing and fastenings. They will also need to develop sufficient fine motor control to use one-handed tools such as scissors and knives, and at the same time begin to understand how these can be used safely. Similarly, they will use the same knowledge and skills to develop their mark-making ability, and the ability to manipulate other small objects such as those found in small world equipment. As their teacher, you will need to find ways to motivate and support children as they rise to these physical challenges. As discussed earlier, physical activity can be highly challenging and engender a high level of frustration. If children are to persist in their efforts, you will need to ensure that the activities you provide are stimulating and motivating. For example, a child struggling to hold a mark-making tool is more likely to persist if the level of challenge is reasonable, and the tools appropriate. You might offer a large felt marker rather than an adult sized pen, a wallpaper pasting brush instead of a standard paint brush. The results will need to be sufficiently rewarding for the effort demanded, producing a vivid thick line rather than a grey pencil line, for example; and you will need to offer genuine targeted praise to produce the motivation for him/her to continue with the task. Remember also that achieving control over large objects, such as a bat or ball, will impact on controlling smaller objects, necessitating that all children are involved in as wide a range of physical activities as possible. You will need to extend these considerations of physical challenge to ICT equipment. Some children will need more support to succeed with fine, highly specific movements. Often ICT equipment can be technically modified; for example, by adjusting the speed of the mouse, or the size of the font on a screen, or even the height of a workstation or chair (see Chapter 8 for more discussion of this).

You will need to maintain a balance between offering opportunities to practise skills; for example the use of scissors, and teaching the learner the skill itself. Both aspects are of equal importance to ultimate success, as is providing the appropriate vocabulary, such as snip, tear, and so forth. Of course you will need to give extra support to any child who is physically challenged; for example, spasticity can affect grip. Rubber tubing can be fixed to cutlery, or specially designed pencils can help to alleviate this. Left-handed scissors will also be useful. At the same time you will need to think about how activities might be differentiated in order to maintain high self-esteem. Children who struggle with manipulative tasks need achievable success criteria, and not to be the one who always struggles. You might consider planning an activity based on tearing instead of cutting for all the children to participate in, thereby allowing less able users of scissors to merge with the rest of the group.

CLASSROOM STORY

Annabelle is four years old. She has special educational needs caused by her cerebral palsy. Movement in her legs is more adversely affected than in her arms and hands. She is very short-sighted and wears glasses, but will still peer closely at objects and bend towards them. She is also very petite, so struggles with large and small equipment. Sometimes her peers are overprotective and fuss around her. Her parents are concerned that she will soon be moving into the Reception class at the primary school and believe that she should be beginning to write. They would like Annabelle to have worksheets to complete at home to practise writing.

What programme of activities might you design for Annabelle that her parents might work with at home, based on the principles outlined above?

Opportunities to handle malleable materials are important on many levels. They are very attractive to children and tend to promote extended periods of concentration, develop imagination, creativity and language use, while at the same time developing manipulative skills. It is important that you provide variety to attract a range of children. You might think about texture, colour, fragrance, where the activity is sited and its scale, and the tools you are providing to work the material. Remember, also, that if this work is to have value in the children's eyes, you will need to be involved, modelling and developing the learning, and avoid the temptation to leave manipulative activities always as self-directed.

Listed below is a range of natural and manufactured materials you might provide in your classroom:

> rice, sand, lentils with small spoons/scoops and small containers to fill; gloop, play dough; strips of material/ribbon to weave; scissors; glue; paper in a variety of sizes and shapes; hole punch; stapler; masking tape; paint; water; small world toys; small construction; train sets and cars.

A SUMMARY OF **KEY POINTS**

In order for you to encourage the children in your class to be active, develop their skills of co-ordination, control, manipulation and movement, and make healthy choices about lifestyle, you will need to ensure that you provide:

> **opportunities for them to be active learners and learn through physical activity across all areas of learning and development;**

> **experiences which lead to an increase in confidence;**

> **experiences that show the benefits of being healthy and active;**

> **opportunities for children gain a positive sense of well-being and begin to build a secure foundation for health and well being in future life.**

MOVING *ON* > > > > > > MOVING *ON* > > > > > > MOVING *ON*

The Primary Curriculum, the children in your care move on to, may provide fewer opportunities for physical activity than they have enjoyed in the EYFS. You will need to support them as they move through the transition to Year 1, and make them and their parents aware of extracurricular activities they might participate in; for example before-school or lunchtime fitness clubs, and school sports teams as well as out-of-school groups such as Rainbows and Beavers. You might also support transition by participating in curriculum development activities which promote more opportunities for physical activity in Key Stage 1.

REFERENCES REFERENCES **REFERENCES** REFERENCES REFERENCES REFERENCES

Barnet, A. and Barnet, R. (1998) *The youngest minds: parenting and genes in the Development of Intellect and Emotion.* New York: Simon and Schuster.

Bruce, T., Meggitt, C. and Walker, J. (2006) *Childcare and Education.* London: Hodder Headline Group.

Davies, T., Goouch, K., Powell, S. and Abbott, L. (2003) *Birth to three matters: a review of the literature.* Research report 444. Nottingham: DfES.

Department for Education and Skills (2007) *Early Years Foundation Stage.* London: DfES.

Gopnik, A., Meltzoff, A. and Kuhl, P. (1999), *How babies think.* London: Weidenfeld and Nicholson.

Karmiloff-Smith, A. (1994) *Baby it's you.* London: Ebury Press.

FURTHER READING FURTHER READING **FURTHER READING** FURTHER READING

Bee, H. and Boyd, D. (2007) *The Developing Child* (11th edition). Boston: Pearson Education, Inc.

Bilton, H. (2002) *Outdoor play in the early years: management and innovation.* London: David Fulton.

Lindon, J. (1993) *Child Development from Birth to Eight – A Practical Focus.* London: National Children's Bureau.

Office of the Deputy Prime Minister (2006) *Developing Accessible Play Space – A Good Practice Guide.* London: Department for Communities and Local Government.

Useful websites

www.jabadao.org
www.ltl.org.uk
www.teachernet.gov.uk
www.activeplaces.com
www.nurturegroups.org
www.everychildmatters.org.uk
www.healthystart.nhs.uk
www.CommunityPlaythings.co.uk

5
Problem-solving, reasoning and numeracy
Norma Marsh and Wendy Baker

Chapter objectives

By the end of this chapter you should:

- **understand the ideas that underpin a relevant mathematical experiences for children in the Early Years Foundation Stage as embodied in the Early Learning Goals;**
- **be aware of ways in which you, as a practitioner, can best support children's mathematical development;**
- **have access to a range of appropriate starting points for activities that encourage development across problem solving, reasoning and numeracy areas of learning experiences;**
- **understand some of the difficulties children may encounter and mistakes they may make;**
- **appreciate the contribution of play as the cornerstone of good provision;**
- **have insights into the planning process for mathematics.**

This chapter addresses the following Professional Standards for QTS:
Q14, Q15, Q23

Introduction

The traditional view of children's mathematical development as a gradual and staged progression from a state of total ignorance to an acceptable level of competence was firmly rooted in the adult perception of competence. Children's earliest efforts at number mastery were therefore measured in terms of their failure to match up to adult expectations. More recent thinking based on developmental psychology and research has concentrated on examining what children can do rather than what they cannot. It is now recognised that right from birth, babies respond to people and objects around them and notice changes in groupings. As soon as they begin to reach towards a person or object, babies are beginning to explore shape and space. By the age of two, many have gained awareness of some number names through joining in with action rhymes and songs.

Carol Aubrey's ongoing project at the University of Durham (1997) has highlighted the levels of mathematical knowledge that children can have on entry to the Reception class, and supports earlier work by Gelman and Gallistel (1978), Starkey (1987) and others. What we now have is the realisation that children, on entering the Nursery, possess a wide range of mathematical abilities and competences based on their existing understanding. As practitioners, our role is to create the right enabling environment, physically, mentally and emotionally, where all children's beliefs will be challenged, their unique opinions and abilities valued and their progress, to the next stage of understanding supported.

This approach will lead to a very different kind of provision. Indeed to the untrained eye it may not appear to be mathematics at all. Rather than teaching mathematics we need to think in terms of encouraging children to participate in activities that allow them to develop problem-solving skills, reasoning skills and begin to develop early numeracy skills. What does that involve? What do mathematicians do?

The nature of mathematics

Calculation is a very important part of mathematics but it is by no means the whole story. Essentially, mathematicians can be seen as people who are striving to understand and make sense of the world and all that it contains. Nature is full of mathematical patterns and shapes and even the weather and other natural and social phenomena can be explained in terms of mathematical theories. Teachers need to be confident in their own understanding of what constitutes mathematical behaviour – otherwise how will they recognise it in others? Mathematical behaviour involves:

- problem-solving;
- investigating;
- collecting data;
- working systematically;
- searching for patterns and links;
- identifying possible cause and effect;
- thinking logically;
- developing explanations;
- convincing yourself and then others;
- developing reasoning skills.

Your task as the teacher is three-fold. The environment you provide, and that includes the personnel, has to be capable of:

- scaffolding children's interpretation of the world through their own experiences, to illuminate mathematical ideas and concepts;
- allowing/encouraging the development of mathematical competence from a sound foundation of experience-based understanding;
- supporting the development of mathematical language.

Play

Mathematical experience offered to children in the Foundation Stage must be relevant and appropriate to their emotional, physical, social and cultural needs as well as being challenging and absorbing. The most appropriate context for this is through play. Without pressure, they further develop and reinforce the very important attitudes acquired from birth to three years that will influence their capability and future approach to education.

- resilience;
- confidence;
- self-assurance.

Mathematical experiences

Whichever area of mathematics is the focus there are three main ways in which you can plan for children's learning.

- You can plan a specific mathematical activity for a child to undertake either individually or in a small group under the direction of an adult.
- You can set up/structure an area of the room, e.g. shop, model-making, so that play will expose children to mathematical ideas, where an adult can intervene to extend the learning.
- You can provide equipment for freely chosen play that encourages certain mathematical concepts. Child-initiated play is of fundamental importance if we are to enable children to develop as independent active learners. The more opportunities we provide for free play, the more children develop skills as decision-makers, taking on responsibilities for steering their own learning. This is a very exciting aspect of learning but can be rather daunting for some teachers as you cannot plan for those moments where the exact opportunity to intervene and extend the thinking of the children occurs. Such spontaneous learning occurs all the time and good Foundation Stage teachers are ever alert to these opportunities.

Breadth of experience

All areas in the setting, from the outdoor play area to the book corner, have the potential to trigger mathematical learning. There are no subject boundaries for the young learner – the extent of your imagination as an innovative provider is the only limit on their experience.

PRACTICAL TASK PRACTICAL TASK **PRACTICAL TASK** PRACTICAL TASK **PRACTICAL TASK**

Think about the sand tray. When children are busy playing, what mathematical experiences are they encountering? How do these differ if the sand is wet/dry? How would you intervene to encourage an understanding of positional language?

Scaffolding children's learning

As in all areas of Early Years provision, knowing what experiences to offer to which children, at what point in time, is crucial for effective learning. For this reason, careful observation and monitoring of children's achievement forms the foundation for informed and appropriate activities. All members of staff need time to observe children in order to keep formative records up to date for use in planning.

The Early Learning Goals

These set out clearly the learning outcomes that children should have achieved by the time they transfer to the Key Stage 1 classroom. They are intended to be the end points, and the Practice Guidance for the Early Years Foundation Stage booklet, provided as part of the EYFS package, breaks these down further to help teachers and other Early Years practitioners to keep track of progress to this end point. It is fundamental to note that children all learn and develop in different ways and at different rates. All the areas of learning and development are of equal importance and are all interconnected. Problem-solving, reasoning and numeracy skills complement and are complemented by all of the other areas of learning and development; nothing is developed or learnt in isolation.

The Early Learning Goals are separated into three groups under the headings:

number – number as labels and for counting;
calculating;
shape, space and measures.

Number

By the end of the Foundation Stage, children should be able to:

- say and use number names in order in familiar contexts;
- count reliably up to ten everyday objects;
- recognise numerals 1 to 9;
- use developing mathematical ideas and methods to solve practical problems.

As adults, we are so accustomed to the notion of number and it fits so naturally into our lives that it is difficult to appreciate the enormity of the task facing young learners. Number is an abstract concept. It takes a vast range of experiences with, for example, two legs, two toys, two cakes, two shoes, two animals, two friends, etc., to reach the realisation that there is a similarity between all of these very different groupings. What's more, this similarity has nothing to do with the objects you are handling but with the quantity of them that you have.

Only after this realisation can any number on its own begin to mean something to the young learner. In addition to this, children need time to acquire a range of skills and ideas that will help them to make sense of and manipulate numbers with confidence. They will need to:

- hear, distinguish and remember the spoken number names;
- count confidently according to the principles (see below);
- recognise 'quantity' in a range of contexts;
- apply this knowledge to a range of situations;
- understand the conservation of number;
- understand the significance of the written symbol;
- write the symbols;
- understand, read and write the number word.

Gelman's principles of counting

Research into the understanding of number led to the identification of a set of principles that govern successful mastery of counting. Of the five principles, the first three relate to the 'How' aspect of counting and the last two to the 'What' aspect.

1. The stable order principle. The recognition that there is a set order to the words that have to be used in the counting procedure.

2. The one–one principle. The procedure for 'tagging' each number word in turn to an object to be counted. In the early stages of counting, children physically move objects as they are counted. This develops through touching to pointing and then to nodding the head in order to keep track of the count.

3. The cardinal principle. The knowledge that the final number you say as you count a set of objects actually tells you how many there are in the set.

4. The abstraction principle. The understanding that counting is a skill that can be applied to any objects, seen or unseen, in any context.

5. The order-irrelevance principle. The order of counting objects in a set does not matter as long as the three 'how to count' principles are applied.

(Gelman and Gallistel, 1978)

Common difficulties experienced by children in relation to these principles

Gelman's principles	Common difficulties
The stable order principle	Children can adhere to this principle and still not arrive at an accurate count. The order of words they use may always be the same but it might not be the correct sequence. In other words, their application of the knowledge is correct but the knowledge itself has flaws.
The one–one principle	Children may: • miss out an object; • tag an object twice; • tag as many objects as there are syllables in the number name, e.g. se'ven.
The cardinal principle	The situation often arises where a child is engaged in counting yet, if asked to say how many there are, will respond, not with a numerical answer, but by starting the count again.
The abstraction principle	Because of the way in which tasks are presented, children sometimes gain the impression that only like things can be counted.
The order-irrelevance principle	Although this may seem self-evident, those who work with young children are aware of the difficulties children have with this aspect of counting. It is extremely difficult for them to keep a track of the tagging when they are not progressing in a logical way through the set of objects.

As teachers, your task will be to capitalise on all opportunities to use the language of number and encourage children to take part in activities that help them to achieve the above.

REFLECTIVE TASK

Although there are eight farm animals in front of him, Omar insists that there are seven. Why might he think this? What errors might he be making? How will you find out? What will you ask him? If you watch his response to tasks you set, what will you be looking for? How are you going to respond in order to help him make progress with counting?

Issues to consider

1. Some number names are in general use within the language either as whole words, e.g. 'to' (2), 'for' (4) or as parts of words e.g. 'tend' (10), 'once' (1), and children need to become aware of the particular mathematical significance of these.
2. There is often a mismatch between the particular idea of counting (which is most usually 'saying the number names in order') and the notion of counting as a process that enables you to find the answer to the question 'how many'? The purpose of counting is often not recognised by young children, (Munn, 1997).
3. Children often have a knowledge of numbers used purely as labels – bus, house and telephone numbers, for example.

PRACTICAL TASK PRACTICAL TASK **PRACTICAL TASK** PRACTICAL TASK **PRACTICAL TASK**

How many songs and rhymes that incorporate numbers or ideas of quantity do you know? Begin now to make a collection of these. Can you alter the words of well-known songs to include number words? Or write new words to familiar tunes?

The following are some ideas of activities that encourage children to acquire the necessary number sense.

Linking the spoken/written number to the quantity

In response to a spoken/written number, children:

- show a number of fingers;
- place a number of objects on a plate;
- collect a number of small objects in a basket, bowl, etc.;
- perform a number of actions (jumps, claps, etc.).

Initially you will model these for children. Through repetition they will become able to respond independently.

Linking the sound to the symbol/numeral

- Use the symbol in conjunction with the spoken word so that children begin to associate the two.
- Discuss and describe the symbols with and to children.
- Use a variety of numerals (e.g. wooden, magnetic, tactile) to encourage children to handle and become familiar with the shapes. Always link to the number name.
- Use a washing line with the numbers pinned up in order. Refer to these when counting orally, singing number songs, etc.
- Use a 'naughty' puppet to alter the numbers while children have their eyes closed. Turn numerals upside down, remove one, progressing to more complex tasks like swapping numerals as the children gain in expertise.
- Use digit cards, so, as you speak the number, children show the correct card.
- Use smiley/sad faces or thumbs-up/thumbs-down responses from the children to agree/disagree as you show a number card/speak the number word.

List the ways in which you could include these activities within the daily routines of the Foundation Stage setting. Decide what practical problems you could set for children that would encourage them to use number skills.

How might you incorporate this into outdoor play?

The child who has had access to a range of experiences such as those detailed above, through adult-initiated, shared activities and in free and structured play contexts will be well on the way towards a sound understanding of numbers. But again, that is not the whole picture.

The number line

There is another aspect of number that contributes greatly to number awareness, and that is ordinality. This hinges on knowing where numbers lie in relation to each other and work on the number line should form a significant part of children's experience once they recognise the number symbols.

The line can be thought of as the written equivalent of intransitive counting. This is the kind of counting where number names are said in order, but with no idea of a particular quantity attached; for example, counting to ten before you go and find someone in 'Hide and seek'. Confidence and competence in using a number line underpins the development of many calculation strategies.

Early activities

Use a number track that is large enough for children to stand on and move along. Before children recognise the numerals, a line with coloured spots or pictures can be used. Children become familiar with the format through taking part in activities where they are invited to:

- choose a particular spot/picture to start on;
- take a given number of steps;
- find out which other spot/picture they land on.

Once they begin to recognise the symbols, asking children to stand on a particular number and displaying that number on a card helps them to match the symbol to the sound and to the position on the track. They could also use cards with spots on and match those to a 'spotty' track initially and later to the number track.

This can progress to giving the number cards to children and asking them to organise either numbers along a blank track or themselves into a line. Once they have mastered the problem of forming a line, there is the opportunity to ask questions and work on activities that will help children to acquire a mental image of the line that will help with calculations.

The development of visual imagery in mathematics is very important. It is the pictures formed inside your head that help to make sense of the information given. Children do need to practise this and games that involve closing eyes and thinking about something will all help; for example, the teacher asks children to think about two of something – then asks a child to say what he/she can see. All children are then encouraged to picture this.

Calculating

- In practical activities and discussion begin to use the vocabulary involved in addition and subtraction.
- Use language such as 'more' or 'less' to compare two numbers.
- Find one more or one less than a number from 1 to 10.
- Begin to relate addition to combining two groups of objects and subtraction as 'taking away'.

Calculating is a natural progression from counting and you should take every opportunity to provide children with practical challenges and problems that allow them to use their developing skills, whatever their level of expertise. The more purpose there is to acquiring skills, the more readily they are learnt.

PRACTICAL TASK PRACTICAL TASK **PRACTICAL TASK** PRACTICAL TASK **PRACTICAL TASK**

What is the language of addition and subtraction?

How many words can you think of that could be included here?

Check your list against the appropriate vocabulary list in the Primary National Strategy.

Mathematical language

Children need to understand concepts in language that is meaningful to them. Once understanding has been established (and this will happen only after many and varied practical experiences), the mathematical terminology can be introduced. As an Early Years practitioner you will need to be a careful listener and skilful negotiator of the possible gaps between their understanding and your meaning, and vice versa.

Observation

The idea of 'less' as the inverse of 'more' is often alien to children. Within their experience the opposite of more, as in 'Can I have some more?', is much more likely to be 'No' or 'No more' or 'None left'. The Practice Guidance for the EYFS stresses the need for practical activities and this is what you should aim for. In the context of games, free play and routines, initiate discussions where quantities are questioned. Use songs like 'Ten green bottles' and 'Five speckled frogs' to introduce ideas of 'one less' and 'taking away'.

Set up outdoor activities where children can throw bean bags into buckets, or knock down skittles and be required to work out their score.

Use snack times to give experience of sharing and needing one more chair or two more pieces of apple, etc.

Play circle games like 'The farmer's in his den' to keep running totals and emphasise the idea of 'one more'.

Extending number line activities

Encourage the use of 'and one more step takes me to ...?' as you or a chosen child move along the line (either a track on the floor, or children holding numbers). Ask, 'What happens if we move the other way along the line?' Once the line has been formed with children holding the number cards, you can begin to set the watching children challenges; for example, 'Can you swap with the person who is holding a number that is more than 5?' '...less than 8?' Progress to 'one more than/one less than' or even 'two/three more/less than' depending on the ability of the children. This is an activity that all children can take part in and achieve success.

Another line of questioning can be based on 'If you start on ___ and move on three more, where will you be?' This forms a practical foundation for the strategy of 'counting on' which comes later.

During activities with children it is tempting to stress words like 'altogether' when adding and 'left' when subtracting. Try to avoid using these words too often as they can become so interrelated with the processes in the children's minds that they listen exclusively for these triggers to identify the mathematics that is needed to solve a problem. This can be a difficulty when they encounter word problems later in their schooling.

PRACTICAL TASK PRACTICAL TASK **PRACTICAL TASK** PRACTICAL TASK **PRACTICAL TASK**

The outdoor area is set up as a garden centre. Make a list of the resources you might need to ensure an inviting and stimulating learning environment.

What opportunities could there be for the children to experience 'addition'?

REFLECTIVE TASK

The above experience is an example of structuring the environment in order to enable independent learning. Think about how this can be enhanced through the support of an adult. Identify two different roles that the adult might adopt in this scenario. What impact would each of these have on the children's learning?

Shape, space and measures

- Use language such as 'greater', 'smaller', 'heavier', 'lighter' to compare quantities.
- Talk about, recognise and re-create simple patterns.
- Use language such as 'circle' or 'bigger' to describe the shape and size of solids and flat shapes.
- Use everyday words to describe position.
- Use developing mathematical ideas and methods to solve practical problems.

Measuring experiences

At this stage, measurement is by direct comparison and it is through the refinement of this activity and the increasingly particular vocabulary used that you will extend children's knowledge. Most children will enter the Nursery with the basic measurement language of 'big' and 'small'. It will be your task to devise scenarios and challenges that will extend this to cover such attributes as length, height, width, weight, girth, etc., and to encompass comparative language rather than simple classification. The outdoor area provides a useful environment for introducing larger scale measuring.

Such activities should always take place in relevant contexts and be accompanied by the appropriate language. You will have to model this use of language for them.

Experiences with pattern

The identification of patterns is an important mathematical skill and one that contributes significantly to the problem-solving process. Being able to recognise a pattern, a repetition of something familiar, depends on the skill of distinguishing between things that are the same in some way and those that are different. Early sorting experiences, many of which may occur prior to starting in the Nursery, involve children in sorting objects according to particular criteria or shared attributes. In this way they learn to discriminate between objects and focus on particular features of the object.

Issues to consider
- Children will often ask, 'Do you like my pattern?', when what they really have is a design. How will you respond?
- The notion of a 'repeating pattern' may be a new idea that you will have to introduce.
- Bead threading, while it can be based on pattern-making, is not a particularly relevant or challenging mathematical activity.

Contexts for pattern-making include:

- clapping games;
- action rhymes such as 'the hokey cokey';
- printing at the art table or in sand;
- follow-my-leader games;
- big shapes on the floor;
- 'people' patterns, e.g. stand, sit, stand, sit . . .

Verbalise the patterns for the children so they can hear as well as see the repetition. Plan for a progression from recognising the patterns in the early stages, through being able to follow on the pattern, to being able to create patterns of increasing complexity.

CLASSROOM STORY
Jen, aged four years two months, spent much of her time playing with the pattern blocks. She started with simple repeating patterns but quickly moved to patterns with bilateral symmetry and then on to designs with rotational symmetry. At the same time, Katie gained equal satisfaction from filling every hole in a pegboard with a coloured peg to make 'lovely patterns'.

Experiencing shapes

The focus here is on the properties of shapes rather than just learning to name any particular shape. Through building, stacking, rolling, sliding and handling shapes of all kinds children will begin to acquire a sense of what exactly constitutes any given shape. Which comes first – 2-D or 3-D shapes? Since 2-D shapes exist only as faces on the 3-D shape or as drawings on a page, I would tend to introduce the language for the two at the same time, but the practical and physical activity that the child has will be through interaction with solid shapes during construction play and while playing on the large apparatus outdoors.

Issues to consider
- Children often internalise irrelevant features as important, e.g. orientation.
- For this reason you should vary the way you present shapes to children.

CLASSROOM STORY

During story time, I became aware that the children were whispering the names of various shapes that appeared on the cover of the book. I abandoned the story and we looked at the shapes. They identified the circle, the square, the oblong and the triangle that appeared as in Figure 5.1.

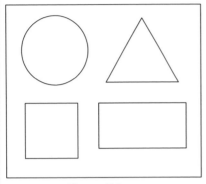

Figure 5.1

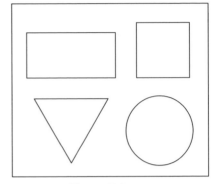

Figure 5.2

I turned the book through 180° and asked again about the shapes (see Figure 5.2). Square, circle and oblong were named immediately, but there was no further response. 'What about this?' I asked, indicating the remaining shape. Still no response. However, Stuart was looking uncomfortable. 'Yes, Stuart?' I inquired. 'Well, if it was the other way up it would be a triangle but ...', he shrugged.

● Children see shapes holistically; they do not understand that the properties define the shape.

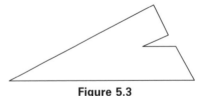

Figure 5.3

For this reason they see Figure 5.3 as a triangle with 'a bite out' (Josh, 4y 1m) or 'with its mouth open' (Annie, 3y 11m).

The thin plastic shapes that are often used as '2-D' are in fact 3-D. Use sticks/string, etc., to outline the shapes on the floor. Children can be set challenges to make as many different shapes as they can using a box of straight sticks of different lengths. Children are much less likely to develop the misconception that a 'proper triangle' is the equilateral one (so often used in illustrations) if they have created a series of triangles for themselves as part of a game called 'Take three sticks'.

Use feelie-bags with shapes hidden inside to encourage children to talk about what they can feel. Use language that the children will understand, such as

'point'   (you can put your finger on it);
'edge'   (you can take your finger for a walk along it);
'flat sides'   (you can rub your hand over it);
'curved'   (you can curl your hand round it).

Use the inside and outside environment to set up 'shape' walks and do not forget to look at natural shapes as well as artificial ones.

Positional language

Many words are familiar to children on entry to the Nursery, others less so. A good time to reinforce positional language is during physical activity, whether outside on the large apparatus or in the hall during movement lessons. Giving precise instructions to the children as part of the session will enable them to gain experience in locating themselves in relation to objects and other people.

Other practical and motivating ideas include the following.

- Circle games where a Teddy is passed around and each child has to follow an instruction as to where to place the Teddy; for example, 'behind you', 'in the middle', 'next to your foot', 'on top of your head', 'in your lap', etc.
- Guessing games where a toy is hidden and questions as to its location are asked.

Within positional language we should also include the idea of a turn and of right and left.

A holistic curriculum

Although the Early Learning Goals have been described separately, each accompanied by suggestions of relevant activities, you must remember that in practical terms, within the Foundation Stage setting, such distinctions are neither necessary nor desirable. Most of the activities cover more than one area of mathematical development and when contextualised within the setting will give access to development across a range of areas of learning.

Recording

You will notice that there is no mention of children's recording of their mathematical experiences in the Early Years Foundation Stage. This does not mean that no recording should take place but rather that there is no expectation that children will record in written form. This leaves you, the teacher, to exercise your professional judgement as to when and how it might be appropriate for individual children to take the first steps towards formal recording. Children should certainly be encouraged at all times to devise such recording as they feel necessary. The work of Martin Hughes (1986) indicates that children can record with meaning but that they have difficulties with standard representations for calculations. The introduction of formal symbols such as + and − and = should not be attempted until a sound understanding of the processes, based on considerable practical experience, has been secured.

So far we have considered what might be termed the building blocks of an appropriate approach. How do you turn this into meaningful and enjoyable classroom activities and experiences?

Planning

The format for planning differs widely between settings as it must do in order to meet the specific needs of particular groups of children. However, there are common threads and the classroom story that follows gives insights into the ways that teachers approach planning.

CLASSROOM STORY

Lisa teaches in an Early Years unit and describes for us how her team embarks on planning.

We find it useful to have an initial 'brainstorming' session to collect all our ideas on a web chart (see Figure 5.4) and we then edit this into a final version for our medium-term plan. This shows all kind of experiences, teacher-led, teacher-initiated (but then left to the discretion of the children) and just ways of setting out areas and resources in the learning base that will stimulate the children's enthusiasm and encourage them to extend their learning through play.

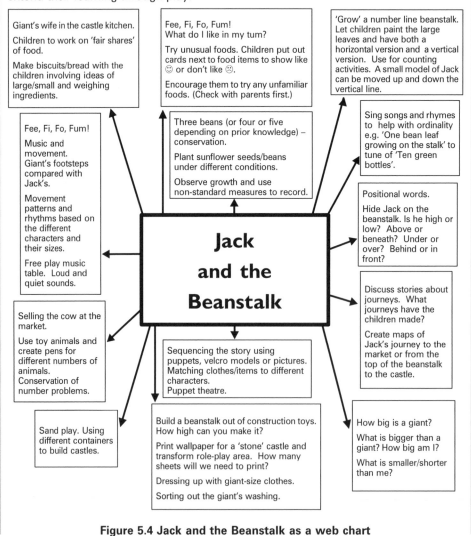

Figure 5.4 Jack and the Beanstalk as a web chart

Sometimes our themes last for some weeks. Other times we may have mini-topics that link together. We often use books or rhymes as a starting point. Children love listening to stories over and over again and we build this into the planning. This way we can use parts of the story to lead directly to the learning experiences we have planned. We make a conscious effort to consider which aspects of numeracy might be promoted through other areas of the curriculum and in this web there are clear links with other areas of learning.

Next, we begin to think about how the environment will promote and enhance the individual activities. What should the room look like? How can we include the outdoor environment? Have we got the right resources? Are they accessible? Is there a preferred order to the activities? What impact does this have on how we arrange the various sections of the room? An important question to resolve early on is, 'Which activities could happen at the same time?' 'Is it possible to work with a small group on a "quiet task" when there is a group of children enthusiastically acting out the "Fee-Fi-Fo-Fum" part of the story complete with musical instruments?' We try to 'troubleshoot' classroom management issues such as this in order to avoid problems later on. One theme rarely covers all aspects of mathematical development so we have to make sure, over the year, that we address all areas. 'Jack and the beanstalk' allows the children access to quite a few of the Early Learning Goals and complements other themes during the year.

We display our web chart on the wall so that we can add other ideas as we go along. This is vital because the children's free play often promotes learning that we had not considered. We observe their play as part of our role and are always ready and willing to make additions and alterations to our planning in order to make the most of their interests and enthusiasm. This observation also helps us to closely monitor the children's achievements so we actually know what to provide next. So our planning is flexible. We have to be led by the children to some extent. After all, teaching and learning is a two-way process. As teachers we have to decide what is appropriate and what is not but we do learn an incredible amount from observing and talking to the children as they go about their learning.

PRACTICAL TASK PRACTICAL TASK **PRACTICAL TASK** PRACTICAL TASK **PRACTICAL TASK**

Look at the web chart.

- Can you identify which Early Learning Goals underpin the proposed experiences?
- Which experiences link with knowledge and understanding of the world?
- Which aspects of mathematical development does this theme favour?
- Which areas are neglected?

Choose one of these areas and identify an appropriate learning objective from the Early Learning Goals. Can you think of experiences/activities that you could incorporate into this theme to address this?

A SUMMARY OF **KEY POINTS**

> **Mathematics provision should build on and relate to life experiences.**

> **Activities should be practical, appropriate and enjoyable.**

> **Play provides the best medium for learning.**

> Children should be encouraged to talk about their mathematical experiences.

> You are not just developing skills; you are encouraging a positive attitude and approach that will sustain the child throughout his/her mathematical education.

> You are enabling a child to become a competent, confident and self-assured learner.

MOVING *ON* > > > > > > MOVING *ON* > > > > > > MOVING *ON*

In this chapter you have been introduced to many important issues related to supporting the development of children's mathematical thinking. With a sound understanding of these underlying principles and a good personal knowledge of the nature of mathematics, you will have a firm foundation for creating the optimum learning environment for the children you teach. The big unknown is always what the particular concerns and interests of the children in the group might be. But, how you harness those concerns and interests to create absorbing and stimulating mathematical learning experiences is the constant challenge and ultimate satisfaction of the effective teacher.

REFERENCES REFERENCES **REFERENCES** REFERENCES **REFERENCES** REFERENCES

Aubrey, C. (1997) Children's early learning of number in school and out, in I. Thompson (ed.) *Teaching and learning early number*. Buckingham: Open University Press.

Gelman, R. and Gallistel, C. R. (1978) *The child's understanding of number*. Cambridge, MA: Harvard University Press.

Hughes, M. (1986) *Children and number*. Oxford: Blackwell.

Munn, P. (1997) Children's beliefs about counting, in I. Thompson (ed.) *Teaching and learning early number*. Buckingham: Open Unversity Press.

Starkey, P. (1987) *Early arithmetic competencies*. Paper presented at the biennial meeting of the Society for Research in Child Development. Baltimore, MD, Aiprl.

FURTHER READING FURTHER READING **FURTHER READING** FURTHER READING

Atkinson, S. (1992) *Mathematics with reason*. London:. Hodder and Stoughton. An exploration of fundamental ideas in relation to helping children to 'emerge' as mathematicians. Includes case studies/teacher stories of such an approach in action.

Aubrey, C. (1997) *Mathematics teaching in the early years*. London: Falmer Press. An examination of classroom practice in the light of teachers' pedagogical and subject knowledge. This book highlights significant issues for teachers within the Foundation stage in terms of effective provision for optimum learning.

Montague-Smith, A. (1997) *Mathematics in nursery education.* London: David Fulton. A comprehensive, practical and easy-to-read guide that covers all aspects of mathematics from planning to assessment. A wealth of anecdotal evidence supports the ideas expressed and 'see at a glance' tables indicate which concepts can be developed through activities across all environments within the setting.

Nunes, T. and Bryant, P. (1996) *Children doing mathematics*. Oxford: Blackwell. Detailed examination of children's acquisition of competence across areas of mathematics. Includes international comparisons and research. The first two chapters give valuable insights into children's difficulties in the Early Years.

Pound, L. (1999) *Supporting mathematical development in the early years.* Buckingham: Open University Press. A clear rationale, linked to research and illustrated by example, gives a sound overview of all relevant aspects. A good starting point for further reading.

Thompson, I. (ed.) (1997) *Teaching and learning early number*. Buckingham: Open University Press. A collection of writings covering recent thinking and research into the current structure of the mathematics curriculum in schools. Several chapters deal specifically with issues relevant to the Foundation Stage.

6
Communication, language and literacy
Rosemary Boys

Chapter objectives

By the end of this chapter you should:

- be aware of the influence of language on social, emotional and academic development;
- recognise the Early Learning Goals for communication, language and literacy as stated in the Early Years Foundation Stage;
- understand the adult/child relationship necessary for language and literacy acquisition;
- understand the relationship between oracy and literacy development;
- be aware of the teaching strategies appropriate to language and literacy acquisition.

This chapter addresses the following Professional Standards for QTS:

Q5, Q14, Q15, Q17, Q18

Introduction

This chapter will address the professional standards required for the area of learning identified as communication, language and literacy in the Early Years Foundation Stage (EYFS) Practice Guidance. It will examine theoretical and pedagogical issues related to oracy (speaking and listening) and literacy (reading and writing), and make explicit their importance for the child's social and emotional development.

There is an important interrelationship between oracy and literacy. This is not only because the knowledge and understanding of one informs the other, but also because of the way in which acquisition takes place. Both literacy and oracy should be learned within a purposeful and social context. Both rely upon other, more competent users to model and provide encouragement, and both require opportunities to practise developing skills.

Examining the Early Learning Goals for this area of learning shows that the first two categories of these (Language for communication and Language for thinking) are explicitly related to oracy development. Further reading will show that these goals recognise the need for direct learning about the social nature of oral communication. These same goals also have implications for all future learning. Consequently, the establishment of effective language and the ability to use this language for such interpersonal processes as questioning, retelling, negotiating and justifying is a priority for early childhood practitioners.

Language for communication	• Interact with others, negotiating plans and activities and taking turns in conversation • Enjoy listening to and using spoken and written language, and readily turn to their play and learning • Sustain attentive listening, responding to what they have heard with the relevant comments, questions or action • Listen with enjoyment, and respond to stories, songs and other music, rhymes and poems and make up their own stories, songs, rhymes and poems • Extend their vocabulary, exploring the meanings and sounds of new words • Speak clearly and audibly with confidence and control and show awareness of the listener
Language for thinking	• Use language to imagine and recreate roles and experiences • Use talk to organise, sequence and clarify thinking, ideas, feelings and events

The Early Learning Goals in categories three to six (see below) are concerned with literacy acquisition, but still have relevance to oracy skills, particularly the development of the young child's auditory skills. These goals are the outcomes of the Early Years Foundation Stage. It is the role of the practitioner to identify each child's developmental needs, continuously monitor children's progress, and provide appropriate learning opportunities for children to move towards these goals.

Linking sounds and letters	• Hear and say sounds in words in the order in which they occur • Link sounds to letters, naming and sounding the letters of the alphabet • Use their phonic knowledge to write simply regular words and make phonetically plausible attempts at more complex words*
Reading	• Explore and experiment with sounds, words and texts • Retell narratives in the correct sequence, drawing on language patterns in stories • Read a range of familiar and common words and simple sentences independently • Know that print carries meaning and, in English, is read from left to right and top to bottom • Show an understanding of the elements of stories, such as the main character, sequence of events and openings, and how information can be found in non-fiction texts to answer questions about where, who, why and how
Writing	• Use their phonic knowledge to write simple regular words and make phonetically plausible attempts at more complex words* • Attempt writing for different purposes, using features of different forms such as lists, stories and instructions • Write their own names and other things such as labels and captions, and begin to form simple sentences, sometimes using punctuation
Handwriting	• Use a pencil and hold it effectively to form recognisable letters, most of which are correctly formed

(*This goal appears twice within the documentation.)

Oracy development

The importance of effective communication skills

In the education of young children the teaching of language skills is far more than a preparation for becoming literate. It is our responsibility to work in partnership with parents to prepare children to become functioning members of our society. It would seem that from birth children are active participants in their own social integration. Trevarthen (1995) holds the view that 'being part of a culture is a need human beings are born with'. The initial stage in the development of social competence is the attainment of intersubjectivity or mutual understanding. This begins in the mother/child interaction starting at birth, and develops as the child's communication and language skills become increasingly sophisticated. It is now recognised that effective language acquisition is essential for both social/emotional and cognitive development. Unless both of these are recognised and addressed, the child will not thrive.

CLASSROOM STORY

Consider a child called Joel. Joel began Nursery for three mornings a week when he was three years three months old. Joel's speech and behaviour soon gave cause for concern. His only form of oral communication was through grunts and gesture. Frustration at not being understood or being thwarted would result in screams and tantrums. He found interaction with his peers and adults difficult and was often withdrawn and socially isolated. He frequently took toys from his peers and would respond with aggression if they tried to retrieve them. He was unable to participate in story time, group activities or role-play situations, and was unable to concentrate on any task for any length of time. He found it difficult to establish trust with his key worker.

The practitioners in the Nursery were concerned for this little boy and were aware that his main problem was an inability to communicate. But why was this child so behind his peers? From their experiences with young children, the reasons could have ranged from a hearing loss to autism. However, a talk with the child's mother gave a quite different story. After Joel's birth she had suffered with severe post-natal depression and found it difficult to respond to her child, so apart from feeding and changing him there was little interaction between mother and son. As the baby became more distressed, the mother became more anxious. Throughout this time the relationship between Joel's parents was deteriorating. Joel's father was convinced his son had brain damage and left the family when Joel was 19 months old. Joel had never been to any kind of playgroup because his mother was embarrassed by her son's behaviour and poor development.

Careful assessment of this little boy showed that his communication and language problems were the consequence of his lack of nurturing and interaction with a caring adult rather than a clinical problem. There is now evidence indicating that children are born with a predisposition to engage and communicate with others (Schaffer, 1996). In Joel's early life his need to interact and participate in constructing meanings with a caregiver was not addressed.

The development of language and communication skills

Learning to communicate and use your own language is the most difficult learning task ever undertaken, but for most children in an appropriate child/caregiver relationship the task is one of mutual satisfaction. Bruner (1983) argues that children are 'geared to respond to the human voice, to the human face, to human action and gesture'. They are also strongly motivated if the reward is a sense of belonging, being able to communicate, and having supportive adults with whom to interact.

Figure 6.1 provides a brief guide to the order in which language and communication behaviours develop in many children. This is not, however, a prescriptive sequence and it is now recognised by practitioners that all children are individuals and that the majority of children will become competent communicators in their own time, and via their own route.

Age	Language skills	Communication behaviours
Birth – 1 mth	The child can hear sounds before birth, and at birth can recognise its mother's voice. Verbal communication is through crying.	The child is addressed continually and directly by adults from birth. New babies have been found to be attuned to the visual patterns common to faces, and begin to imitate the facial expressions of others. Different cries have different meanings and range from distress to contentment; these are responded to and reinforced by caregivers.
2–3 mths	The child maintains the sensitivity to sound. They can tell the difference between several pairs of consonants and vowels. The child listens more carefully and responds to the voices of others. Cooing becomes more varied and extended as the child gains control of vocal organs and breath.	They respond to adult tones of voice, e.g. anger, soothing tones. They will listen before responding with own interjections. They are becoming interested in objects.
4 mths	The child is beginning to use vocal play in which they produce a wide range of noises which are more controlled and often repeated.	The child begins to engage in protoconversations with caregiver, and will practise these alone. They enjoy joining in musical songs and rhymes, e.g. 'This little piggy'. The child still very self-oriented.
6 mths	Babbling develops with inflections in the flow of sound as the child becomes aware of the rhythm of language. Turns head to whoever is speaking and responds to the tone and inflection in a voice.	Ready to play lively games with familiar people, e.g. peek-a-boo, active nursery rhymes. Becoming aware that their actions will cause different responses from adults. Becoming aware of utterances with social conventions, e.g. 'bye-bye'. Beginning to develop an awareness of others, e.g. will follow a finger pointing at something a caregiver has seen.
9 mths	Babbling becomes more sophisticated with greater variety in the consonants and vowels. The inflection in continuous babble is beginning to resemble the adult form. Protowords –where the sound is clear, but not the meaning – are common.	The child understands many adult gestures and will use them in simple contexts, e.g. waving, clapping.

Figure 6.1 The development of language and communication skills

Age	Language skills	Communication behaviours
12 mths	Beginning to say first words but will continue to babble. The first words are familiar words used to express needs. The child is able to understand individual words. Hearing is acute and the child enjoys rhymes and songs, trying to join in. They can hear and understand a simple requests or command, e.g. 'Put it down.'	The child uses protolanguage to engage others in conversation. Conversation includes vocalisation, gestures and facial expression. Conversations rehearsed as the child plays. Words are acquired during purposeful shared activities.
18 mths	The ratio of words understood to words used is 5:1. They are beginning to put words together, these are mainly names (nouns) and action words (verbs). Talk is in the present tense They can hear and understand simple instructions, e.g. 'Give the car to daddy'.	Child is beginning to assert independence and use the word 'No'. Conversations include vocalisations with increased expression. The child responds to non-verbal communication. In play together children perform similar pretend actions but without negotiation. The child enjoys sharing and interacting with a book and adult.
2 yrs	The child can actively use about 200 words. They are beginning to use short, simple sentences. By 2½ there is evidence of language rules.	The child begins to use simple language to talk about people and things not present. Pretend play with peers still does not have a shared intention. Play includes enactments in which partners engage in sequenced pretend activities that require social exchanges but not negotiation.
3 yrs	There is a huge growth in vocabulary development to over 3000 words. Using longer sentences but will miss out less important words. Is using a wider range of words including adjectives and adverbs. Some developmental errors, e.g. confusion of pronouns, I/me; she/her. Will use past tense verbs but make errors with their endings. Will listen to and follow favourite stories and join in the familiar parts.	The vocabulary explosion is related to the child's need to share ideas and experiences. Shared play includes imitative pretend activities in which children will have similar themes, but the actions of the partners are still not integrated. The number of questions children ask increases. The child will enjoy sharing tasks with a supportive, more competent person. They will initiate and maintain conversations.
4 yrs	The child's speech gives evidence of growing control over grammar, vocabulary and phonology. Verb endings are used with increasing accuracy, but generalisations are sometimes overused, e.g. We wented to see Nan.	In play children now negotiate play themes and intentions by arguing, talking and story telling. Play is represented with complementary pretend roles. The child enjoys sharing nursery rhymes, retelling stories and events and inventing their own stories.

Figure 6.1 The development of language and communication skills (continued)

Initial assessment

Children's successful integration into their Early Years community can permanently influence their attitude to school and education. To provide the optimum learning opportunities for each child it is essential that an accurate assessment of a child's ability to use language and communicate is made as soon as possible after their admission. As the purpose of assessment is to become aware of a child's skills and competences, and to establish an accurate profile of the child, assessments should:

- be unintrusive and non-threatening for the child;
- be done within the context of familiar and purposeful tasks;

- be based upon observations during interactions with peers or familiar adults;
- include observations of language use and communication with familiar people;
- focus on the positive aspects and achievements of the child's language use and communication skills.

What is actually assessed will depend on the focus of assessment observations. This could be based upon a perceived need, or to monitor progress or to gauge the success of learning, and will be decided upon by the practitioner. Figure 6.2 categorises and lists some aspects that can be observed, but this is not a finite list, nor should more than one item be assessed at a time. The level at which these will be assessed will also depend on the age, experience and competence of the child.

Speaking	Listening	Communication skills
Articulation Can pronounce words that can be understood as approximate versions of the correct form. *Oral syntax* (grammar) Is combining words together to provide meaning. *Speaking for different purposes* Can use a range of oral genres, e.g. to inform, to question, to describe, to inform, to imagine. *Vocabulary* Is able to use an increasing range of words in the right context. *Recounting and retelling* Can relate and retell events, experiences, stories in the right sequence of events.	*Auditory discrimination.* Can hear sounds such as initial sounds and rhymes as appropriate. *Auditory syntax* Can identify the type of sentence by its grammar and inflection, e.g. question, instruction, command or statement. *Vocabulary* Is able to understand an increasing range of words. *Auditory memory* Is able to remember and recall events, experiences, songs, stories and rhymes.	Can be understood by others. Responds appropriately in conversations. Can follow and respond to instructions, question, etc. *Semantics* (meaning) Can express need and wants. Understands when others express needs and wants. Can take turns in conversation. Is aware of the need for appropriate language in different contexts and with different people. Is able to understand the nuances of language, i.e. does not take things literally.

Figure 6.2 Aspects of oracy that can be assessed

The adult/child relationship in the learning environment

Language acquisition is as much a social process as one of cognition, and children's development depends largely on their interactions with others. From birth, the child and primary carer are both participants in the generation of mutual understanding. Although a very young child has little competence as a communicator and language user, there is the expectation that the child will become adept.

This collaboration extends beyond language acquisition, and also includes joint involvement in wider learning events. As the child grows and develops, collaboration will be with a wider range of supportive companions, but the quality of the learning event will be dependent on the quality of the language used in the interaction.

So, can the collaborative adult/child relationship be translated into the early childhood setting where the practitioner's role is to promote communication, language acquisition, and the use of language as the vehicle for learning?

In their analysis of interactional roles in early childhood settings Hughes and Westgate (1997) found that both during teaching tasks, and in more leisurely contexts, nursery nurses and community workers consistently used a more interactive and supportive style of communication with young children than did teachers. This was characterised by the reciprocal nature of the interactions during which children were given the opportunity to have some control of the discourse, and were given time to experience and use a wider range of functions.

While the Early Years Foundation Stage does not explicitly describe or recognise this relationship, it does identify some principles that should enable practitioners to practise collaborative learning. These include the recognition that effective teaching requires the following.

- Communicating and being with others helps children to build social relationships which provide opportunities for friendship, empathy and sharing emotions. The ability to communicate helps children to participate more fully in society.
- To become skilful communicators, babies and children need to be with people who have meaning for them and with whom they have warm and loving relationships, such as their family or carers and, in a group situation, a key person whom they know and trust.
- Babies and children use their voices to make contact and to let people know what they need and how they feel, establishing their own identities and personalities.
- Help children to communicate thoughts, ideas and feelings and build up relationships with adults and each other.
- Provide time and relaxed opportunities for children to develop spoken language through sustained conversations between children and adults, both one-to-one and in small groups and between children themselves. Allow children time to initiate conversations, respect their thinking time and silences and help them develop the interaction.
- Talk to children and engage them as partners in conversation.

Interacting with young children

To elicit a wider range of responses from children will depend on the effectiveness of your own language. Consider some of the techniques found in the talk of teachers that have been found to enhance the quality and richness of children's responses. Consider also how some of the techniques can be used together, for example a confirmation and an elaboration.

To elicit information from children

Direct elicitation	These are open and closed questions e.g., Why did he run away?
Cued elicitations	Providing strong visual clues and verbal hints e.g., How do birds fly? (flapping arms)
Reflective observation	e.g., I wonder why she is crying?

To respond to what children say

Confirmations	Providing positive feedback e.g., Yes, I think you are right.
Elaborations	Encouraging children to extend their response, or extending it for them and modelling sentence structure and vocabulary. e.g., Could you tell us a bit more about it?
Repetitions	To restate what the child said to the child itself or to peers. e.g., Yes, he is climbing a very tall tree.

Reformulations	This can provide a positive way of providing a correct sentence structure for the child, or make a sentence comprehensible to peers.
Rejections	A wrong response is usually ignored, and the question or instruction reworded e.g., Are you sure it goes next to the blue one?

To describe significant aspects of shared experiences

'We' statements	To encourage children to bring past knowledge and experiences to the present task e.g., What did the baker we visited make as well as bread?
Recaps	To recap what has been done already in the lesson. e.g., Remember how Sammy sprinkled the glitter very gently so it doesn't get all lumpy.

Adapted from Mercer (1995)

PRACTICAL TASK PRACTICAL TASK **PRACTICAL TASK** PRACTICAL TASK **PRACTICAL TASK**

Look at these two conversations and consider the quality of the discourse. Why is one teacher able to elicit so much more discussion from the child?

Conversation 1

T: What's the hen doing?

P1: She's sitting on the floor.

T: Why is she sitting on the ground?

P1: 'Cos she's a bit tired?

T: No, look carefully, what is she sitting on?

P1: It's some grass.

T: It's called straw. Why do you think she is sitting on it?

P1: I don't know.

T1: Well, she's sitting on some eggs. Turn over and look at the picture. The hen has laid these eggs. What will happen next?

P1: I don't know.

Conversation 2

T2: Oh look at this hen sitting on this warm soft straw. I wonder what she's doing?

P2: I think she's very tired and she likes it 'cos it's warm and soft.

T2: You could be right. Let's turn over. Oh look at them.

P2: It's eggs. Look at this one it's got a hole

T2: I can see a little tiny beak poking out. Do you think it's trying to get out?

P1: It's a baby hen like what we had before.

T2: You mean when we had the eggs in the incubator and they hatched into little chicks.

P2: Yeah, but they didn't have a mum. We got them from a man, and put them in that, er, that (pointing at the incubator).

T2: Incubator.

P2: Yeah the incubator, to make them warm, to be little chicks ... You can eat eggs too you know.

Providing the appropriate conditions and environment for language acquisition

The learning conditions provided through the collaborative relationship were identified in the seminal work by Cambourne (1988). He maintained that children need to be immersed in meaningful and purposeful interactions, and given opportunities to practise their growing skills. The way in which adults accept the child's approximations, provide positive feedback and model the correct form of the language provides a supportive learning environment in which children can take risks and accept responsibility for their language.

For these conditions to be met, careful thought needs to be given to the environment in which the learning will take place. If children are to be encouraged to take risks and practise their developing skills, their security within the learning environment also needs to be considered. The learning environment that practitioners should seek to provide for young children should therefore include:

- a high child/adult ratio so that children have opportunities to practise their developing skills with competent users of standard English;
- a routine that includes opportunities for young children to use their language skills for a range of social functions; for example, greeting people, engaging in conversation with a variety of people, negotiating with adults and peers, sharing and co-operating;
- a range of interactive activities and tasks that provide opportunities for explicit modelling and demonstrations, informal practice of skills and imaginative play;
- the availability of resources to promote speaking and listening; for example, books, audio tapes, puppets, role-play areas, games for two or more children;
- well-planned and purposeful learning tasks that will engage children;
- differentiation of tasks to address the individual language needs of young children;
- positive and focused assessment based upon observation of children engaged in relevant tasks.

Organising for oracy development

To be effective in the organisation of oracy development it is necessary to know precisely what needs to be addressed and the most appropriate way of providing learning opportunities. Oracy learning can be categorised into three main areas, as shown in Figure 6.3. Each of these is purpose-driven and therefore needs a context for the learning.

Language for communicating	Language for learning	Speaking and listening skills
• To express feelings and needs. • To be aware of the feelings and needs of others. • To make and maintain friends. • To negotiate and collaborate in play and group activities. • To initiate and participate in conversations. • To be aware of the need for appropriate language in different situations and with different people. • To share and take turns. • To be aware of non-verbal communication.	• To continue to extend vocabulary. • To consolidate and extend grammar usage. • To continue to develop articulation and pronunciation. • To promote auditory memory and discrimination. • To be aware of the rhythm, rhyme and intonations of language. • To enjoy listening to stories, rhymes and songs. • To enjoy participating in stories, rhymes and songs. • To participate in learning tasks involving listening and speaking. • To engage in collaborative play. • To take risks practising their developing competence.	• To ask and respond to questions. • To recall and recount. • To inform. • To make connections. • To formulate meanings. • To speculate. • To negotiate. • To justify. • To respond to suggestions. • To give and follow instructions.

Figure 6.3 Purposes for oracy development

In many cases this learning will not be within a specific language or literacy lesson, but will be embedded within other areas of the curriculum. It is the practitioner's role to recognise and plan for both the explicit and implicit teaching of oracy.

Literacy acquisition

Just as social relationships have been recognised as the foundation of oracy acquisition, so literacy acquisition can be described as a social process embedded in children's relationships with significant others who serve as models of literate behaviour.

CLASSROOM STORY

Consider a child called Kate. Kate began at her Early Years setting for five mornings a week when she was four years one month old. On her first day she could recognise her name on her own coat-hook and tray. She was able to join in the nursery rhymes and most of the songs that were sung together. In story time she listened to the story with concentration and was willing to make predictions about the plot. As her first week progressed it was found that she could write her own name, read most of the environmental print in the room, 'write' a prescription for one of the patients in the role-play doctor's surgery and 'read' familiar books to herself and her new friend. Kate enjoyed word and sound games, and could make alliterative strings for the names of her peers ('Sophie sits on Sarah's sofa'), and recognise and identify rhyming words. She also recognised most letters and some words. It could seem that Kate's precocious ability was the result of ambitious parents and some serious tutoring. This, however, was not the case. Kate is the older of two children in a single parent family. Her mother is a nurse and, more importantly, an avid reader. She has been sharing books and stories with Kate since Kate was tiny. As Kate loves making up her own stories, her mother has written these stories down, and made them into little books for Kate to illustrate and read for herself. Because Kate's mother works, Kate and her sister have been cared for during the day by their maternal grandmother. This home confirms the literate behaviour that is evident in Kate's own home. Kate sees both her mother and grandmother writing shopping lists, cheques, emails, text-messages, letters and messages; using telephone directories and train timetables; reading books, newspapers, letters, messages and recipes. Because Kate is aware that print is meaningful and is encouraged to use it herself, she is aware of how other people also use it. She has been encouraged to find things in the supermarket, read environmental print and symbols, write her own shopping lists and visit the local library.

Just as babies are born ready and willing to communicate orally with their family, so Kate entered this setting ready and willing to communicate through print. This readiness is evident in her awareness that print is meaningful, and that reading and writing are enjoyable and purposeful. Kate did not acquire her knowledge and skills through formal teaching, but through the same collaborative relationship as was evident for oracy acquisition. Within this relationship she was also provided with the appropriate conditions for becoming literate. She was immersed in enjoyable and purposeful print. Reading and writing were modelled for her by competent, literate adults. She was given opportunities to try reading and writing herself, and her efforts and approximations were supported and valued. She was encouraged to take risks with her reading and writing, and decide for herself what she would do.

The literacy process

It is now recognised that reading and writing are more than decoding and encoding symbols on a page, though these are an important and integral part of the literacy process. Reading and writing are complex processes during which the participant brings a wide range of knowledge and skills to the task, and actively interacts with the text. If you examine Figure 6.4 you will see that it is the interaction between each level that will give coherence and understanding.

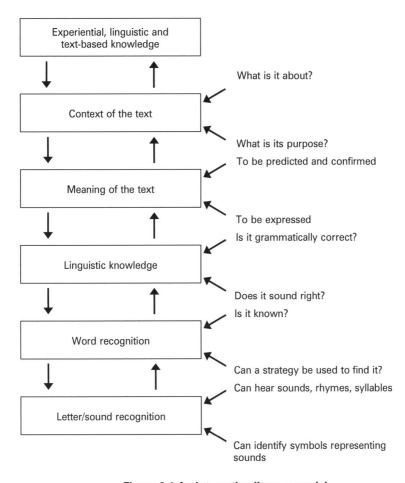

Figure 6.4 An interactive literacy model

Implementing an interactive literacy model

To beginning practitioners, even the thought of teaching literacy skills to young children with differing experiences and abilities can be daunting. This concern has probably been exacerbated by the current perceived overemphasis placed on phonological awareness and grapho-phonic knowledge. This is the outcome of the controversy that has arisen in England as a result of the Clackmannanshire Synthetic Phonics Initiative (Johnston and Watson, 2005) and the subsequent release of the Rose Report in March 2006. The recommendations of both the research and the review have led to the introduction of the prescriptive teaching of one specific form of phonics – this being synthetic phonics. It could however be argued that England is following a trend already begun in the USA, Australia and New Zealand several years ago. It could also be argued that although the initiative has been accepted by some, there is by no means a consensus from practitioners, educators or researchers (Meyer, 2002; Hynds, 2007; Ellis, 2007).

In his report, Rose presents the simplistic view that learning to read effectively and spell correctly is the outcome of phonic decoding through blending sounds to read and segmenting words to spell or encode. It could be argued that this is based on the false assumption that in the English language we have an alphabetical writing system. True alphabetical writing systems such as those are characterised by having each sound in language represented by one letter. In English, which is a derived language, we have 26 letters (graphemes) that have to represent 44 sounds (phonemes), and even our simple vowels and consonants can be inconsistent (so/do; sit/circle; get/ginger). Negotiating vowel digraphs (e.g. Phoebe thought the bough would break) is far more problematic, and can challenge the most enthusiastic young reader if using synthetic phonics is the main decoding/encoding strategy.

From your own studies as a trainee, you will be aware that reading and writing acquisition is a far more complex process than could be addressed by a narrow and formal literacy model. Such a model would disadvantage many children entering the Early Years Foundation Stage classroom, particularly those with little experience of engaging with text. These children need the opportunity to discover the enjoyment and purposefulness of print before embarking on learning that for many will seem both purposeless and difficult. Such a model can also have a negative effect on children who are already experimenting with reading and writing and come from literacy-rich homes. For these children, the non-confirmation of their understanding about literacy will inhibit future progress and undermine their perceptions of themselves as successful literacy user.

For effective literacy teaching, a practitioner needs to adopt a broad approach based on well-written books and purposeful experiences. The practitioner's role is to plan, to model, to inspire, to enjoy and to interact with young children in exciting and interesting literacy events. Reference to the Early Learning Goals will show that these practices are still valued in what remains an experiential and rich programme of literacy learning. To do this there are explicit aspects of literacy teaching that need to be considered and addressed. These include:

- developing a rich literacy environment;
- developing opportunities to utilise play as a learning context;
- developing an awareness of books;
- developing metacognitive strategies;
- developing phonological awareness and graphophonic knowledge;
- developing fine motor skills (this is addressed in Chapter 4).

The literacy environment

It is the practitioner's responsibility to consider the environment that will encourage and promote literacy. It has been suggested that children learn to become literate by being surrounded by print. If children are expected to learn to read, then the environment should be structured to support and encourage them. Young children need to be immersed in environmental print, books, games and writing materials. The home languages of all children should be evident. It is also recommended that other languages should be represented to accommodate children from non-English-speaking backgrounds. This is endorsed by the Early Years Foundation Stage document that recognises the need to 'develop children's awareness of languages and writing systems other than English' (2007, p40).

It is not only the physical environment that must be considered; people also constitute an important part of the literacy environment. It is essential that those working with children are confident and enthusiastic literacy users, and that they are willing to share their skills and experiences. As early childhood settings tend to have predominantly female staff members, practitioners must recognise the need of young boys to have literate male role models. Bilingual children also need to see and hear members of their own communities as proficient literacy users. The modelling can be in the home language or English as it is the behaviours and attitudes to texts that children need to be aware of. This can be done through the practical involvement of members of the whole community and access to bilingual children's books will support this process.

PRACTICAL TASK PRACTICAL TASK **PRACTICAL TASK** PRACTICAL TASK **PRACTICAL TASK**

Take this opportunity to reflect on the early childhood settings you have experienced.

- How did these contribute to the literacy environment?
- How did the practitioners give evidence of their literate behaviour?
- How will you establish an exciting and relevant literacy environment in your own setting?

Developing opportunities to utilise play as a learning context

It is recognised that one of the most important aspects of the literacy environment is the way in which it facilitates play. The role of play in the education of young children and its recognition within the current Early Years curriculum is dealt with in Chapter 1. However, the relevant aspects identified here need to be considered.

- Through play children are engaged in complex communication involving such oracy skills as recalling, recounting, negotiating, directing, sequencing, explaining, justifying and planning.
- Through play children have an opportunity to explore a range of non-fictional texts within an appropriate context, for example, using cookery books in the home corner.
- Play provides a context for writing development. During play children have been found to write in a wide range of non-fictional genres, and write for a wide variety of purposes (Hall and Robinson, 1995; Lancaster, 2007).
- Books and stories provide a model for drama, role play and puppet work that has a clear benefit to reading. Through dramatic play children interpret character roles, develop an awareness of story sequence and plot, come to understand dialogue, and begin to generate their own stories from favourite and familiar texts.
- During free play children who use the book corner have the opportunity to practise reading familiar and favourite books. This often includes retelling the story from memory while pointing to the text and using the illustrations as a prompt.
- Play provides the opportunity for young children to integrate their literacy and oracy skills (Grugeon et al., 2005).
- Play situations can also provide rich assessment evidence of both literacy and oracy development.

Developing an awareness of books

While many children arrive in an early childhood setting familiar with books, for some sharing a book and enjoying a story will be a new experience. Even very young children need the opportunity to listen to and enjoy as many stories as possible. Browne (2004) argues that the exposure of watching and listening to a skilled adult will demystify literacy. Barriere et al. (2000) maintain that reading to children and modelling how enjoyable it can be from a person whom the children value can be beneficial.

During the more informal storytime, books should therefore be read with enthusiasm, expression and sound effects. It is also important that all of the text is read in one sitting so that children can develop a concept for a story. During story time the emphasis of the lesson should be placed on enjoyment and a sense of shared participation. When appropriate books are chosen, storytime can be an opportunity to engage children's concentration and listening skills. Favourite books need to be reread regularly. These are often the books children will attempt to read alone.

The more focused adult/child shared reading experience can be established in the classroom with the use of big books. These large texts ensure that all children have clear access to the text and illustrations, and enable both the practitioner and children to identify specific features of the book. For practitioners, big books are excellent teaching tools as they enable them to imitate the shared intimacy with a book that is a feature of the child/carer literacy event. While e-books are available for young children, and should also be used, big books provide opportunities for children to give evidence of book-handling skills.

For children to begin to interact with a book they need to understand how it is organised. To do this young children must develop concepts about print. Figure 6.5 lists those needed by children at the conclusion of the Early Years Foundation Stage.

Children need to be aware that:
- *print contains meaning and that the meaning is permanent;*
- *the title of the book is on the front cover;*
- *the book has a title page that also gives the title and the names of the author and illustrator;*
- *the book opens from right to left;*
- *you read the left page first on a double page;*
- *you begin at the top of the page;*
- *you make a return sweep at the end of a line;*
- *pictures contain (semantic) information;*
- *the words are in a familiar (syntactic) order;*
- *symbols (graphemes) represent sounds (phonemes);*
- *the symbols are grouped to make words;*
- *the words are grouped to make sentences.*

Figure 6.5 Print concepts

These can be taught during shared reading through the context of the big book, and reinforced each time a book is shared. When children are reading they should be encouraged to follow the text with their finger. Thorough understanding of these concepts will be evident in children's play writing. Although most young children can follow a text with their finger, it takes longer for them to use these conventions in their own writing. This is one reason why children need free and easy access to writing materials including small, blank, stapled books.

Developing metacognitive strategies

To be effective and fluent when interacting with a text, readers and writers need explicit knowledge which will enable them to work strategically using what is referred to as meta-cognition. Working in a thoughtful way through a deliberate selection of strategies gives the literacy user the opportunity to exploit all of their skills and knowledge.

By using big books it is possible to provide young children with enough strategies to function metacognitively. This is done initially through a combination of modelled and shared reading and writing. Modelling is when a practitoner reads or writes alone in view of the children, and gives a commentary of what they are thinking and the strategies they will try using. During shared reading and writing the practitioner and children work together and together employ the strategies previously 'modelled'. The strategies that can be modelled and shared with young children include:

Grapho-phonic cueing	Once children begin to develop an awareness of the sound–symbol relationship they will attempt to use it if they are encouraged and supported. It is usually first used to decode nouns in conjunction with picture cues. After seeing this strategy modelled, young children will look at the illustrations for semantic information, then they will confirm their prediction using the initial letter of the word.
Prediction	This strategy requires the reader to make an educated guess using their experiential knowledge and knowledge. Children should be asked, 'What do you think will happen next?' They should also be encouraged to explain the reason for their prediction.
Picture cues	Illustrations are the first text-based semantic (meaning) cues a young child can access. They can be used for predicting and for decoding individual words.
Repetition	Both events and language can be repeated in stories. Once children recognise the repetition in a text they can predict what will happen next, and can join in the reading of the text, at first relying on their memory of the repeated text or refrain.
Intertextual skills	Children need to be aware that they can bring knowledge of the structure and content of one book to the reading of another.
Semantic cueing	Individual words such as nouns, verbs, adjectives and adverbs can be read from the context of their sentence. If these words are left out when the whole sentence is read and the children are asked, 'What would make sense?', children can predict the word from the sentence meaning.
Syntactic cueing	Individual words such as different parts of a verb (e.g. jump/jumped) and adjectives (big/bigger/biggest) can be read from

the grammar of the sentence. Young children have enough knowledge of sentence structure to be able to make a prediction. Even if the word is not correct it will probably be one from the same word group as the deleted word. Children should be aware that you can read past a word, then go back and try a word that makes the sentence 'sound right'.

It is obvious that to promote and encourage the use of these strategies a practitioner needs access to good-quality texts. Figure 6.6 identifies some of the characteristics that should be used to help in the selection of appropriate books.

A text appropriate for young children should include:
- *a meaningful and enjoyable text;*
- *a predictable story line;*
- *illustrations that support the text;*
- *language and grammar appropriate to young children;*
- *appropriate vocabulary;*
- *clear, bold, well-spaced print;*
- *repetition (and in some texts rhyme);*
- *freedom from gender, ethnic and cultural bias;*
- *interactivity;*
- *ways to encourage children to draw on their own experiential and linguistic knowledge.*

Figure 6.6 Characteristics of a book

PRACTICAL TASK PRACTICAL TASK **PRACTICAL TASK** PRACTICAL TASK **PRACTICAL TASK**

Make a selection of four or five children's books. Using the criteria in Figure 6.6, assess the quality of these books.

Which strategies could you explicitly model or share with each book?

Developing phonological awareness and grapho-phonic knowledge

As well as an explicit knowledge of print concepts and strategies, young children need to be able to understand and use the sound–symbol relationship, segmenting, blending and analogy. These should be established through children's development of phonological awareness. Phonological awareness is the metalinguistic ability that enables children to reflect on the features of a spoken language. As a result of this reflection, children come to understand that words can be segmented into component sounds. Conversely, they also recognise that through blending, words can be constructed and changed. This segmenting and blending is the basis of synthetic phonics.

Children also need to be able to recognise and use alliteration and rhyme. It is through these that children will develop the ability to categorise words. By becoming adept at recognising words that rhyme, children will be able to use the strategy of analogy. Through this they will understand that by knowing one word, they can generate others (show, blow, know, throw).

The constituent parts of words or syllables used in analogy are linguistically termed onset and rime. In her seminal work on children's use of analogy, Goswami (1993) found that a child who is good at rhyming will also realise that shared sounds often mean shared spelling patterns, and that words like 'cat' and 'hat' not only rhyme, but also share the same orthographic unit '-at' (which is termed the 'rime'). The use of analogy is the basis of analytical phonics.

In any effective phonic programme both synthetic and analytical phonics should be taught because they complement and support each other. As is indicated in the communication, language and literacy curriculum for the Early Years Foundation Stage, all phonics should initially be taught through immersion in rich and varied auditory experiences that will develop children's auditory perception and discrimination. Without these skills, children will find it difficult to engage successfully in any phonics programme.

Formal and informal activities that will promote auditory skills include:

- matching objects and child by their initial sounds;
- saying and inventing tongue-twisters;
- sorting groups of objects by their initial sounds;
- listening to, saying and learning poems, songs and rhymes;
- reading stories with rhyme;
- reading stories with alliteration;
- making up own versions of familiar rhymes and poems;
- games such as 'I hear with my little ear something rhyming with _____ .'
          'I spy with my little eye something beginning with _____ ';
- clapping the rhythm to songs and rhymes;
- clapping the syllables of children's names.

PRACTICAL TASK PRACTICAL TASK **PRACTICAL TASK** PRACTICAL TASK **PRACTICAL TASK**

See if you can generate four other activities young children could participate in for:

1. alliteration;

2. rhyme;

3. segmentation;

4. blending.

A SUMMARY OF **KEY POINTS**

This chapter has recognised that as practitioners we must:

> **acknowledge that competency in language and communication influences cognitive, social and emotional development;**

> **have an awareness of the development of language and communication skills in all of the children in our care, based upon careful observations and interaction with each child;**

> **plan explicit opportunities for children to use and extend their developing language skills with supportive adults;**

> **recognise the strong links between competence in oracy and the successful development of literacy skills;**

> organise the learning environment so that children can be immersed in purposeful print, and engage in purposeful and appropriate literacy tasks;

> provide a model of literate behaviours for young children to emulate;

> recognise the role of the practitioner as central to children's development and the quality of provision.

The role of parents/carers in literacy education has not been explicitly discussed in this chapter (see Chapter 2). However, their importance must be recognised.

MOVING *ON* > > > > > > MOVING *ON* > > > > > > MOVING *ON*

The Communication, Language and Literacy area of learning and development is not only complex, but in many ways it also underpins the five other areas. It is for this reason that practitioners must seek to ensure that their own awareness and understanding is kept up to date, and that the enjoyment of participating in and contributing to children's linguistic and literacy development is maintained. This is most effectively done through involvement in in-service education, examining and engaging with appropriate initiatives and collaboration with colleagues. Membership of professional associations will also enable us as practitioners to engage more actively in the decision making processes that influence the curriculum that we teach.

REFERENCES REFERENCES **REFERENCES** REFERENCES **REFERENCES** REFERENCES

Barriere, I., David, T., Gouch, K., Jago, M., Raban, B. and Ure, C. (2000) *Making sense of literacy*. Stoke on Trent: Trentham Books.

Browne, A. (2004) *Developing language and literature*, (3rd edition). London: Paul Chapman.

Bruner, J. (1993) *Child's Talk; learning to use language*. New York: Norton.

Cambourne, B. (1988) The whole story: natural learning and the acquisition of literacy in the classroom. Auckland: Ashton Scholastic.

Department for Education and Skills (2006) *Independent review of the teaching of early reading: final report*. London: DfES.

Ellis, S. (2007) Policy and research: lessons from the Clackmannanshire Synthetic Phonics Initiative. *Journal of Early Literacy*, 7 (3), 281–97.

Goswami, U. (1993) Toward an interactive analogy model of reading development: decoding vowel graphemes in beginning reading. *Journal of Experimental Child Psychology*, 56(3), 443–75.

Grugeon, E., Hubbard, L. Smith, C. and Dawes, L. (2005) *Teaching Speaking and listening in the primary school*. London: David Fulton.

Hall, N. and Robinson, A. (2003) *Exploring writing and play in the early years*, (2nd edition). London: David Fulton.

Hughes, M. and Westgate, D. (1997) Teachers and other adults as talk partners in nursery and reception classes. *Education*, 3–13, March.

Hynds, J. (2007) Putting a spin on reading: the language of the Rose Review. *Journal of Early Childhood Literacy*, 7 (3), 267–79.

Johnston, R. and Watson, J. (2005) *The effects of synthetic phonics teaching on reading and spelling attainment: A seven year longitudinal study*. Edinburgh: SEED.

Lancaster, L. (2007) Representing the ways of the world: how children under three use syntax in graphic signs. *Journal of Early Childhood Literature,* 7(2).

Mercer, N. (1995) *The guided construction of knowledge: talk amongst teachers and learners*. Clivedon: Multilingual Matters.

Meyer, R. (2002) *Phonics exposed: understanding and resisting systematic direct intense phonics instruction.* NJ and London: Lawrence Erlbaum Associates.

Schaffer, H. R. (1996) *Social development: an introduction*. Oxford: Blackwell.

Trevarthen, C. (1995) The child's need to learn a culture. *Children in Society*, 9(1).

7

Knowledge and understanding of the world

Elaine Spink, Brenda Keogh and Stuart Naylor

Chapter objectives

By the end of this chapter you should:

- **have developed an understanding of the ways in which children learn about the world and what knowledge and understanding of the world (KUW) means for them;**
- **be able to support children effectively in developing KUW;**
- **have examined the key principles of the Early Years Foundation Stage in relation to developing KUW;**
- **be able to identify the next steps for you as a professional working with Early Years children.**

This chapter addresses the following Professional Standards for QTS:

Q3(a), Q8, Q10, Q14, Q15, Q25(a), Q25(b)

Introduction

> *Children must be supported in developing the knowledge, skills and understanding that help them to make sense of the world. Their learning must be supported through offering opportunities for them to use a range of tools safely; encounter creatures, people, plants and objects in their natural environments and in real-life situations; undertake practical 'experiments'; and work with a range of materials.*
>
> (DCSF, 2007a, p14)

Even before birth we are exploring and interacting with our world. We respond to sounds; recognise our mothers' voices; see light and shade; taste the fluid which surrounds us; feel the confines of our environment; and begin to make sense of the plethora of experiences which life comprises. 'Learning' is a lifelong process of making sense of the world and children must be supported in developing the knowledge, understanding and skills which enable them to do this. This is the premise upon which knowledge and understanding of the world (KUW), an area of learning within the Early Years Foundation Stage (EYFS) (DCSF, 2007a), is based.

Knowledge and understanding of the world is made up of six aspects:

1. exploration and investigation;
2. designing and making;
3. ICT;
4. time;
5. place;
6. communities.

These aspects form the foundations for later learning in science, design and technology, ICT, history and geography but here, in the EYFS, they are closely related. Every aspect has a significant contribution to make towards delivering the outcomes of *Every Child Matters* (DfES, 2003).

In this chapter, the ways in which children learn about the world, what KUW means for them, and the ways children may be supported effectively in developing KUW will be discussed; the key principles of the EYFS examined; and the next steps for professionals working with EYFS children identified.

Learning about the world

We all seem to be born with the miraculous capacity to extract from (early) experiences and begin the process of sorting our world into some sort of order.

(De Boo, 2000, p2)

Children are born with innate capabilities – innate 'knowledge' if you will – which enable them to meet their needs and to begin manipulating their environment from the moment of birth. A newborn baby, placed on her/his mother's abdomen, can make the journey to their first fast-food takeaway within minutes of being born, totally unaided by the adults around her or him. They wriggle and squirm in a seemingly unco-ordinated way but their movements take them straight to the mother's nipple. How do they 'know' how to do this? – truly a miraculous capacity.

Learning occurs when these innate abilities are tempered by experience, expanded and changed by it so that, as De Boo says above, our world slowly becomes more ordered and understandable. The processes of learning enable us to accrue knowledge, acquire and refine skills and develop understanding. In discussing KUW we are perhaps considering the most holistic and all-encompassing area of learning since it concerns, quite literally, life, the universe and everything. It will therefore be necessary to consider those elements which are specific to developing KUW and which distinguish it from the other EYFS areas of learning, while emphasising that 'all areas of learning and development are connected and all are equally important' (Practice Guidance Card 3.2, DCSF, 2007b).

How do children learn about the world? They learn through interacting with it and being active in their exploration of it. We are not making any distinctions here between how babies learn, compared with young children, adolescents or even adults, since the evidence points to the same principles underpinning the learning of all of us. We learn through play and, as discussed in Chapter 1, it is the most powerful vehicle for learning in EY education. Characteristics of play which resonate particularly with developing KUW are that:

- it is about possible, alternative worlds and involves being imaginative, creative, original and innovative;
- it actively uses first-hand experience, including struggle, manipulation, exploration, discovery and practice;
- it can occur in partnerships, or groups of adults and/or children.

(adapted from Bruce, 1991)

Similarly, it is fascinating to note that the features Janet Moyles highlights in defining play apply so readily and aptly to learning in science and technology, two curriculum areas which have their foundations in the KUW area of learning. According to Moyles, play is investigative; exploratory; experimental; energised by curiosity; real and first hand; a chance to practise skills, to know and understand concepts (Moyles, 2002, p14).

We learn through forming ideas about the world and then testing these ideas out or changing them when exposed to the ideas of others. Models of learning about the world have developed a long way from the 'jugs and mugs' approach to education where the teacher is the jug and the children are the mugs, waiting to be filled with the knowledge which pours forth from the teacher.

You will already be aware that constructivism is a philosophy of learning which says that individuals build (construct) their own views and ideas about the world. These ideas, or concepts, are formed from the individual's everyday experiences but some will be misconceptions such as 'all heavy things sink' or 'air has no weight because there is nothing in it'. Knowledge and understanding develop when we are exposed to alternatives. Therefore, learners' ideas are central to the learning process. Effective teachers enable us to challenge our ideas, sometimes directly through questioning ('Why do you think that? Do all heavy things sink?'); sometimes through providing focused activities ('Find out which of those objects float and which sink.'); by providing resources which challenge thinking ('This candle is very heavy. What happens when you put it in the water tray?'); or by enabling us to talk with others who have different ideas. This applies equally well to learning in history and geography: many notions will not accord with actuality and as an effective practitioner you will need to challenge children's views.

We learn about the world through developing awareness of the learning process itself: thinking about thinking. Developing metacognition, the ability to reason about your own thinking, is crucial to making sense of the world. You will need to encourage this by enabling children to be involved in planning learning tasks and activities, to describe their progress through activities and to evaluate the outcomes. Recent research by the Effective Provision of Preschool Education Project discussed in Chapter 1, suggests that where adults participate in sharing their thoughts with learners, described as 'sustained shared thinking', high-quality learning is most likely to take place.

In developing KUW you will have a lot to aim for. Gaining knowledge is relatively straightforward. Learners can be told something, shown something or experience something. However, there is a vast difference between knowing something and understanding it. Knowing how to operate a DVD player does not guarantee an understanding of the way in which it works. Knowing that Napoleon lost the Battle of Waterloo does not guarantee an understanding of the complexities of the politics and strategies which produced that outcome. There is gathering strength in the argument that knowledge transmission is no longer appropriate at any stage of education, since the pace of change is too great for any statutory curriculum or framework to keep up with. For children who reached the age of five in 2008, it is estimated that over 60 per cent of the jobs they will do as adults have yet to be invented (Barrett, 2006). The availability and rapidly increasing quantity of information means that as an Early Years practitioner, your efforts with children must focus on how to access that knowledge, how to interpret and question it, how to make decisions based on it and how to use it to solve problems, rather than how to absorb and retain it. 'Learning is for living, not merely for knowing' (Hayes, 2006, p9).

So what does KUW mean for children? The Practice Guidance for the EYFS (DCFS, 2007b) specifies four key features.

1. Finding out about the world through exploration and a variety of sources.
2. Opportunities to learn about different ways of life and to develop positive and caring attitudes.
3. Opportunities to learn to respect and value all people.
4. Involvement in practical applications of knowledge and skills, making decisions about what to investigate and how to do it.

Echoing themes which have featured in this discussion so far, Ofsted highlighted characteristics which made settings outstanding: adults understand how children learn and develop; children engage enthusiastically in challenging activities that promote their learning; children show confidence in their play and learning (Ofsted, 2007, p14).

The question now is, how can you implement these features effectively?

Supporting children effectively in developing KUW

At the heart of this is recognising the uniqueness of every child and understanding that each child develops at a different rate and in an individual way (DCSF, 2007b). The first principle of the EYFS – a unique child – is the overarching theme in the discussion which follows when the three remaining principles, positive relationships, enabling environments, learning and development, are put into practice in supporting children's development of KUW.

Positive relationships

The practice guidance for the EYFS suggests that as a practitioner, you should give particular attention to: using parents' knowledge to extend children's experiences of the world; helping children to become aware of, to explore and to question differences in gender, ethnicity, language, religion, culture, special educational needs and disability issues; and supporting children with sensory impairment by providing supplementary experience and information. However, 'positive relationships' encompass a broader remit than this and have a profound impact on learning about the world.

KUW comes from learning about people, as well as places, times, events and objects. As an Early Years practitioner, you may acknowledge that children are social beings, perhaps without examining the implications of this for the ways in which learning is organised. Babies are 'pre-wired' to respond to the faces and sounds of people. Not only do they become more animated when shown black-and-white images with shapes corresponding to the areas of light and shade of faces,but they are also pre-wired to take part in conversations. If you hold a newborn baby at a distance at which they can focus on your face (interestingly, the focus distance is the distance from a mother's face to her nipple) and then slowly stick your tongue out and in, far from being thought impolite, this action will instigate a copying response from the baby who will pull tongues back at you. You will be involved in a tongue-pulling conversation!

It seems that all learning must involve social contexts and many and frequent opportunities to interact with others. These learning interactions take place between children, between children and their parents, families and carers; with adults from within the setting; and with those external to it. People can be the greatest resource for developing KUW in the EYFS, not just employed staff in the setting but any adults and older pupils who are willing or able to spend time with the children. They bring the depth and breadth of experience needed in this very wide area of learning.

As an effective practitioner, you will support learning about the world by encouraging children to talk to each other, about what they have found out, to speculate on future findings or to describe their experiences. This will enable reflection on learning and on new knowledge gained (DCSF, 2007b, p76). In the best settings, adults show children that they value their ideas (Ofsted, 2007) (and by implication, these are the settings in which children's ideas are elicited and then developed, along constructivist lines). In these outstanding settings, the children participate in decision-making; they learn to approach different cultures and religions through 'activities and lively discussions' (op cit), often centred on visitors who share experiences; and the providers recognise the fact that parents know their children best, ensuring that they (the parents) remain actively involved.

Classroom Story
Involving visitors to enrich learning

Joseph's grandad visited the nursery regularly. Talking to the teacher one day he happened to mention that he had noticed how difficult the children found learning to use tools and how it seemed difficult for them to produce anything interesting or creative. He had an idea that he would like to try out that combined his love of gardening with his skills as a joiner. The next day he brought in a large bag full of fruit and vegetables. With the help of the children he cut them into chunks. Now the children were able to use long nails to hammer the chunks together to make animals, trees, buildings, monsters, in fact anything that their imagination and skills would allow them to make!

At the core of learning about the world is a reciprocal relationship between children and adults, as illustrated in Figure 7.1.

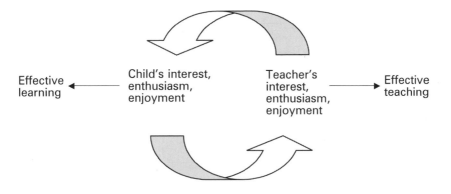

Figure 7.1 Reciprocal relationship between children and adults

It is your role to be the catalyst for generating and sustaining this relationship. This can be achieved through the following.

- Modelling appropriate behaviours and responses – enthusiasm, curiosity, questioning, observing closely, showing surprise, showing wonder, using more technical vocabulary, responding positively to children's ideas, exploring ways of finding answers.
- Working alongside children to illustrate an enthusiasm for learning – 'I'm really excited! I didn't know that we had two kinds of ladybirds in the garden until Thomas found them today.'
- Connecting learning to the outside world. 'Look how we can make the Roamer work by pressing the buttons. What do you have at home that you can programme like this? A washing machine – what a good idea Anjani!'
- Valuing ideas of all people in the learning environment. 'Roisin said that the piece of wood is really big so it will sink. She has watched carefully and noticed that all the big things have sunk. Let's see what happens - what a surprise, it floats!'
- Helping children to be aware of and reflect on their learning. 'Who has learnt something new today? Sally? Sally's brick wall kept falling over and now she says that she has learnt how to make it stay up. How did you do that Sally?'
- Being flexible, willing to catch the moment, recognising that routines help young children but that surprise and spontaneity are also loved by them. 'Monika has just seen a rainbow outside – let's all go and look at it.'

The adult must recognise and praise 'effort as well as achievement so that all children develop positive attitudes to themselves as learners' (Practice Guidance card 1.1, DCSF, 2007b). Ofsted endorses this view but, with their prevailing focus on measuring and assessing achievement, omits the celebration of 'effort': 'In outstanding settings, children are proud of what they do. Adults celebrate children's success and offer praise for their achievements' (2007).

Enabling environments

Listen to the children: the magic comes from them.
(Nursery practitioner when asked why the setting was such an exciting place to be)

An enabling environment offers a range of activities which will encourage children's interest and curiosity (DCSF, 2007b, p75). It will support developing KUW through stimulating interest and provide a wealth of opportunities to share new ideas and experiences. Ofsted look for environments which are planned thoughtfully so that children can choose what they do from a range of interesting resources, natural materials and exciting activities. A rich indoor learning environment:

- invites observation; for example 'Have you seen the old coins that Sam's uncle brought in? Are they like the ones that we have today?'
- stimulates curiosity; for example 'What do you think this is?' (an artefact/object brought into the setting) 'What does it do? Where might it be from?'
- poses problems; for example 'How can I stop my ice lolly from melting so quickly?'
- provides opportunities to build on prior learning and experience; for example 'I've put some seeds and compost in our garden centre. Can you make some plants grow like we did before?'
- reflects the interests and achievements of the children; for example 'Tom and Kalindi have found lots of conkers and now they're finding out which is the biggest.'
- involves the children in deciding what to do and where.

However, even when thoughtfully planned, the indoor setting cannot substitute for active experimentation out of doors when developing KUW. Some learning can happen only outside; for example, finding out where mini beasts live; learning to use bicycles and wheeled toys; experiencing different weather conditions. One of the strengths of outdoor learning is that it can take place on a larger, messier and noisier scale (HGfL, 2007) than is possible indoors, extending, not only complementing, indoor provision.

A rich outdoor learning environment for developing KUW can be created by:

- growing plants (in tubs if necessary); providing bird feeders;
- using a log to create a habitat for mini beasts; marking out a timeline; marking out compass directions and pointers to local landmarks;
- highlighting different textures; creating a 'treasure hunt'; making a weather station.

Inside or outside the setting, the range and quality of resources will have a significant impact on the children's learning about the world.

Her Majesty's Chief Inspector of Education, Children's Services and Skills stated in the 2006/ 07 Annual Report that improvements were noted by inspection teams in settings which 'used a more varied range of resources and opportunities to promote children's understanding of their own communities and the wider world' (p21).

The EYFS Briefing Pack for Local Authorities (www.teachernet.gov.uk, updated July 2007) states that learning about the world is facilitated when resources are provided in response to a child's interest and when materials enable children to follow their own ideas. The question for you is, how can children's ideas be anticipated and resources readied for the moment when a child seeks to explore their own interests? Experience will facilitate accurate prediction and you will begin to be prepared for the more unusual events. For example, you could collect resources for a snowy day comprising containers for collecting snow, bottles of coloured water for squirting patterns in the snow, objects for printing with, buckets and spades, a magnifying glass, and then be ready for an immediate response when the snow begins to fall.

Effective Early Years practitioners make best use of resources available and build up a supply of materials to support the development of KUW. Parents and other friends of the setting, including local businesses and community groups, can often provide a surprising range of items. In this way, a wide range of resources can accumulate which reflect the diversity within the community and within our society. Most of the resources will be everyday objects, with the exception of ICT resources which should include (for developing KUW) cameras, CD players, tape recorders, and programmable toys in addition to computers (see Practice Guidance and discussion in Chapter 8).

If children are to learn to work independently and with autonomy in developing KUW, as reflected in the ELG for KUW with the requirement for children to select tools, techniques and appropriate resources, they need opportunities to access resources without adult intervention/support. This necessitates their becoming familiar with what resources are available, how to use them and where they are stored (requiring clear labelling or colour-coding). The practitioner must also consider how to build progression into the use of certain resources. For example, a Nursery teacher provided dough for playing with; the next day, the dough was textured with sand; the day after it was coloured and scented; after that it was accompanied by tools for cutting, rolling and printing; finally, baked dough was provided and the children requested the resources they needed to explore this.

Learning and development

For effective learning and development in KUW, the EYFS (DCSF, 2007b, card 4.01) recommends that particular attention is given to planning, based on first-hand experiences; teaching, through practical activities; communicating, particularly children communicating; supporting children in the use of ICT; and challenging stereotypes. To this list, addressed elsewhere in the Practice Guidance but worthy of discussion in relation to the focus area of learning here, will be added assessing development and learning in KUW.

Planning

Planning underpins effective practice and is discussed in more detail in Chapter 9. Not surprisingly, Ofsted emphasises planning a great deal in making recommendations to or requirements of EYFS settings ('develop the planning arrangements', 'plan for next steps' (2007, p36) and yet there is a contrasting position to this. Many experienced practitioners point to the serendipitous events that led to great leaps in understanding and it is certainly true that for a child, learning about the world cannot always be planned, controlled or systematic. As previously discussed, the world changes almost too rapidly for an education system to keep pace with, and opportunities for learning present themselves continuously. Gaining KUW may be coincidental, random and at times unsystematic. It may be initiated by those who have not been involved in the planning: by the child, another child or another adult.

The EYFS Practice Guidance eloquently puts it thus:

> *No plan written weeks in advance can include a group's interest in a spider's web on a frosty morning or a particular child's interest in transporting small objects in a favourite blue bucket, yet it is these interests which may lead to some powerful learning.* (p12)

The Guidance also identifies planning as the source of particular challenges and dilemmas, including ensuring flexibility for groups while keeping a focus on individuals, planning time for regular observations of children who do not attend regularly and involving parents in the planning cycle.

The answer lies, as is so often the case, in the 'middle ground' between the two positions of to plan or not to plan. Planning is essential, but the plans must be flexible enough to adapt to circumstances. Being spontaneous does not imply a lack of planning or preparation and opens up possibilities such as those illustrated by the following example.

CLASSROOM STORY

One afternoon it began to hail. The Reception class teacher quickly gathered the children in the 'home bay' where the windows slid open to allow enough room for 25 hands to reach outside. The children described the feel of the hail, watched it bouncing on the ground, made it melt in their hands and listened to the sound of it hitting the windows and roof. This prompted the teacher to fetch metal trays to hold outside and the class listened to 'hail music'. The children later had opportunities to replicate the hail music with musical instruments.

A flexible approach to planning will facilitate the involvement of the children and their families in the planning process. For example, 'That's a good idea, Sami. What would you like to do to find out about that?' In later learning, the investigative cycle in science, the designing and making process in design and technology, the research process in history, for example, all require the children to apply planning skills and to have the autonomy to follow their own paths of enquiry. These capabilities are ones which are often fostered very well in EYFS settings.

The requirements for the EYFS place much emphasis on the planning of first-hand experiences, practical activities and opportunities for exploration and experimentation. In an example of good practice in the EY being recognised and of attempts being made to transfer it to later stages of education, HMCI Christine Gilbert, in her Annual Report 2006/07 pointed out the need to plan and teach skills through practical activity.

Planning effective starting points can open up rich veins of enquiry in all aspects of developing KUW. Your starting point may arise from a display, a role-play area, from visitors and artefacts, from unusual or interesting objects, from programmes used on the computer, TV or radio. Your starting point may also be that incidental occurrence when a child brings in something to share, or a rainbow appears.

As children learn in different way, it is important that you provide a variety of routes into learning for them. Table 7.1 shows a range of activity starting points used by a Nursery for developing KUW around the theme of 'I am special'.

Person	Unusual object	Everyday object	Question	Book	Display	Visit/ outdoor learning	ICT
Visit from a health visitor	A child's special possession (included great-grandad's medal, a dead tarantula in a glass case, a bamboo table decoration from an Indonesian wedding)	Large mirror	What is special about you?	'Guess how much I love you?'	Group photos. Poster of children from around the world	To the camera shop; use of digital camera	Digital camera + computer to compile group photos; record children singing.

Table 7.1 Example of activity start points

PRACTICAL TASK PRACTICAL TASK **PRACTICAL TASK** PRACTICAL TASK **PRACTICAL TASK**

Think of starting points under the following headings to support developing KUW within the theme of 'Homes'.

Person	Unusual object	Everyday object	Question	Book	Display	Visit/ outdoor learning	ICT

How would you use the building of new houses next to the setting/school as a starting point?

Teaching

What comes first, learning or teaching? Can you have learning without teaching? What is your role as an educator – teaching or facilitating learning? Your responses to these questions will serve to contribute to the wider debate which rumbles – and sometimes rages – along. Phillip Beadle has called for a recognition of the importance of teaching over facilitating learning. 'Real teachers know that while learning may sometimes happen accidentally, without great teaching, it doesn't happen with any degree of regularity or with much joy' (2008, p6).

And yet an 'at the front, directing the proceedings' role is often less appropriate in the EYFS than in any other stage. The practitioner is more subtle in their directing of the learning, through the organisation of time, activities, resources and intervention. However, there is a place for direct teaching. The EYFS Practice Guidance states that practitioners should teach skills and knowledge. An important yet sometimes overlooked fact is that children will rarely just 'know' how to do something; skills must be taught through instruction, demonstration and opportunities to practise. For example, teaching how to use tools or equipment. Practical activities, as emphasised by the EYFS Practice Guidance, provide the contexts for the teaching of skills and knowledge (for example, 'this is called a magnet') but we are, at the same time, facilitating learning through providing resources, involving other adults/other professionals, managing and organising the environment and communicating with children and parents.

Your teaching – or facilitation of learning – will require you to model appropriate learning behaviours and responses, particularly enthusiasm, questioning, close observation to notice details, showing surprise and wonder, responding positively to ideas (particularly those which differ from your own) and exploring ways of finding answers. HMCI has emphasised the significance of the teacher's approach, across all stages. 'In outstanding lessons, the teachers' enthusiasm for their subjects is infectious and they engage pupils' interest through lively presentation and a brisk pace of learning' (HMCI, 2007).

Questioning is of particular importance in developing KUW, so while it undoubtedly forms a significant element of effective communication, discussed later, it is essential to consider its contribution to effective teaching. Questioning builds the climate of enquiry upon which KUW is based. EYFS settings must provide environments in which raising questions and seeking answers are encouraged and promoted (see Harlen, 2006, for guidance). Ofsted point to the need for settings to develop understanding of how to question effectively (2007, p36). This involves understanding the difference between subject-centred questions – those which appear to require a right answer, such as 'How do you fasten these?' – and a person-centred question, such as 'How do you think we can fasten these two things together?', which invites opinion, is less threatening and can lead to exploration. It also necessitates an understanding of the difference between productive questions, those which lead to further enquiry, and unproductive questions, which tend to close possibilities down.

We must encourage children to raise their own questions and we must use questions to model investigative behaviour, for example 'What do you think will happen if I put glue on this button and put it there?' 'What do you think this is and how could we find out?' Strategies for handling children's responses to questions are also very significant. How do you invite responses? 'Hands up to tell the teacher' will not always be appropriate. The children can, and should, be invited to share their responses with others, such as a 'talking partner', or in non-verbal ways such as manipulating objects or pictures. A subject-centred question may provoke a misconception (or a 'wrong' answer if you have a particular response in mind). For example, a teacher asked, 'What town is our school in?' A child responded with 'London' (which was 250 miles away). At that point, many teachers would have shown that it was not the answer they were expecting and moved on to another child. The skilled teacher in this case adapted her questioning to enable this child to succeed, asking 'Where do you live, Ryan?'. As well as effective questioning and teaching, the practitioner was demonstrating effective communication.

Communicating

There are excellent ideas suggested in the EYFS Practice Guidance (page 77 onwards) which emphasise communication and purposeful interaction between children and with the adults in the setting. For example:

- plan time when children can discuss past events in their lives;
- display and talk about photos of favourite places;
- plan time to listen to children.

The last is a particularly interesting and pertinent one as, in our busy working lives we often need to be reminded to make time (implying a conscious action, not leaving it to chance) for listening. As developing KUW centres on children collecting and reflecting upon ideas (of their own and those of others) we must avoid the temptation to 'put words in their mouths'. In outstanding settings, adults engage children in discussion by asking open-ended questions and waiting for the children to think about their reply (Ofsted, 2007, p15). Their thoughts and words may take a long time to formulate and we must wait. It is also important to plan time for children to develop their listening skills with each other, to be able to respond to each other's ideas and begin to wonder about alternative views, beliefs and conceptions of the world. The aspects of learning within KUW have particular vocabulary associated with them: the vocabulary of time and place; scientific terminology; ICT-specific meanings; the vocabulary of designing and making. We should not attempt to shield children from subject-specific vocabulary by oversimplifying or replacing recognised terms with something we deem more child-friendly. Most children readily acquire new vocabulary and with relatively little practice, will use it appropriately in correct contexts.

Assessing

As stated in the EYFS Practice Guidance, 'all effective assessment involves analysing and reviewing what you know about each child's development and learning' (p12) and then planning accordingly. You will find a detailed discussion of this in Chapter 9. A particular concern for the KUW area of learning is that, with the emphasis being on practical, first-hand experiences, assessment must be 'in the moment'. Our observations must capture the sometimes fleeting evidence presented in an exploratory activity or discussion. This means that activities focused on developing KUW must be the focus of frequent observations and also feature periods of regular sustained observation and assessment. Your learning plans for each child will be based on the information you gain about their KUW from talking to them, their parents and your colleagues and from observing them (Practice Guidance card 4.2, DCSF, 2007b).

For further guidance on the general principles underpinning assessment in the EYFS, see Chapter 9.

Manageability is a key challenge for an area as broad and disparate as KUW. It is essential to make sure that the quality of the children's experiences is not gained and maintained at the expense of your sanity! In order to keep a balance between what is ideal and what is achievable, it is important to plan with manageability in mind. This will involve: initially identifying short, simple activities which can be built upon gradually as confidence in this area of learning grows; avoiding being overambitious – young children bring lots of ideas with them but so much in their KUW is new to them and will need time to develop; taking time to linger over experiences; valuing repetition – not all experiences have to be new; drawing upon the knowledge and expertise of others; making best use of local resources; and having experiences/activities in reserve. You and the children should be enjoying while achieving in teaching and learning.

REFLECTIVE TASK

Use the questions below to reflect on how well you are doing and to identify how you may further improve your practice.

- How do you promote children's enjoyment and achievement in developing KUW?
- How do you plan improvements and review their success?
- Do you know what children are achieving and what progress they are making?
- How do you plan to develop the children's learning further?
- Do you involve children and parents in planning and reviewing the children's learning and development?
- How do you ensure that all adults involved are continuing to develop their understanding of how children learn about the world?
- Do you provide opportunities for children to learn and challenge views about differences in gender, culture, religion, language and ethnicity?
- Do you plan first-hand, practical, exploratory activities?
- Do you use a range of ICT to support children in developing KUW?
- Do you use vocabulary specific to this area of learning?

Involve the children in reviewing your provision, find out what they think and feel. The questions which follow are offered as a guide to reflective conversations with children.

- What do you like doing best?
- What can you do by yourself?
- What have you been doing today/this week?
- What would you like to do tomorrow/next week?
- What makes you happy when you are here? What makes you sad?
- What do you like finding out about?

(based on Ofsted, 2007, p41)

And finally,

- What three things will you do next to further improve your practice in facilitating children's development of KUW?

A SUMMARY OF **KEY POINTS**

> Children develop knowledge and understanding of the world in active, investigative and exploratory ways.

> Children's ideas are at the heart of the learning process and must shape our planning, teaching and assessing.

> Learning about the world should happen in a social context based on talk and interaction.

> Variety is vital – in starting points, resources, adult involvement, roles, environments and teaching strategies.

> Questioning and challenging are essential to developing understanding of the world.

MOVING *ON* > > > > > > MOVING *ON* > > > > > > MOVING *ON*

As your children move from the EYFS, the knowledge, skills and understanding they have gained will be continued in the National Curriculum subjects of science, history, geography, ICT and design technology. In order to support learners at this point of transition, you will need to be familiar with the programmes of study for these areas and their related assessment. You will also need to work closely with colleagues and parents to ensure continuity and progression are maintained. You might also encourage parents to seek out extra-curricular opportunities for developing learning in this area, either that available as clubs accessible at lunchtime or before and after the school day, or within the community in places such as libraries and museums.

REFERENCES REFERENCES **REFERENCES** REFERENCES REFERENCES REFERENCES

Barrett, N. (2006) Creative partnerships: Manchester and Salford. www.ioe.mmu.ac.uk/cue/seminars/ BARRETT%20Urban%20seminar1.doc. (accessed 21 July 2007).

Beadle, P. (2008) Teachers: Go to the front of the class. *Education Guardian*, Tuesday 15 January.

Bruce, T. (1991) *Time to play in early childhood*. London: Hodder and Stoughton.

DCSF (2007a) *Statutory Framework for the Early Years Foundation Stage*. London: DCSF.

DCSF (2007b) *Practice Guidance for the Early Years Foundation Stage*. London: DCSF.

DfES (2003) *Every Child Matters*. London: TSO.

De Boo, M. (2000) *Science 3-6: laying the foundations in the early years*. Hatfield: ASE.

Harlen, W. (2006) *The teaching of science in primary schools*. London: David Fulton.

Hayes, D. (2006) *Inspiring primary teaching*. Exeter: Learning Matters.

HGfL (Hertfordshire Grid for Learning) (2007) *Knowledge and understanding of the world*. www.thegrid.org.uk/learning/foundation/areas/knowledge (accessed 13 January 2008).

HMCI (2007) *The Annual Report of Her Majesty's Chief Inspector of Education, Children's Services and Skills 2006/07*. London: TSO.

McBratney, S. (1994) *Guess how much I love you*. London: Walker Books.

Moyles, J. (2002) *Just playing?* Oxford: OUP.

Ofsted (2007) *Early Years: getting on well: enjoying, achieving and contributing*. London: TSO. www.ofsted.gov.uk/publications (accessed 20 December 2007).

Briefing Pack for Local Authorities www.teachernet.gov.uk, updated July 2007 (accessed 12 December 2007).

FURTHER READING FURTHER READING **FURTHER READING** FURTHER READING

Cooper, H. (ed.) (2004) *Exploring time and place through play: foundation stage – Key Stage One*. London: David Fulton.

Palmer, J. (2004) *Geography in the early years*. London: Routledge Falmer.

8

ICT in the Early Years Foundation Stage
Tony Poulter

Chapter objectives

By the end of this chapter you should:

- **have an understanding of how ICT can enhance learning in the EYFS across the six areas of learning;**
- **have an overview of the learning theories applicable to the use of various ICT tools;**
- **know the importance of promoting ICT so that pupils become confident users of it.**

This chapter addresses the following Professional Standards for QTS:

Q17, Q23, Q25(a)

Introduction

According to Hall and Higgins (2002, p293):

> *The burning questions are not **whether** computers should be used but **where** and **how** ICT can be used to enlarge and enrich young children's experience of learning.*

This categorical conclusion was reached by the authors after examining research into the impact of information and communication technology (ICT) on teaching and learning in the Early Years and it is the last two questions that we shall be focusing upon in this chapter. Of course, it must be acknowledged that ICT does have its detractors. Cuban (2001, p67) refers to use of ICT in pre-school settings as a 'benign addition', and Plowman and Stephen (2003, p149) comment that 'Its use does not transform practice'. However, there is a large and growing body of evidence that contradicts these views, indicating that the positive impact of ICT on the teaching and learning process has been substantial, particularly in recent years. The often-quoted motivational value of ICT (see the Becta website for more on this) is no less relevant to children in the Early Years Foundation Stage (EYFS). Its potential ability to enhance teaching and learning is often stated and cannot be denied.

A perusal of the *Statutory Framework for the Early Years Foundation Stage* (DCSF, 2007a) shows that ICT can play its part in all four overarching themes, their underlying principles and supporting commitments. It may not be initially obvious but ICT can play a major part in developing a unique child as a competent learner, can aid in the building of positive relationships at home and in the learning setting, and certainly has its place as part of an enabling environment for learning. However, it is in the learning and development theme that ICT will be most relevant and it is the use of ICT in the 'interconnected' areas of learning and development that will be examined in the remainder of this chapter.

ICT can make a substantial contribution in all six areas of learning and development, although the most overt references to ICT can be found in the knowledge and understanding of the world (KUW) section of the *Practice Guidance for the Early Years Foundation Stage* (DCSF, 2007b).

In the guidance (pages 81/82) practitioners are advised to:

- talk about ICT apparatus;
- incorporate technology resources in children's play;
- draw young children's attention to ICT apparatus in the setting or the locality;
- teach children to click on icons to make things happen;
- provide a range of programmable toys and other ICT equipment including computers;
- ensure safe use of all ICT apparatus.

This chapter will discuss how this might be done and offers some practical advice about resources that are available and how they might be used.

When they first arrive in the Nursery class, children should begin to develop their basic ICT skills. Many children may actually already be confident users of the technologies but some will not and you should be prepared to quickly address this difference. The instilling of mouse and keyboard skills should be a top priority if children are to have access to learning opportunities right across the six areas of the EYFS (and subsequent key stages). There are alternative input devices to help younger children; for example, touch screens, switches, even a smaller mouse. However, the ability to connect mouse movements to the pointer on-screen is a particularly important skill and many of the software packages mentioned in this chapter will promote the acquisition of this skill.

ICT in knowledge and understanding of the world

Although it is clear that ICT should be used to develop skills across the areas of learning and development, it is the knowledge and understanding of the world strand alone in the statutory framework that makes direct reference to ICT. Practitioners should be aware, however, that when children are using ICT in other areas of learning, for example in the development of early literacy or mathematics skills, they will, by default, also be addressing KUW. Computers are seen as one among many ICT 'tools' that can help the young child to learn. For instance, when gathering information children might utilise CD-ROMs or other ICT devices such as digital cameras, video cameras and audio equipment such as a tape recorder. ICT is seen as an invaluable tool to both teacher and learner.

PRACTICAL TASK PRACTICAL TASK **PRACTICAL TASK** PRACTICAL TASK **PRACTICAL TASK**

Resource audit

According to the guidance, practitioners are required to 'Support children in using a range of ICT to include cameras, photocopiers, CD players, tape recorders and programmable toys in addition to computers' (page 76). Iram and John Siraj-Blatchford in their booklet *More Than Computers* (2005), list these and many more resources that come under the umbrella term 'ICT'. It would be most useful to carry out an audit of ICT equipment in your setting. Is there a wide range of devices and apparatus including computers, printers, programmable toys, a digital camera, CD-ROMs, DVDs, a karaoke machine, TV and video camera? What about internet access? Is an interactive whiteboard or plasma screen installed? Visit other settings, well resourced in terms of ICT, and see how these are being used.

Furthermore, as a practitioner you are responsible for planning and implementing equal access to ICT resources for both boys and girls, and those children with special needs. The computer is particularly good at giving the latter group access to the curriculum. You will also need to address inequality with regard to home background and be aware of the 'digital divide'. Many homes today are ICT-rich environments that produce 'computer whizz-kids'. However, some children will come from ICT-poor homes and practitioners should ensure that various differentiation strategies are in place to develop their skill

As well as in ICT, knowledge and understanding of the world is the area responsible for laying the foundations for learning in science, design and technology, history and geography. ICT can support the young learner in all of these areas. One of the early learning goals (ELGs) in this section of the statutory framework (the ELG for ICT) stresses that children should 'Find out about and identify the uses of everyday technology and use information and communication technology and programmable toys to support their learning' (p5). The 'Development matters' strand of this ELG, in the guidance, suggests that children should:

- show an interest in ICT;
- seek to acquire basic skills in turning on and operating some ICT equipment;
- know how to operate simple equipment;
- complete a simple program on the computer;
- use ICT to perform simple functions on ICT apparatus;
- use a mouse and keyboard to interact with age-appropriate computer software.

You are provided with appropriate (if not in-depth) guidance on how to aid children in achieving these objectives and accomplishing the overall goal. The rest of this chapter will put some meat on the bones offered in the guidance.

ICT devices

Many ICT devices are of use in the development of skills in this area of learning. As well as the programmable toy (mentioned quite often in the guidance), the tape recorder, video/DVD player and television, and the digital camera could all prove to be very useful. John Stringer (2001) makes a good case for using ICT apparatus, other than the computer, in science. He suggests using cassette tape recorders to record observations of experiments, using the telephone to find out the latest local weather forecast, and using the fax machine to contact another school and compare the progress of plants. Most EYFS settings will have access to a computer but it may not be a state-of-the-art machine, or may not have appropriate software. As a teacher, you should be ready to take advantage of the huge variety of ICT-related devices around today and to stimulate your learners' interest in them.

Software

Certain types of content-free software packages could be of great benefit to the EYFS child in the KUW area of learning and development. This includes software such as word processors, data-handling programs and presentation packages. We shall explore these in more depth as we consider other areas of learning. There has been a huge explosion of content-specific CD-ROMs and websites (about a certain topic within a given subject) in recent years, aimed specifically at the EYFS age range, and these will also be well worth utilising in this area of learning, whether it is based around science, design and technology, history or geography.

Role-play

Opportunities for including ICT devices in a role-play situation should not be missed. The computer and other ICT equipment can be a part of various scenarios – the school office, the library, the shop and so on. Purposeful play is stressed in the guidance and play seems more authentic to the children if real (not 'pretend') apparatus is used. As 'scene setter', you have an important part to play too. By taking part in such activities children are not only learning about ICT but learning through ICT as well (Cook and Finlayson, 1999).

PRACTICAL TASK PRACTICAL TASK **PRACTICAL TASK** PRACTICAL TASK **PRACTICAL TASK**

Planning role-play

Plan a lesson in which you design a role-play scenario of 'the travel agent'. The equipment you use could include a digital camera for passport photographs, a computer with word-processing software to record customer details, and an atlas on CD-ROM to explore the world looking for holiday destinations. Relate the lesson to objectives in the knowledge and understanding of the world section of the guidance. Other areas of learning may also be covered. Identify possible opportunities for assessment.

Interactive whiteboards

One piece of ICT hardware that will be appearing more and more in the EYFS setting is the interactive whiteboard (IWB). This has been heralded in various quarters as some sort of panacea for the all the ills that besiege education. While this may be an exaggeration, IWBs are the latest invaluable ICT 'gizmo' in the teacher's toolkit and will certainly pay dividends if installed in your classroom. Supporters of the visual, auditory and kinaesthetic (VAK) learning styles model in particular may well find them an attractive proposition. IWBs, many claim, promote learning using visual, auditory and kinaesthetic senses with children being able to see, hear and touch a variety of engaging multimedia content. IWBs are here to stay and can allow any practitioner to deliver exceptional lessons in any area of learning and development, as will be seen.

ICT in communication, language and literacy

There are many instances where ICT might be helpful in developing communication, language and literacy (CLL) skills. ICT can help young children to become 'skilful communicators', to learn 'through activities and experiences that engage all the senses' and help 'to communicate thoughts, ideas and feelings' (page 39 of the guidance). If you are teaching at the end of the EYFS you should look at the *Primary framework for literacy and mathematics* website where you will be able to navigate to a most helpful document (available online or as a hard copy) which details how to use ICT in the 12 strands of literacy with EYFS children. Furthermore, it lists ten different ICT applications that you might use in delivering these activities – a 'must-have' resource! However, in this section we will look at how multimedia computers can be used in this area of learning to develop:

- reading through the use of talking books on CD-ROM and at websites;
- early writing through the use of talking word processors with word bank facility;
- speaking and listening skills by playing adventure games;
- early literacy skills through content-specific software.

Talking books

Talking books, which could exist only in ICT-format, are now commonplace in the Early Years setting. Titles such as *Talking stories* (2Simple*), Planet wobble* (Crick) and reading scheme-based CD-ROMs such as the *Oxford reading tree* (Oxford University Press/Sherston) have become familiar sights but have lost none of their power to be instructive and engaging. Programs like this allow pupils see and hear text being spoken in the context of colourful illustrations and also allow them to interact with the story through 'hotspots' that, when clicked, set off entertaining and engrossing animations. Research over the past decade has shown that the benefits of using such packages with EYFS children are manifold.

- They can be used like printed material to support a range of approaches to reading.
- They are fun and easy to use, providing motivation.
- Interest in, and concentration on, the text are sustained and increased.
- They provide particular support to early readers, reluctant readers and the less able.
- They give a simple introduction to the skill of reading from the computer screen.
- The interactive nature of the screen enhances the story and aids understanding of the text.
- They are an excellent precursor to reading the printed version of the book.
- They promote the increase of word accuracy and word recognition.
- The relationship between the written word and the spoken word is clearly shown.
- They stimulate the all-important 'talk' about the story.

Talking books are designed to be used by young children without the assistance of an adult. Because the text can be spoken to them, the program is in effect modelling the process of an adult reading aloud to the child, thus negating the need for an adult to actually be there.

> **RESEARCH SUMMARY** RESEARCH SUMMARY **RESEARCH SUMMARY** RESEARCH SUMMARY
>
> Grenier and Thornbury (2001) carried out a small-scale study looking at the joint attention of adults and Nursery children at the computer. This is a particularly worthy area of study as many educational researchers and theorists contend that it is always preferable to have an adult at the computer with the child/children to provide the all-important guidance and support (what Bruner called 'scaffolding') essential to effective learning. This added value to past studies by Medwell (1996) and Collins et al. (1997) that suggested guided participation and purposeful intervention by adults when children are sitting at the computer in the Early Years setting are something that practitioners should always plan for.

So, although talking books can be used independently by children, the talk they promote between teacher and learner is of greater value. Further support can be gained from the presence of another (perhaps more able) child at the computer. The teacher must get involved if young readers are to be active learners and not just passive recipients of text, no matter how 'edutaining' it is. It is as well to be aware that all the whistles and bells offered by this type of multimedia software (for example, eye-catching animations and noisy sound effects) can distract some children from the narrative, and possible gains in reading ability may suffer as a consequence if not guided by an adult.

Many excellent talking books can be found online. *Story bear* has some delightful stories at *The little animals activity centre*. *Tweenies – story time* and *Fimbles – comfy corner* are both excellent too. You may notice that these are all BBC sites but we make no apologies for that as they are all engaging, entertaining, CD-ROM-quality resources. However, many more can be found on the Web and a good place to begin looking is at this 'Literacy links' page (www.btinternet.com/~tony.poulter/links/kidlit.htm). Just scroll down to the 'Reading websites' box and explore the links. You will be amazed at what is out there in cyberspace.

Talking word processors

Word processors? For children who, perhaps, cannot write even their own name legibly? Surely we jest! Well, believe it or not they could be a very useful tool, not just for writing development but in promoting reading as well as speaking and listening skills. The Teacher Training Agency (now renamed the Training and Development Agency for Schools, TDA) published exemplification material for English (1999, p19) and clearly favours the use of word processors, where children are:

> ...using simple word processing software, to communicate in images and writing and recognise the value of written communication, even before they have developed the fine motor skills required for legible handwriting.

Note the reference to a 'simple' word-processing program. Use does not have to be made of the full-blown version of a program like Microsoft Word (though arguably it could). There are plenty of child-friendly word-processing packages on the market with facilities to help the emergent writer along. Writing activities with word processors need to be well thought out by the teacher. They need to be short, simple, focused but meaningful exercises, especially in the beginning. More often than not they should be collaborative tasks with two, perhaps three, pupils involved, and your intervention as the teacher, or assistance of an adult helper, is desirable and preferable.

There are many strategies that can be used to get young children writing, even if keyboard familiarity and mouse control are poor (although word-processing programs will, as a by-product, assist in the development of these all-important ICT skills). Overlay keyboards (sometimes referred to as 'concept keyboards') seem to be used very little these days and have been replaced by 'wordbank' programs that can be used in conjunction with the traditional QWERTY keyboard. One such program is *Clicker 5* (Crick) with its many 'grids' (essentially on-screen overlays or wordbanks) containing words and pictures (even sounds and animations) which offer a way of building up sentences on-screen quickly without resorting to time-consuming and frustrating sessions of 'hunt and peck'.

There are grids on many topics to choose from (which may be useful in other areas of learning and development) and it is very simple to create your own grids. New grids can be purchased, but why not register (it's free) at the LearningGrids website and any amount of *Clicker* grids can be downloaded free of charge? You will notice that pictures can appear with text, which always provide extra motivation for young writers. Differentiation is easily incorporated into the grids according to the ability of the children. One nice feature of this package is that support for popular reading schemes such as *Oxford Reading Tree* and *Planet Wobble* is available, thus making the link between reading and writing clear.

The value of the wordbank facility cannot be overstated. The vocabulary and spelling ability of early writers can often be quite limited and can deter writing. This facility allows users to right-click on a word, if they are not sure about it, to hear it first. If the child decides to use the word it simply has to be clicked on to be inserted in their writing. There are ready-made wordbanks but you can input your own lists of words that are perhaps difficult to recall and/or to spell, on a given topic before the children come to use the program.

But perhaps the most telling advantage of this particular word processor, with regard to supporting early writing, is the 'talking' facility it possesses. And it is not alone. As well as *Clicker 5,* there are other packages around, such as *Textease CT* (Softease) and *Talking First Word* (RM) where the typed word is actually spoken as the text is being composed. With these programs, letters, words, sentences or whole paragraphs and texts can be read back to the child. Young writers get the benefit of immediate feedback. Words are highlighted as they are spoken, enabling the children to follow the passage. Research evidence seems to show that talking word processors, using synthesised speech as feedback, lead to increased confidence and concentration, to improved punctuation and spelling, and to dramatic gains in reading ability. The case for using such software packages with EYFS children would seem a compelling one.

When using any of the word processors mentioned, and the impressive facilities they offer to the young writer, the activity should be a collaborative one. Once again, the importance of the talk that goes on around the computer should not be underestimated. The writing being composed on-screen can be the focus for much quality discussion. Many argue (Hardy, 2000; Riley, 2003) that computer use is a social activity and through co-operative learning the greatest gains are made. This can be particularly true of collaborative writing with word processors. Composing text at the keyboard with a peer, and more importantly with the teacher or assistant, provides an excellent opportunity for talk and collaborative learning in what Vygotsky called the zone of proximal development (ZPD), the gap between a child's present knowledge and their future learning potential. The support given to children by the software, their peers and the teacher all provide the 'scaffolding' needed to enable the children to bridge that gap.

Adventure games

One type of software that is designed specifically to promote discussion between children and the adults who inhabit the EYFS environment is the adventure game. This type of software is a simulation or model of a sometimes real but often imaginary world, a 'micro-world'. As groups of children explore this world they have to discuss alternatives, solve problems, make decisions and offer predictions. They have to learn from mistakes and ultimately achieve their goal – escape the maze, find the treasure, rescue the princess (or prince) and so on. Decisions are made based on reading simple text with picture clues and sound support. The sound aspect of multimedia programs like these should not be under-estimated. Aural, as well as oral skills are being developed.

These games have been around for 25 years now and have become more sophisticated, entertaining, engrossing and motivating since the advent of the CD-ROM. Enchanting titles such as *Casper – Mystery in the Castle* (Focus), *Noddy and the Toyland Fair* (Focus) and *Rainbow Fish and the Whale* (Dorling Kindersley) will do a fine job of challenging and inspiring children to think in creative and flexible ways. Here the literacy skills of speaking clearly, putting forward a point of view and justifying it are being developed. Listening to the perspectives of others and commenting sensibly are equally important. As a bonus, reading skills will often be further developed by use of this type of software as they become a part of the story.

Vygotsky's socio-cultural, communicative view of how young children learn through inter-action with others (in this case their peers and their teacher/helper) and through objects in their learning environment (in this case the computer and its software) applies to the use of adventure games particularly well. According to this theory, language is paramount. The communicative aspect of teaching and learning is very much to the fore.

This has a lot in common with constructivist theorists such as Piaget and Bruner, who espouse active interaction with the environment and the people within it to build up increas-ingly complex understandings over time. Adults provide support or scaffolding in the form of, for example, guided participation and purposeful intervention. The interactive, multime-dia facilities of today's adventure games would no doubt gain their approval having, as they do, the potential to develop problem-solving, thinking and communication skills.

In using adventure programs, individuals in the group see different aspects of a problem. Thus, together the group arrives at a solution to that problem. They can then progress, perhaps with a little practitioner prompting, to the next stage and ultimately the achievement of their goal. Studies seem to strongly suggest that computer use has a great deal of potential to enhance collaborative learning. It provides the structure and direction needed to make collaborative learning effective. The practitioner's role as an active participant in the learning process becomes central. They must give guidance, offer explanations and steer the group in the right direction by intervening purposefully but sensitively – in short, provide scaffolding.

Literacy software and websites

There are many CD-ROMs and websites that address the promotion of early literacy skills such as alphabet familiarity, letter recognition, letter shapes and sounds, phonics and spel-ling. And the beauty of many of them is that they are whiteboard-friendly, which is always a bonus. The games are often introduced by popular TV, cartoon and book characters for added motivation. A few of our favourite CD-ROMs include *Alphabet Soup* (2Simple), *Clicker Phonics* (Crick) and *ABC-CD* (Sherston).

Recommended websites would include *ICT Games – Literacy*, *Early ICT – Games* and *The Hoobs – Activities.* Of course there are many more CD-ROMs and websites out there. A 'try before you buy' policy is always a good idea before paying out for expensive CD-ROMs, and always check the appropriateness of the content of websites before introducing them to children.

ICT and problem-solving, reasoning and numeracy

There is great scope for using ICT in the problem-solving, reasoning and numeracy (PSRN) area of learning and development. Again, practitioners teaching children at the end of the EYFS are encouraged to visit the *Primary framework for literacy and mathematics* website where they will find assistance in using ICT to seek patterns, make connections, recognise relationships, work with numbers, shapes, space and measures, and develop skills in counting, sorting and matching. In this section we will look at how:

- the collaborative use of programmable toys can be utilised to explore position, direction, angles, shape and space, and to encourage the development of mathematical language;
- the use of simple graphing programs can develop data-handling skills;
- the use of certain CD-ROMs and websites can aid the development of early number skills.

Programmable toys

Both the statutory framework and the guidance make specific reference to the use of 'programmable toys' and it is a fact that these devices are very useful in PSRN. They could be remote-controlled, radio-controlled models of some kind but the term usually refers to programmable robots with a built-in keypad such Pixie (Swallow Systems) or perhaps Roamer (Valiant Technology). BeeBot (TTS) is the 'new kid on the block' and is particularly appropriate to this age range (see Figure 8.1).

Figure 8.1 BeeBot (plus accessories)

These floor robots (or turtles) were an innovation of the constructivist Seymour Papert, who developed the Logo computer language. Like Piaget, he believed that children work through concrete experience to develop conceptual understanding. Thus, before children could be exposed to the screen turtle in Logo they had to use the floor turtle to prepare the way. So using a 3-D toy like the Roamer, and becoming confident with it, is excellent preparation for using an early Logo program such as RoamerWorld (RM).

By its very nature, use of a robot can encourage the development of mathematical language in young children because it can address so many areas of the subject. Instructional language is promoted because the toy must be given a sequence of commands before it will move. Numeracy skills are fostered, as a numerical input is required to specify how far you want the toy to travel or turn. Number recognition and the value of a given number will occur through the use of the Roamer because this actually has numbers on the keypad, whereas with Pixie or BeeBot there are no numbers and counting comes into play (for example, three presses of the 'Forward' arrow means move forward three lengths of the toy). By experimenting, concepts such as direction, angle, shape and space, and the language associated with those concepts, are introduced to the young child. As with literacy, the value of talk in a numeracy setting should not be underestimated and should of course include the practitioner and/or assistant.

There are many good reasons for making use of a programmable robot such as the Roamer. Donahue, at the Valiant Technology website, lists numerous pedagogical advantages, and concludes by saying:

> *In sum, the Roamer can serve as the basis of a powerful problem-solving curriculum that will help young children begin to develop the habit of creative, independent problem-solving while introducing them to the key technologies of the modern Information Age.*

There are limitless innovative and creative ways that the teacher can use the Roamer. The Becta website suggests using the Roamer in the context of a story. Many stories are suggested: *Rosie's Walk, Don't Forget the Bacon, The Shopping Basket, The Little Red Hen.* The children really enjoy dressing up the Roamer as a character from a story (removable covers for the Roamer can be purchased) and then programming it to travel around a specially created environment (perhaps a grid with painted-on scenes from the story or one of the many playmats that can be purchased). When the Roamer appears as Postman Pat and has the challenge of delivering letters to doors or as Santa Claus with the task of visiting all those chimneys, the learning taking place will be much more meaningful to the children.

CLASSROOM STORY

The QCA published some excellent guidance in 2005, called *ICT in the Foundation Stage*, which was made up of a number of case studies showing how ICT has been used successfully in the EYFS. One such example is called *Programmable toy – delivering letters:*

> *Edward puts the post van on the number line by the post office. He counts how many squares it needs to move to reach the first house he has a letter to deliver to. He presses the forward button the right number of times, presses Go and the post van moves along the road to the first house. The children count out the numbers on each square as it travels over them. When the post van stops at house number four Daniel counts how many squares it now needs to move to house number seven.*

The practitioner had set up the number line beforehand (it is possible to buy these for certain toys on the market) and placed numbered houses along it. They show the children how the post van (programmable toy) delivers the letters. The children then try and on occasion questions are asked of them such as, 'The van is at house number four. How many more squares do we need to move to deliver the next letter to house number seven?' Having been set a problem, the children discuss what instructions to input before actually doing so.

Robots such as the Roamer are much more than toys for learning about going forward and backwards, left and right. They are open-ended, interactive devices that can promote learning in all sorts of areas, not just PSRN. Work on the computer using the screen turtle with older, more able EYFS children will go much more smoothly if they have covered the all-important groundwork with a programmable toy.

Data handling

Data-handling activities are not beyond the capability of EYFS children and the software packages available make things quite easy for both teacher and children. Data-handling skills should be promoted from an early age by setting straightforward exercises such as counting the different coloured sweets in a packet. Simple surveys can be introduced, for instance 'Our Pets', 'Favourite Colours' or 'How We Get To School'. These surveys, perhaps in the form of tally charts, can be taken across to the computer and, following teacher modelling, the data can be entered. The presence of an adult at this stage will be important and even more critical when it comes to generating a graph and discussing what it shows.

There are many easy-to-use graphing programs on the market suitable for use in the EYFS. *Counter for Windows* (BlackCat) contains a program called *Counting Pictures* and introduces young children to data handling, offering the facility to generate different infant-friendly pictograms or alternatively block graphs. *Starting Graph 2* (RM) also offers simple surveys (tables) and the opportunity to produce pictograms (and other chart types) all at the click of a mouse (no need to use the keyboard in 'touch mode').

Suites of programs are now coming onto the market and one such, designed for the 3–7 age group, is *Infant Video Toolkit 2* (2simple). The programs in this suite include *2count* (a simple data-handling program to make pictograms), *2graph* (for producing block graphs, bar charts, etc.) and *2question* (used to make simple branching databases). Working at a very basic level, a software kit like this can cater for all the children's data-handling needs and is easy for young children to master as there is no need for any great skill in reading.

Numeracy CD-ROMs and websites

There is an abundance of software packages and websites available for use in the PSRN area of learning and development. Here are some favourites. Many CD-ROMs on the market will help in the development of early numeracy skills such as number recognition, counting, adding, subtracting and the exploration and creation of number patterns. Most are of the 'edutainment' variety, all-singing, all-dancing, multimedia extravaganzas. Motivation will rarely be a problem when using these content-specific, content-rich programs with their engaging animations and all-important sound prompts. Titles such as *Maths City 1* (2Simple), *123-CD* (Sherston) and *Fizzy's First Numbers* (Sherston) are excellent examples of this type of software, but there are many more titles to choose from. A browse through a catalogue such as that at the *R-E-M* website (for numeracy packages or any other type of educational software) will lead to many useful discoveries.

As with CD-ROMs in this area, there are many appropriate websites for EYFS children that will aid the development of number skills. There are some excellent maths games to be found in the 'Mathematical development' section of the *BGfL – Foundation Stage* website, at the Early Years section of the *Crickweb* site and the *Numberjacks* website (another winner provided by the BBC). Once again, all of these (and many others) make superb interactive whiteboard resources.

ICT and personal, social and emotional development

Although use of the computer is most obvious in the three areas discussed above, there is plenty of scope for ICT in the three remaining areas of learning and development. In the personal, social and emotional development (PSED) area your aim, among other things, is to develop a child's confidence through building positive relationships with peers, working well in various group situations, instilling a positive disposition to learning and promoting problem-solving skills. ICT can, as has already been made clear, help develop all of these attributes.

Practitioners should be willing to look for links between statements in the guidance in this area of learning and ICT (as stated in KUW). Under this area, according to the guidance, practitioners will have the opportunity to encourage children 'to develop autonomy' (p23) which could be linked to 'Know how to operate simple equipment' (p81).

REFLECTIVE TASK

Peruse the statutory guidance for personal, social and emotional development. Can you see possible links to ICT? These might be quite obvious but not always. You may have to be creative.

Certainly use of ICT can promote interaction between children who are knowledgeable about various devices and those who are not. For example, a child from an ICT-rich household may know how to operate a DVD player and how to make its contents appear on the TV screen. Why not ask this child to put on a DVD and show another child, perhaps from an ICT-poor background, how it is done. Children often delight in showing off their expertise and helping others to learn. Opportunities like this abound when using a variety of ICT equipment. Using ICT will also aid the achievement of the PSED Early Learning Goal in the framework that refers to being able to 'Work as part of a group' and to 'taking turns and sharing fairly' (p12).

RESEARCH SUMMARY

Pange and Kontozisis (2001) carried out a study of Greek pre-school children and the collaborative use of computers. Basing their work on Vygotsky's socio-cultural theory of learning, where pupils' communication with their teachers and their peers is paramount, they found a positive correlation between using computers in this way and learning new concepts or gaining new knowledge. By collaborating in a variety of ways with, around and through the computer, the child is more able to make progress in their learning. One of the major outcomes of this study was the 'collaborative patterns that children developed while working with the computer'. More experienced children helped those with little or no experience. The latter children were not afraid to ask their 'mentors' questions. Other studies bear this out and practitioners (and trainees) will do well to take note.

In the guidance, it states that practitioners should 'Support children in using a range of ICT to include cameras, photocopiers, CD players, tape recorders and programmable toys in addition to computers' (p75). We see no reason why that support, on many occasions, cannot be given by another child as practitioners seek to develop their charges socially.

ICT and physical development

Looking for links to ICT is relatively easy when examining the physical development (PD) area of learning in the guidance. For example, if the children are to 'Respond to rhythm, music and story by means of gesture and movement' (p93 of the guidance) there will be an excellent opportunity to introduce the children to cassette or CD players (in fact the guidance makes it clear that practitioners should provide these devices). Another section suggests that children 'Use whole-body action rhymes such as "Head, Shoulders, Knees and Toes"' (p95), which could easily be linked to use of audio CDs, CD-ROMs and websites such as the *Tweenies – Song Time*.

A more obvious link to ICT is 'Take photographs to put in a book about "Me and the things I can do"' (p95). Performances could be recorded with digital cameras or, better still, with digital video cameras. The Digital Blue cameras are very popular in schools today, being inexpensive, robust, easy to use and effective. The whole package (digital still/video camera, software, teaching resources etc.) is called *Digital Movie Creator* (see Figure 8.2; as we write, version 3.0 is now available). EYFS children would find these simple to use but they would need help in putting their 'movies' together and adding lots of special effects. Their delight upon playback is assured.

Figure 8.2 Digital Movie Creator 2.0

Using CD-ROMs and other computer software in the course of their meaningful play will ensure that children, as stated in the guidance, 'Engage in activities requiring hand–eye coordination' (p102) through extensive use of the mouse and the keyboard. The mouse itself, of course, is an excellent example of a 'one-handed tool' (p102). Letting young children explore the computer, which should be as natural a part of the EYFS setting as it is in the home setting of many children, is often a good idea. They will enjoy pressing keys, and moving and clicking the mouse, and seeing the effects of their actions on-screen. As Smidt (1998) puts it, this is not 'messing about' but is essential physical exploration.

ICT and creative development

In the creative development (CD) area of learning and development you will not be surprised to learn that ICT can help to enhance art and music activities. In fact, budding artists and musicians will find them very motivating and will use them as a springboard to greater things in the future. So when the framework states that children should, 'Express and communicate their ideas, thoughts and feelings' (p16) artistically and musically, practitioners should realise that ICT has an important part to play.

Art software

Children will thoroughly enjoy exploring, as the guidance states, 'colour, texture, shape, form and space in two dimensions...' (p110) using any of the major paint packages available for children. *2Paint* (part of 2Simple's *Infant Video Toolkit 2*) is one of the most popular of this type of program, as well as *Clicker Paint* (Crick) and *Colour Magic* (RM). There are many more. These packages have many simple, yet powerful, tools (some complete with helpful audio prompts and engaging sound effects) that enable children to be very creative and to develop their artistic skills. A colour printer is essential if the 'hard copy' is to be as impressive as the on-screen creation and self-esteem is to be increased. Even use of *Paint*, the basic package that comes with Microsoft Windows, is perfectly adequate for exploring shapes and colours, and for early 'mark making' where children might, for example, attempt to write their name with the mouse.

PRACTICAL TASK PRACTICAL TASK **PRACTICAL TASK** PRACTICAL TASK **PRACTICAL TASK**

Photography plays a big part in today's art curriculum and there is no reason why EYFS children cannot make use of digital cameras. You could use one of these devices to take photographs showing 'The Adventures of Teddy' around the school (both inside and outside). The children, with your help, can download these photographs to a computer and put them into a slideshow program like Microsoft's excellent free package *PhotoStory3* (downloadable from www.microsoft.com). Various visual effects can be applied as well as captions explaining what Teddy is doing. Add a soundtrack to finish the slideshow and then run it in Windows Media Player. You will be as impressed with the final result as the children!

Music software

According to the guidance, children must 'Recognise and explore how sounds can be changed' and 'recognise repeated sounds and sound patterns' (p112). An exceptional piece of software for addressing these development matters is *Music Toolkit* (2Simple). This suite of programs is suitable for use across the primary age range but *2Explore* and *2Beat* are particularly appropriate for young children of 3 to 5 years old. They can even begin to compose their own little tunes. This is simple but powerful software that will illicit impressive results.

Music cassettes and CDs are ubiquitous in today's EYFS setting and will often be used in achieving ELGs in this particular area of learning and development. Tape recordings or video recordings of performances (perhaps as they 'match movements to music') can be made and played back, much to the delight of the children.

Web resources for EYFS practitioners

Hopefully, this chapter has made clear that there are many excellent websites suitable for use with children in the EYFS whatever the area of learning and development being addressed. But what about sites for practitioners? Happily, there are many websites that we would wish to recommend to practitioners and we think that you will be surprised at the quality of the resources on the internet. A lengthy list of EYFS and ICT-related sites can be found at the *Primary Teacher's Toolbox – Early Years Links* web page (www.btinternet.com/ ~tony.poulter/links/eylinks.htm). However, a few deserve a special mention.

The *Becta Schools* site has many excellent pages about developing ICT in the Early Years that could prove to be very enlightening for practitioners. *The Standards Site* has an interesting section entitled *Improving the use of ICT in the Foundation Stage*. If you want a copy of the *ICT in the Foundation Stage* guidance (with its various case studies), find it at the QCA website.

Finally, the *ICT in the Early Years* site is well worth a visit, with useful documents available and helpful tips on planning ICT usage in all six areas of learning and development. The site also points to research by DATEC (Developmentally Appropriate Technology for Early Childhood), whose findings resulted in seven guiding principles concerning the effective use of ICT in the EYFS. In conclusion, when using ICT with young children, we offer these excellent guiding principles to adhere to.

1. Ensure an educational purpose.
2. Encourage collaboration.
3. Integrate with other aspects of the curriculum.
4. Ensure the child is in control.
5. Choose applications that are transparent.
6. Avoid applications containing violence or stereotyping.
7. Be aware of health and safety issues.

For more details on these principles see the booklet by Iram and John Siraj-Blatchford entitled *More Than Computers* (2005).

A SUMMARY OF **KEY POINTS**

There is little doubt that ICT can be of great use in the EYFS.

> It can motivate young children and enhance their learning experiences.

> Though applicable to all six areas of learning, it is particularly useful in developing literacy and numeracy skills and in promoting knowledge and understanding of the world.

> Practitioners would do well to utilise generic software packages such as word processors, data-handling and graphics packages, as well as a range of CD-ROMs and websites especially designed with EYFS children in mind.

> Other ICT equipment, notably programmable robots, digital cameras and interactive whiteboards, should also be introduced at this stage.

> The advantages of collaborative, co-operative learning should be exploited when using ICT, with the practitioner or assistant intervening in a purposeful way to encourage meaningful talk and to provide scaffolding.

MOVING *ON* > > > > > > MOVING *ON* > > > > > > MOVING *ON*

For further information about planning ICT, and also assessing it, in the EYFS see *Primary ICT: knowledge, understanding and practice* by Allen et al. (2007, 3rd edition) in the Achieving QTS series by Learning Matters. Also see *Using ICT in Foundation Stage teaching* by Poulter and Basford (2003), Learning Matters.

REFERENCES REFERENCES **REFERENCES** REFERENCES REFERENCES REFERENCES

Collins, J., Hammond, M. and Wellington, J. (1997) *Teaching and learning with multimedia.* London: Routledge.

Cook, D. and Finlayson, H. (1999) *Interactive children, communicative teaching.* Buckingham: Open University Press.

Cuban, L. (2001) *Oversold and underused: computers in the classroom*. Cambridge, MA: Harvard University Press.

DCSF (2007a) *Statutory Framework for the Early Years Foundation Stage*. London: DCSF.

DCSF (2007b) *Practice Guidance for the Early Years Foundation Stage*. London: DCSF.

Donahue, T. *Pedagogical advantages of the Roamer.* www.valiant-technology.com/

Grenier, J. and Thornbury, M.L. (2001) Adults and children at the computer in the Nursery, in *Beyond the school gate*. (MAPE) Northants: Castlefield (Publishers).

Hall, E. and Higgins, S. (2002) Embedding computer technology in developmentally appropriate practice: engaging with early years professionals' beliefs and values. *Information Technology in Childhood Education*, (1), 301–20.

Hardy, C. (2000) *Information and communication technology for all.* London: David Fulton Publishers.

Medwell, J. (1996) *Talking books and reading.* Oxford: Blackwell Publishers.

Pange, J. and Kontozisis, D. (2001) Introducing computers to kindergarten children based on Vygotsky's theory about socio-cultural learning: the Greek perspective. *Information Technology in Childhood Education*, (1), 193–202.

Plowman, L. and Stephen, C. (2003) A 'benign addition'? Research on ICT and pre-school children. *Journal of Computer Assisted Learning*, 19, 149–64.

Riley, J. (2003) *Learning in the early years*. London: Paul Chapman.

Siraj-Blatchford, I. and Siraj-Blatchford, J. (2005) More than computers – information and communication technology in the early years. *Early Education*.

Smidt, S. (1998) *A guide to early years practice*. London: Routledge.

Stringer, J. (2001) We haven't got a computer. *Primary Maths and Science*, January, 35–36.

TTA (1999) *Using information and communications technology to meet teaching objectives in English.* London: TTA Publications.

FURTHER READING FURTHER READING **FURTHER READING** FURTHER READING

What the research says about ICT and motivation:

http://publications.becta.org.uk/display.cfm?resID=25798

Siraj-Blatchford, I. and Siraj-Blatchford, J. (2005) More than computers – information and communication technology in the early years. *Early Education*.

Useful websites

Primary framework for literacy and mathematics
www.standards.dfes.gov.uk/primaryframeworks/
The Little Animals Activity Centre
www.bbc.co.uk/schools/laac/story/sbi.shtml
Tweenies – Story Time
www.bbc.co.uk/cbeebies/tweenies/storytime/

Fimbles- Comfy Corner
www.bbc.co.uk/cbeebies/fimbles/comfycorner/index.shtml
ICT Games – Literacy
www.ictgames.com/literacy.html
Early ICT – Games
www.kented.org.uk/ngfl/games/
The Hoobs – Activities
www.channel4.com/learning/microsites/H/hoobs/activities/index.jsp
LearningGrids
www.learninggrids.com
Valiant Technology
www.valiant-technology.com/
R-E-M
www.r-e-m.co.uk/
BGfL – Foundation Stage
www.bgfl.org/bgfl/4.cfm
Crickweb
www.crickweb.co.uk/Early-Years.html
Numberjacks
www.bbc.co.uk/cbeebies/numberjacks/
Tweenies – Song Time
www.bbc.co.uk/cbeebies/tweenies/songtime/
Digital Blue
www.playdigitalblue.co.uk/
Primary Teacher's Toolbox – Early Years Links
www.btinternet.com/~tony.poulter/links/eylinks.htm
Becta Schools
schools.becta.org.uk/
The Standards Site
www.standards.dfes.gov.uk/
ICT in the Foundation Stage guidance
www.qca.org.uk/libraryAssets/media/QCA-05-2237.pdf
ICT in the Early Years
foundation.e2bn.net/

9

Observation, assessment and planning

Lynne Clarke

Chapter objectives

By the end of this chapter you should be able to:

- **understand the role of assessment in learning and teaching within the Early Years environment;**
- **recognise the importance of observation in the assessment process;**
- **know what should be assessed and how purposeful records can be maintained;**
- **recognise the place of formative and summative assessment and implementation of the Foundation Stage Profile;**
- **be aware of the importance of working in partnership with parents and others in supporting the assessment process;**
- **understand the benefits of quality assessment for children, teachers, parents and the whole school.**

This chapter addresses the following Professional Standards for QTS:

Q11, Q12, Q13, Q22, Q25 (b), Q26 (a), Q27, Q29

Introduction

The arrangements for observation, assessment and planning in the Early Years Foundation Stage Practice Guidance (2007c) bring together the principles outlined in the Curriculum Guidance for the Foundation Stage and those in the Birth to Three framework. They emphasise the importance of using regular daily observation as the key assessment tool.

The principles in KEEP (Key Elements of Effective Practice) (DfES, 2005) draw attention to the importance of practitioners' understanding of observation and assessment underpinning their practice through the following principles:

- understand the individual and diverse ways that children develop and learn;
- develop and continuously improve their practice in meeting children's needs, learning styles and interests;
- use their knowledge and understanding to actively support and extend children's learning in and across all areas and aspects of learning.

These principles also recognise the contribution that parents and other professionals can make to the observation and assessment process in supporting you to develop your work with children in ways that are sensitive, positive and non-judgemental.

The Early Years Foundation Stage Practice Guidance builds on these principles. It sets out four columns of guidance which represent the ongoing cycle of thinking about development and assessing children's progress. Each area of learning and development, within the practice guidance, identifies the following.

- A 'development matters' column which states the skills, knowledge, understanding and attitudes a child needs to develop in order to support their progress towards the Early Learning Goals.
- A 'Look, listen and note' column which will help you in identifying specific aspects of children's behaviour to be observed. These observations will help you gain a better understanding of the children's development and use the information from these observations to plan for children's future learning.
- An 'Effective practice' column which identifies activities or experiences you will be able to provide to support and extend children's learning and development based on the process of continuous observations.
- A 'Planning and resourcing' column which will help you in developing and sustaining a stimulating and vibrant environment in which all children's interests and learning needs are accommodated. The planning of such an environment should take account of spontaneous learning interests and needs, and as such should be flexible and ongoing.

The role of observation in the assessment and planning process

Assessment begins with careful observation. As an Early Years practitioner, you are committed to ensuring that you provide young children with quality learning experiences that involve and engage them in the learning process.

Observation helps you to:

- put the child at the centre of your practice;
- find out about specific likes or dislikes and see how each child reacts to change or new situations;
- see each child as an individual and find out about his/her specific needs;
- ensure that planning is based on meeting the needs of each child.

Through regularly reviewing and analysing your observations you will be making an assessment about children's learning and identifying new skills, knowledge, understanding and attitudes that have developed and, therefore providing information for planning the next steps in children's learning.

Nutbrown (2006) emphasises the importance of this process of observation and assessment to the planning process: 'Part of any practitioner's role is to assess children's learning, their developmental needs, their need for support, their achievements and their understanding.'

Clearly then, as part of your everyday teaching you will be carrying out assessments of children's learning. These assessments are the judgements you make about a child's learning and draw on your own observations to make that judgement. In this way your observations will help you to come to a conclusion about the areas of learning in which children are doing well, and those areas of learning where they may need extra support.

On a daily basis, you will need to make judgements about a wide range of aspects of children's learning, including their ideas, knowledge, motivation, abilities and thinking. You will then need to consider how their interests and ideas might be developed. Using your knowledge of the children in your class you will be able to ensure that the resources and activities (indoor and outdoor) are planned to inspire, challenge and intrigue each child.

Such judgements are based more upon what teachers in early education see children do and hear children say rather than formal assessments. Ongoing assessment begins with careful observation. (p127)

Taking time to watch and listen to children and, looking at examples of work or models they have made will help you to identify what children can achieve.

> *Observation can help practitioners to identify children's achievements and their learning needs and strategies, including their schemas. Worthwhile curriculum contents can be matched to children's learning once those needs have been identified.* (p127)

CLASSROOM STORY

David comes into class on Monday morning and tells you about a trip at the weekend when he visited a castle with his parents. During the morning you observe him spending a sustained period of time in the construction area, building. He brings you the model he has made and describes the walls and turrets of his castle.

Once outdoors, he plays in the large wooden block area building. He enlists the help of a friend and together they set about building the walls of the castle and making a drawbridge.

- How could you build on David's interests?
- Might you ensure that box-modelling materials are available to help him expand on his technology skills and build using a range of materials?
- Could you pose questions such as 'How can you make the drawbridge go up and down?'?
- Might you encourage mark-making skills by drawing maps or plans of his castle?
- Could you ensure a range of books is available to support his interest?

Planning an environment to support assessment

Observation and assessment are central to the learning process as they support you in:

- focusing on the child's strengths and areas for development;
- ensuring that children are making progress and highlighting those who may require additional support;
- analysing whether your teaching is successfully meeting each child's individual learning styles and needs;
- considering how successful your classroom organisation and management are in supporting and encouraging independent and autonomous learning;
- identifying both child involvement and adult engagement.

Therefore, assessment provides you with a process for collecting information about each child which should inform and support future planning. You will need to think beyond the traditional notion of planning activities, as it is equally important to think about how you plan and to organise the physical environment to take account of children's needs and interests.

The following story identifies how one teacher uses her knowledge of children's interests to develop aspects of the environment which will both inspire and challenge the boys while also developing their interest in mark-making.

CLASSROOM STORY

Mrs Smith notices that several boys were not accessing either the role-play or the mark-making areas indoors, but were involved in imaginative play outdoors using the vehicles and taking them to the garage for repairs. As part of the topic of 'helping others', she discussed with the class ideas for creating a role-play area outdoors. They decided to set up a garage with overalls, clipboards, worksheets, order forms, etc., all of which would stimulate interest. The teacher included large construction equipment in the area to encourage design, making and repairing skills. She met with two mechanics from the local garage who agreed to spend some time with the children supporting boys (and girls) in the role-play area, and encouraged them to act as role models for the play and to demonstrate writing for a purpose.

REFLECTIVE TASK

You will want to encourage children's curiosity and autonomy in your setting. How will this impact on the choice of materials/resources you use and the way you arrange your environment? Which factors will you need to consider ensuring that the environment you create is inclusive and appeals to all the children in your class?

Ferre Laevers (2002) refers to ten action points for practitioners to consider when planning for and organising an enabling environment. These points support the development of an effective learning environment.

1. Rearrange the classroom in appealing corners and areas.
2. Check the content of the corners and replace unattractive materials by more appealing ones.
3. Introduce new and unconventional materials and activities.
4. Observe children, discover their interests and find activities that meet these orientations.
5. Support ongoing activities through stimulating impulses and enriching interventions.
6. Widen the possibilities for free initiative and support them with sound rules and agreements.
7. Explore the relation with each of the children and between children and try to improve it.
8. Introduce activities that help children to explore the world of behaviour, feelings and values.
9. Identify children with emotional problems and work out sustaining interventions.
10. Identify children with developmental needs and work out interventions that engender involvement within the problem area.

How would you use these action points to support you in developing your classroom environment?

Chapter 2 refers to Laevers's well-being and involvement scales as useful tools for assessing children's attitudes and dispositions to learning. Laevers's use of the term 'well-being' is concerned with the extent to which children feel at ease, are comfortable within their environment and have their physical needs and their emotional needs met. He is concerned that all children feel valued and recognised as individuals.

Laevers refers to involvement as a quality of human activity characterised by concentration and persistence; a high level of motivation; a high degree of satisfaction; and intense mental activity. He argues that, when involved, the child is functioning at the limits of their mental capacity, in their 'zone of proximal development'. Clearly then, the provision of an effective environment can enhance a child's level of well-being and involvement, which in turn will have an impact on the quality of learning taking place.

Formative and summative assessment

You will already be aware that assessment can take either of two forms: formative and summative.

Formative assessment

This is assessment to inform planning. It should be based on observations of the children in action in both self-chosen play and adult-planned activities. It involves you in using the following skills:

- observing;
- questioning;
- challenging;
- supporting;
- intervening;
- discussing.

This form of assessment involves constant dialogue between you the teacher or other adults or partners and the child. It will support you in making decisions about the extent of the child understanding and the path for their future learning. Sharing such assessment information with the child can be motivating for them and help them recognise both their own potential and the part they play in their own learning journey.

The EPPE (DfES, 2004) research makes reference to sustained shared thinking – the skill of supporting children's interest and involvement in activities by posing questions, sharing ideas or thoughts, and giving them the opportunity to voice their ideas. The relationship established between the child and adult is fundamental, if sustained shared thinking is to prove effective.

The EYFS card 4.4, Learning and development (DCSF, 2007c), states:

> In the most effective settings practitioners support and challenge children's thinking by getting involved in the thinking process with them. The adult shows genuine interest, offers encouragement, clarifies ideas and asks questions. This supports and extends children's thinking and helps to make connections in learning.'

Formative assessment will also involve you in not only recording the information from incidental or spontaneous observations, but also gathering information from planned observations. Incidental or spontaneous observations could be recorded in note form and are not only a useful way of recording information but will also help build up a picture of the child's interests as well as achievements. These recordings require sufficient information so that they could be easily understood by others and should include the date and time of the observation.

Carrying out planned observations of individual children will enable you to look at specific aspects of a child's development including how they access activities independently and whether there are differences in behaviour at different times of the day. You will need to collect a range of evidence to support your judgements. This will include your own observations, learning stories, observational evidence from other staff or parents, annotated samples of children's work, and photographic evidence of a child's involvement and interest in activities. This will allow you as the teacher to systematically build up a picture of each child, which will support your short-term planning and facilitate further learning and development. This is generally known as assessment for learning.

Recording your observation will involve you in drawing on a range of techniques. You might use narrative, time or event sampling, anecdotal recording on sticky notes, or learning stories or journeys. Learning stories are increasingly being introduced into the EYFS, based on work of Margaret Carr, and the development of the New Zealand Early Years curriculum – Te Whariki. Te Whariki focuses on the importance of promoting children's positive dispositions to learning, their interest and motivation and their social and emotional development, and has influenced the themes and principles of the Early Years Foundation Stage.

The format of the learning story links to the five overall principles and goals in the Te Whariki curriculum, which are:

- well-being;
- belonging;
- contribution;
- communication;
- exploration.

Each strand links to five learning dispositions:

- well-being – trust that this is a safe place to be involved and playfulness that often follows from deep involvement;
- belonging – courage and curiosity to find an interest here;
- contribution – responsibility for justice and fairness and able to take another's point of view;
- communication – confidence to express ideas or point of view;
- exploration – perseverance to tackle and persist with difficulty or uncertainty.

These dispositions are linked to the assessment processes of:

- describing – what learning is taking place;
- documenting – some of the actions;
- discussing – with other practitioners and learner;
- deciding – what to do next.

Some EYFS settings use the Te Whariki principles in their assessment frameworks. Examples can be found on the Early Years Foundation Stage CD-ROM or in the Primary

National Strategy booklet, *Confident, capable and creative: supporting boys' achievements*. Other EYFS settings have adapted the format to fit the Early Years Foundation Stage as the following example shows. This example illustrates the richness of evidence which can be gathered from one simple ten-minute observation. The areas of learning and development which Emily is experiencing can be clearly tracked. Additionally, there is substantial evidence linked to the key reference points which also highlight her attitudes and dispositions to learning (see Chapter 2).

Area of learning	Reference points	Learning story
Personal, social and emotional development Communication, language and literacy Problem-solving, reasoning and numeracy Knowledge and understanding of the world Physical development Creative development	Choices made (interests or schemas) Relationships (being involved) Skills/attitudes (persistence) Communication (expressing ideas and feelings) Contribution (responding to others) (Circle any of the above where dispositions are identified in the observation)	*Emily is playing in the outdoor area, in the bark area, which has wooden stepping stones, tyres and wooden planks. She spends ten minutes in this area, moving the planks around onto the stepping stones and tyres as if she is making an obstacle course. She walks along the planks and then moves them around and tries to jump from one stepping stone to another. Another child joins her and the two of them take it in turns to walk or run along the planks, moving the planks around to change the walkways. They collect a ball and try to roll it along one plank. They discover that if they place a plank from a stepping stone onto the bark the ball rolls faster down the slope. They continue this play for another ten minutes. One of the adults asks them what is happening and they describe what happens to the ball when they roll it along the plank.*
Short-term review *Both girls were absorbed in their play, developing an awareness of positional language. They are developing their physical skills and are able to play co-operatively They discover the ball rolls faster down an incline.*		**Possible lines of direction** *Encourage positional language through action games outdoors.* *Using a range of objects to roll on different surfaces and different gradients.*

What learning did I think took place? i.e. main points of observation
use of positional language
developing their skills of walking and running along a narrow object
recognising that a ball moves quickly down an incline
working together
		How might we build on this interest/ability/ situation to
		   – be more complex
		   – extend learning
		   – appear in different areas?
		
		How we might encourage next steps in the learning journey?
		Building a more complex obstacle course.
		Providing a range of objects to roll, and finding out what happens if the gradient is changed.

REFLECTIVE TASK

Amy has been in Nursery for one term. She enjoys listening to stories and regularly seeks out an adult to read her favourite story. She is starting to show an interest in the text and to recognise some of the letters in her name. What might be the 'next steps' in teaching and learning for Amy?

If you are to remain fresh, motivated and positive in the classroom, it is important that the assessment, recording and reporting aspects of your work are:

- valuable and valued as a tool for managing teaching and learning;
- useful and accessible to all stakeholders, including the child;
- time-efficient and manageable;
- ongoing and focused.

Therefore the information you eventually record must be significant. The following points may help you to decide whether achievements are significant:

- The child has demonstrated a skill for the first time.
- You feel the child has consolidated a concept after demonstrating proficiency on several occasions.
- The child has demonstrated clear understanding of a process, i.e. as a result of a problem-solving activity.
- The achievement may be significant for one particular child and should be defined for that child. For example, a child with speech and language difficulties may initiate a conversation with his peers for the first time.
- It involves talking with children about their achievements. Do they feel they are significant too?
- If it is truly a significant achievement, there will be implications for the planning of future teaching and learning opportunities for that child.

Involving others in the process

In order for your assessment to capture a picture of the whole child, you will need to ensure that you incorporate as many views in the process as possible. This might include staff from the previous setting a child has attended, teaching assistants, welfare staff, outside agencies such as speech therapist, health visitor, educational psychologist, learning support staff or EAL staff. The child's parents will have significant information to contribute since they will know the child better than anyone else, and of course not forgetting the child him or herself. All the above will be able to provide information which will help to give the most rounded picture of the child, his or her interests and achievements. Further discussion of this aspect may be found in Chapter 1, Chapter 10 and Chapter 11.

PRACTICAL TASK PRACTICAL TASK **PRACTICAL TASK** PRACTICAL TASK **PRACTICAL TASK**

Think about the useful information parents or staff from the previous setting could provide about a child prior to entry to your setting. What information would you find helpful to support you in getting to know the child? How would you approach the setting staff or parents to gather appropriate information?

Summative assessment

This provides a summary of children's learning and development at a specific point in time. It is a summary of all the formative assessments carried out over a period of time and is used to produce a measurement of achievement. This is generally assessment of, rather than for, learning.

However, there is not a simple split between the two forms of assessment. Summative assessment can also be used to inform planning; for example, at the end of a phase or period of learning such as at the end of a topic, when it informs subsequent plans.

Linking assessment to the principles of the EYFS

Guidance in *Creating the picture* (DCSF, 2007a) describes approaching the four themes of the EYFS: the unique child, positive relationships, enabling environments, and learning and development in a holistic manner. Therefore it is vital that within these themes assessment is not reduced to tick-lists. The key to effective assessment in the Early Years Foundation Stage is high-quality observation and anecdotal recording. This is a skill which you may find you need to develop in order to become adept at capturing significant moments in a child's learning, some of which are planned, and some of which are not.

Linking assessment and planning

Planning for specific curriculum areas has been covered in other chapters. However, it is important to emphasise that planning, observation, assessment and evaluation must all work together if you are to ensure you provide a quality teaching and learning environment. The Early Years Foundation Stage emphasises the importance of planning as:

> *key to making children's learning effective, exciting, varied and progressive. It enables practitioners to build up knowledge about how children learn and make progress. It also provides opportunities for you to think and talk about how to sustain a successful learning environment.*

It may be helpful to think about planning and assessment as part of a cycle, as depicted in Figure 9.1.

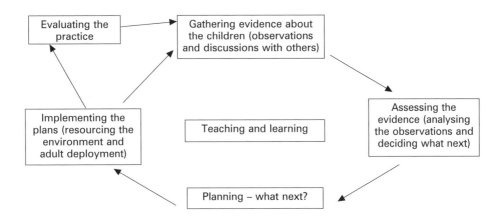

Figure 9.1 Planning and assessment cycle

The Early Years practitioner is required to document children's learning experiences using a variety of methods. This has been explored earlier in this chapter. Nevertheless, what learning experiences you actually intend children to have also needs to be recorded. Your school or local authority may well provide you with specific guidance on what information to include in your medium- and short-term planning. There is a range of exemplar guidance which can also be found on the EYFS CD-ROM which you may find useful as a starting point.

It is important to remember that owing to the unique nature of how young children learn, and the fact that the EYFS is process driven, it is not always easy to define a particular learning objective. Phrases such as 'possible outcomes' or 'possible learning intentions' are common phrases used when defining learning intentions in the EYFS. The key to successful planning documentation is that it is a flexible document, which indicates your responsiveness to children's responses to planned and unplanned learning experiences.

Statutory assessment requirements

Alongside the assessment procedures prescribed by your school assessment co-ordinator or Local Authority, you will also be required to record each child's attainment against the Early Learning Goals and identify their learning needs at the end of the Foundation Stage. The Foundation Stage Profile (FSP) is the statutory means of recording this information.

For most children, this is at the end of the Reception year in primary, infant or first schools – but the FSP must be completed in any government-funded setting, including private, voluntary or independent, in which children complete the EYFS.

Each child's typical developments and achievements will be recorded on assessment scales which are derived from the Development Matters statements and the Early Learning Goals. The summary profiles must be completed for each child reaching the end of the Foundation Stage, during the summer term. Your local authority will inform you when the information is required and how it is to be collected.

Information from the profiles is used to inform Year 1 teachers about the individual child's learning and progress. You are also required to report to parents about their child's progress. This information is collected annually by the DCFS, and from 2008 Local Authorities will have to agree statutory Early Years targets based on the EYFS as part of their duty to improve the outcomes of the young children in their area to reduce inequalities.

The profile provides useful information about, for example:

- attainment in the six areas of learning;
- the attainments of children born in different months of the year;
- the attainments of boys and girls;
- attainments in settings educating children from similar socio-economic backgrounds;
- other analyses based on matching children with their school census data.

All teachers involved in completing the FSP are expected to take part in moderation activities within their Local Authority. These moderation activities will support you in ensuring you are familiar with best practice in terms of the assessments you are recording.

Further guidance can be found on the QCA website regarding the assessment requirements.

Conclusion

Throughout this chapter, the importance of observation, assessment, recording and their importance in supporting you in planning for and providing a stimulating and creative environment has been emphasised. In this environment children will thrive socially and emotionally as well as academically.

A SUMMARY OF **KEY POINTS**

> Be clear about the terminology used in assessment.

> Have a focus for your assessments and be clear why you are carrying out particular assessments.

> Make observation and assessment a part of the daily routine.

> Ensure that the outcomes of your assessments are reflected in your planning.

> Consider the impact of assessment on the quality of the teaching and learning opportunities.

> Consider the role of others who can support you in the assessment process, for example, parents, classroom assistants.

> Remember, whatever recording system you use, ensure that is manageable.

> Recognise the achievements of all your pupils and celebrate and their success with them and others.

MOVING *ON* > > > > > > MOVING *ON* > > > > > > MOVING *ON*

You will be required to collect evidence for the Early Years Foundation Stage Profile during the academic year. At the end of Reception it is a statutory requirement to complete the profile. Spend some time becoming familiar with the documentation which supports this process. Your school or local authority may have devised their own additional support materials which you will also need to be acquainted with. Finally, you may also find it useful to look at the 'e-profile', which is an online tool which can be used for this process.

REFERENCES REFERENCES **REFERENCES** REFERENCES REFERENCES REFERENCES

Carr, M. (2001) *Assessment in early childhood settings*. London: Paul Chapman.

DCSF (2007a) *Creating the picture.* Primary National Strategy. London: DCSF.

DCSF (2007b) *Confident, capable and creative: supporting boys' achievements*. Primary National Strategy. London: DCSF.

DCSF (2007c) *Practice Guidance for the Early Years Foundation Stage*. London: DCSF.

DfEE/QCA (2000) *Curriculum Guidance for the Foundation Stage*. London: Qualifications and Curriculum Authority.

DfES (2002) *Birth to three matters*. London: DfES.

DfES (2004) *The effective provision of pre-school education project: findings from pre-school to end of Key Stage 1. Final report*. London: DfES/Surestart.

DfES (2005) *KEEP: Key elements of effective practice*. Primary National Strategy. London: DfES.

DfES (2006) *Improving outcomes for children in the Foundation Stage in maintained schools*. Primary National Strategy. London: DfES.

Hutchin, V. (2007) *Supporting every child's learning across the foundation stage*. London: Hodder Education.

Laevers, F. (2002) Research on experiential education reader: a selection of articles. Leuven: Centre for Experiential Education.

Nutbrown, C. (2006) *Threads of thinking* (3rd edition). London: Paul Chapman.

Taylor, J. and Woods, M. (eds) (2005) *Early childhood studies: an holistic approach*. London: Hodder Arnold.

10
Positive relationships: parents as partners
Wendy Whittaker

Chapter objectives

This chapter focuses on the importance and relevance of the relationship between parents and Early Years practitioners. The Early Years Foundation Stage emphasises the value that is created for children's learning, development and care from birth to five when there is a positive relationship between parents and practitioners.

By the end of this chapter you should:

- **appreciate the important role that parents and carers play in supporting their children's well-being, development and learning;**
- **understand and acknowledge the range of roles that parents and carers can play inside and outside the setting;**
- **recognise the knowledge and expertise that parents and carers bring to their children's learning and care;**
- **realise the importance of effective two-way communication and liaison with parents and carers;**
- **recognise the impact of positive relationships with parents and carers on children's transition and learning;**
- **understand the barriers that parents and carers may face in becoming actively involved in the setting/school;**
- **be able to reflect on examples of practice which demonstrate parents as partners.**

This chapter addresses the following Professional Standards for QTS:

Q4, Q5, Q6

EYFS themes

One of the themes of the Early Years Foundation Stage is 'positive relationships' (see Chapter 1 for discussion of the structure and overview of the EYFS). 'Parents as partners' [2.2] is a key component of this theme. The focus is on how settings and schools view and treat parents, and how they value the part that parents and carers already play in the learning and development of their child. The wide range of family structures, and the inherent cultural diversity in the UK, are highly relevant here, as too, is the way these are authentically valued in the practice of the school.

Introduction

This chapter seeks to examine various notions of parental involvement in learning and how and why you will need to address this issue with well-informed practice. What is meant by involvement is also examined. Some difficult questions are asked along the way, such as:

- Are settings prepared for the realities of involving parents?
- What about parents who are seemingly uninvolved?
- How can settings lower barriers to involvement?
- Why is it important to involve parents at all?

Some case studies are included to help you.

The Early Years Foundation Stage (EYFS) framework highlights the significance of creating a partnership with parents, but parental involvement is not simply about recruiting volunteers to clear up the paint pots. In many settings, parental involvement has become a bit of a catchphrase, encouraged as yet another way to raise educational standards, without recognition of the real value and opportunities that parents bring to their children's learning. The rhetoric of involvement and participation has often foreshadowed the reality – leaving many schools wondering how to actively engage parents without making them feel like part-time helpers. Giving parents a real voice in the running of the school and using families' backgrounds and perspectives to inform the curriculum is still an area that schools struggle with. This chapter is intended to give some practical guidance on this and space for reflection on how partnership with parents is indeed possible. Settings that have addressed the concept and understood the implications in policy and practice have found that parental involvement is not just another strategy to support children's learning and development – it is a way of ensuring that the setting promotes learning for all within the local community.

CLASSROOM STORY

Blackmore Infants School Nursery department wanted to increase parental involvement and develop deeper relationships with parents of Nursery children. They were particularly keen to understand more about the children's cultural and home background, so that this could be used in their observations and understanding of the children's play. The Nursery teacher invited three parents to talk to her about what approaches they thought might work. The parents suggested giving disposable cameras to the children to record their home life. The three parents devised a letter to the rest of the parents and agreed to distribute the cameras to all those who were willing to take part. Parents were asked to take care of their camera and return it to school by a certain date, and also their permission was sought to share the content of the photos; in return their children were asked to take photos of the significant features of their home life – hobbies, activities, TV programmes they watched, family members, pets, preferred play objects, and food that they ate.

Not all cameras were returned; some got lost, some were damaged. Of the ones that were returned, the photos were developed and the children created a large, child-height display. Some were also included on the school website. The Nursery held a special open coffee morning when parents were invited to come in and chat to the staff about the relevance of certain photos. The Nursery teacher phoned those parents who couldn't come in and asked them about the photos. Together they were able to explore the way home experiences influenced Nursery play. Parents were then asked to write with their child, a description of each photo taken – either in English or in their own home language, and these were then displayed alongside the photo. By chatting to the school staff about their home and cultural background, parents felt more comfortable discussing issues and the sustained shared thinking taking place in both the home and the Nursery. For one parent it was the first time they had felt really valued in their role. Another realised how important the home was in shaping and influencing their children's play. One staff member recognised how little she really knew about certain children within the setting. A parent suggested repeating the project in a few months' time to chart the learning and development of the children and to observe any changes in the photographs that were taken. Gradually a learning set was developed between staff and a number of parents using the photographs that the children took as an impetus for provision, planning and observation. Staff realised the benefits as they were able to deepen their understanding of the children's worlds outside school, and parents began to appreciate the value of observation and documenting their child's learning.

The potential of parental involvement

In early education, the notion of parental involvement and partnership with parents has gained tremendous ground in the last 15 to 20 years. Despite the variety of types of organisation involved in early education and care – pre-schools, day nurseries, playgroups, maintained Nursery provision – there has been a universal awareness and acknowledgement that a genuine partnership with parents is vital for a young child's well-being and development. Since the publication of the Plowden report (Central Advisory Council for Education, 1967) there has been significant research into the benefits of involving parents and carers in the education and learning opportunities of their children. The Plowden report highlighted how parental attitudes towards their child's education vitally influenced the child's school performance. During the 1980s a number of research studies showed the effectiveness of directly involving parents in their children's learning, such as the Haringey Reading Project (Tizard et al., 1982) and the PACT project (Griffiths and Hamilton, 1984), which focused upon the parents assisting in the development of children's reading skills. Indeed, one of the more straightforward ways of conceptualising parental involvement has been around communication, language and literacy, and support within the home to undertake these activities.

Legislative frameworks

The 1986 Education Act, followed by the 1988 Education Reform Act, extended parents' involvement with their child's education by providing them with opportunities to become members of the school governing body. It extended parents' involvement in schools by providing them with an ability to make an important contribution to governance and leadership.

Parents' right to information about their child's progress was extended in the 1997 White Paper, *Excellence in Schools*, which required that schools:

- consult with parents as part of the inspection process;
- provide information about a child's progress in the form of an annual report;
- enable access to a pupil's educational record and information about the school curriculum, including a school prospectus;
- produce an annual report outlining the steps taken by the governing body to discharge its functions;
- hold an annual parents' meeting to discuss the report.

However, there has been some criticism of the one-way nature of this flow of information, particularly with regard to home–school contracts, which have been described as 'protocols for policing parent and child compliance with professional values' (Vincent, cited in Crozier and Reay, 2005, p98). Wider legislative developments have since emphasised the importance of the recognising the influence of family and home on the learning and development of children.

The Children Act 1989 refocused attention on the responsibilities of the parent, once more stressing the importance of the role of parents in caring for and educating their child. The Act also makes it clear that parents have the right to be consulted and informed about the progress of their children, and thus, outlines the way institutions involved in the care and education children are responsible to parents. *Every Child Matters* (2003) and the Children Act 2004 highlighted the central role that parents have in promoting and supporting the five outcomes for children, which are:

- staying safe;
- being healthy;
- achieving economic well-being;
- enjoying and achieving;
- making a positive contribution.

Within this Act, local authorities are directed to 'have regard to the importance of parents and other persons caring for children in improving the well-being of children' (DfES, 2004). Parents are seen as vital partners in the process of change, who as well as giving support are also expected to receive support. Schools are expected to change the way they work 'by personalising learning to suit the individual aspirations, circumstances and talents of each child' (DfES, 2004, p38) and by offering extended services that reflect the needs of families in the local community.

RESEARCH SUMMARY RESEARCH SUMMARY **RESEARCH SUMMARY** RESEARCH SUMMARY

The Effective Provision of Preschool Education (EPPE) Project (2003) highlighted the impact that the home environment can have on children's learning and development, stating that 'what parents do with their children is more important than who parents are' (Sylva et al., 2003, p4). Settings that had higher involvement levels from parents and shared the educational process with parents were found to be more effective for children's learning and development. The Researching Effective Pedagogy in the Early Years (REPEY) study (Siraj-Blatchford et al., 2002) also found that settings did better overall when they proactively worked with parents to address pedagogical approaches to learning within the home.

In 2002 the DfES (now DCSF) commissioned a report by Professor Charles Desforges with Alberto Abouchaar on the impact of parental involvement on pupil achievement and adjustment, and among the key findings they discovered that 'differences between parents in their level of involvement are associated with social class, poverty, health, and also with parental perception of their role and their levels of confidence in fulfilling it. Some parents are put off by feeling put down by schools and teachers' (Desforges, 2003, p5). Schools can be an important resource for parents to access information and advice about their child's learning, development and well-being, and can be an important influence in strengthening the home as a place of loving support and security. Your role as an Early Years teacher facilitating and proactively engaging and supporting parents is, therefore, critical to ensuring effective and meaningful involvement and maximising opportunities for children.

By working with parents and their children in the Early Years you will have a unique opportunity to develop strong, successful relationships with parents. This positive beginning to the school experience can impact on the rest of the child's life. Schools that choose to develop their partnerships with parents also find that it has massive benefits within their day-to-day practice; for example, with increased attendance, higher pupil motivation and self-esteem, fewer behavioural challenges and more meaningful learning opportunities for children.

What do we mean when we refer to parents or carers?

On the surface this seems to be a simple question, but when looking in more depth, it is a much more complex issue. The Parents' Charter was first issued in 1991 and signalled the start of an information revolution to extend parental choice and raise standards. Since then important changes have taken place and parents' rights have been strengthened, leading to the updated Parents' Charter of 1994. It explained what parents can expect and how to become effective partners in their children's education. However, the status of parents extends, according to Houghton and Colgan (1995, p95), to others involved in the care and upbringing of children: 'Thus extended family members, grandparents, step-parents, childminders or foster parents may be considered as sharing parental responsibility'.

In terms of legislation, section 576 of the Education Act 1996 defines a parent as:

- all natural (biological) parents, whether they are married or not;
- any person who, although not a natural parent, has parental responsibility for a child or young person;
- any person who, although not a natural parent, has care of a child or young person.

The law regarding who has parental responsibility was revised in 2003. In relation to children born after 1 December 2003, both of a child's legal parents have parental responsibility if they are registered on the child's birth certificate. This applies irrespective of whether or not the parents are married. Prior to this, if a couple were not married, only the mother automatically had parental responsibility. A child's biological parents are the child's legal parents unless the child has been adopted. However, parental responsibility can be acquired through:

- being granted a residence order;
- being appointed a guardian;
- being named in an emergency protection order (although parental responsibility in such a case is limited to taking reasonable steps to safeguard or promote the child's welfare);
- adopting a child.

The general principle is that:

> *Everyone who is a parent, as defined above, has a right to participate in decisions about a child's education; even though, for day to day purposes, the school's main contact is likely to be a parent with whom the child lives on school days. School and LEA staff must treat all parents equally, unless there is a court order limiting an individual's exercise of parental responsibility.*

> (DfEE, 2000, p5)

Consequently the title of 'parent or carer' could refer to a large number of people associated with the child.

You will also already be aware of the huge diversity in family life in the UK. Teachers and practitioners need to get to know the child's family make-up and be aware of the wide variety of home situations in which children live. By getting to know those who care for the child, you will be able to collaborate with them appropriately and understand their background and particular needs. The same approach will not necessarily work for all, so it is vital that teachers understand the individual child's family before attempting to engage and co-operate with their parents and carers.

Another issue that has become more prevalent is that of a father's involvement in his children's education. Often, when we refer to 'parental' involvement, this is a shortcut for 'maternal' involvement, when in fact fathers play a huge part in contributing to a child's sense of identity and emotional stability in learning. Research undertaken by Eirini Flouri and Ann Buchanan (2001) based on information from the National Child Development Study found that the involvement of fathers improved children's prospects at school; children were less likely to be involved in anti-social behaviour than those whose fathers were not involved; and children had better mental health long-term, even after controlling for fathers' socio-economic status and education. Many factors affect fathers' involvement in Early Years settings – from the gender bias of staff (usually predominantly female in Early Years) to the size of the furniture. Unless staff make a positive effort to understand and recognise the barriers to paternal involvement, many men remain an unseen yet highly influential factor in their children's lives. As an Early Years teacher you need to be aware of any stereotypes that might exist in your own mind or in the practice of your setting. For example, it might be that staff feel more comfortable discussing children's learning with mothers than with fathers, and therefore unwittingly ignore men who come into the setting with their partners. Times of parents' evenings and open days might not be suitable for men – offering twilight sessions or alternative times could be organised for men who work shifts or office hours.

CLASSROOM STORY

Reesa started Nursery half-way through the term, so her parents had missed the opportunity to attend the open day. This was also the time when staff would get to know the parents a little before their child started Nursery. Each day either her mother or father would collect her from Nursery, taking it in turns. Each was always punctual, but preferred to stand in the playground and wait for her than come into the building. Neither of her parents said much when they collected her, and staff found them each to be reticent to discuss Reesa's progress. They did not stay and talk to the other parents or involve themselves in the nursery activities.

The Nursery teacher noticed that Reesa's reading book was often missing from her bag, and that she did not always return permission slips for trips and other activities. The teachers were keen to involve parents and carers in the Nursery by inviting them to help with activities or baking on a Friday, and to accompany them on trips with the children. However, Reesa's parents never responded and seemed not to be interested. Reesa settled well into Nursery, making a number of friends, and occasionally she would go home to play with another child and their parent.

At the end-of-term parents' evening, Reesa's mother came alone. The Nursery teacher mentioned her concerns to Reesa's mother, who explained that actually she and

Reesa's dad had separated shortly before Reesa had started Nursery and they were now not on speaking terms. It had been an upsetting time for them all, and she acknowledged that they had struggled to ensure consistency for Reesa. This meant that letters, books and other items from Nursery often got lost in transit between the two homes, and that the school did not have the contact details for Reesa's father. They discussed practical solutions such as duplicate letters, and separate reading bags, and agreed to see if this helped. A few weeks later, Reesa's father approached the nursery staff, offering to help with an IT project that the Nursery was involved in. The staff noticed over time that both parents seemed more relaxed and communicative, and there was far less confusion over the things Reesa needed while at Nursery.

REFLECTIVE TASK

When have you experienced discrimination or been misunderstood because someone did not take time to find out about your personal circumstances? How could the misunderstanding have been avoided? As an Early Years teacher, what steps could you take to ensure that you know as much as possible about the children in your class to avoid making assumptions and mistakes?

Why involve parents?

Involving parents and carers and creating a partnership with them holds many significant benefits for the child, the setting and school, the parents and the wider community. These include the following.

- Creating the best learning opportunities for the child. Parents and carers have hugely valuable knowledge and understanding about their children – and practitioners and teachers can learn a great deal about children from their parents and carers and vice versa. By developing relationships that enable real sharing between the school and the home, meaningful dialogue is encouraged that can be extended to support the child's learning. This can happen in two ways:
  - Developing a relevant curriculum and learning environment within the setting. Understanding and knowing more about the children in their care allows schools to reflect the cultural diversity of their children in an authentic way and to address and discuss issues that are pertinent to those particular children. It also allows them to extend learning for children individually if they have insight into a child's particular learning interests and motivation.
  - Helping parents to understand their child's play behaviour and how they can support their child's learning at home. The expertise parents already hold about their child is a good starting point, but they may feel unnecessary pressure to help their child 'achieve'. Schools and settings can assist by sharing information and practice about the importance of play in the Early Years.
- Providing wider support for parents and carers in their role by offering advice, signposting to additional services or simply acting as another listening ear. *Every Child Matters* (2003) stresses the importance of working with other organisations and providers to ensure parents have access to information and advice when necessary. Not all settings and schools can provide these directly, but local authorities will have a compendium of services that schools and settings can access. (This is discussed further in Chapter 11).
- Giving parents a voice in the design and running of the school/setting. Again, it is stipulated in *Every Child Matters* (2003) that parents and carers are to be consulted and allowed to express their views about services. This might mean that parents review policy, or even write the policies for the school, ensuring that the school reflects the needs of the families and communities it serves.

- Providing support for staff and children by utilising the skills and expertise of parents and carers within the school. Parents and carers are often willing to help out if they feel that they can be useful and contribute in a purposeful way. This may be by simply accompanying children on a trip, or by offering particular creative or technical skills to the school. Schools do need to be aware of avoiding creating unnecessary stereotypes, though, by inviting all parents of either sex to participate and offer skills of all varieties.
- Being a valuable experience for the parents themselves. Nurseries have been described as outposts for adult education and indeed for some parents and carers, contact with their child's Early Years setting can be the first positive experience of schooling that they have had for some time. Once trust has been established, parents and carers might find that working in the setting can lead to a growing confidence and to developing a new career. Certainly this is the case at Pen Green in Corby, where the impact of their innovative work on the lives of parents and carers and the wider community is described in Chapter 7 of Whalley et al. (2001).
- Easing issues of transition for children. When parents and carers work closely with settings, staff have a deeper knowledge of and understanding about the children in their care. This, in turn, impacts on the ability of the setting to help children settle in quickly and confidently and to reduce issues of separation and change. For children who may be in the care of a childminder for parts of the day, or access other childcare provision, it is vital that they are able to make the transition easily and with the minimum of disruption. Familiar and responsive adults (key workers), availability of resources (continuous provision) and sensitive awareness of the child's needs are all helped by a close relationship with parents.

Other benefits that arise from working with parents and carers include:

- ensuring continuity between home and school and enhancing a child's opportunity to 'stay safe';
- developing closer relationships outside and within the setting;
- allowing children to experience the lives of other adults and to learn additional skills;
- allowing for some individualised input – and for children to experience quality time alone with an adult;
- helping the setting to gain knowledge about the local community and the cultural backdrop of children's lives;
- enhancing the opportunities for the school to be involved in the life of the community.

The guidelines provided for schools preparing for an Ofsted inspection highlight the need for schools to form good working relationships with parents and the community. These guidelines promote the need for schools to actively involve parents and carers in their child's education more than simply communicating with parents and carers about their child's educational progress.

What is meant by a partnership with parents?

By definition, the notion of partnership with parents implies equality. However, achieving a real partnership with parents takes determination, energy and time and requires both partners to be willing to be committed to the relationship. There is an assumption that teachers know what parental involvement means and that there is a shared understanding of the meaning of involvement and that it is unproblematic and is viewed unquestioningly. For Early Years practitioners who may not have worked closely with parents before, it can be a difficult and exasperating area of practice, and requires skills and abilities that do not necessarily come naturally or by accident. The reality of parental involvement is highly complex and needs a level of competence that may not have been developed through training.

The home influence

One of the first concepts for practitioners and teachers to recognise is that parents are their child's first teachers, and home is their first school. The home influence is the most enduring and has more impact than any other on a child's life (Belsky, 1984; Bronfenbrenner, 1979). Creating a purposeful and effective collaboration between home and school is therefore vital if it is to affect a child's outcomes, and if schools are to provide a relevant and personalised approach to learning. Parents themselves are not always aware of how important their input is, and it may take time for some parents to recognise the importance of their role in their child's learning. This unfortunately has been reinforced in the past by teachers who have conveyed the message that they are the educational 'experts' and therefore the role of the parent is to ensure that the child can manage to go to the toilet on his or her own, or tie his or her shoelaces. The REPEY (Siraj-Blatchford et al., 2002) research emphatically demonstrated that children do better in settings where practitioners share a pedagogical approach with parents, and where this happens most effectively is where the curriculum is jointly shared.

Models of parental involvement

It is perhaps helpful here to introduce a model of involvement which breaks down the various stages and points of entry for parents, and which may reflect the various levels of involvement in your own setting (Figure 10.1). This is taken from Pugh and De'Ath (1994). They split the levels into active and passive to show the differences in the early stages of involvement.

Contact point of entry	Level of activity
Non-participation	Early stages may be active or passive depending on circumstances, levels of confidence, purpose of use/scheme
	Substitute, respite, relief from childcare
	Active non-participation, e.g. shopper, working mother
	Passive non-participation, e.g. by default, too scared, language barrier
Being there	Receptive and responsive
	Active attending functions
	Passive coming in for coffee, chat and fags
Co-operation	Overtly contributing to or for the group/scheme
	Active going on the rota, working in the group/scheme; usually under supervision, following instructions, doing 'chores' or providing servicing, e.g. mending furniture
	Passive providing particular materials when asked, e.g. yoghurt cups, newspaper
Collaboration	Joint activity with workers
	Taking part in planning, initiating and assisting in activities, defining objectives, e.g. users'/parents' committee; parents take some responsibility, e.g. toy library; involvement in assessment
Partnership	Joint planning and execution with workers
	As above but extended to equal access to information and resources, e.g. management committee; decisions or acceptance of referrals; formulation of goals and objectives. Parents may substitute for workers in running group or visiting homes; parents as educators, authors, evaluators, project workers
Control	Parents determine and execute decisions
	Planning of activities, resources, budgets, selection of personnel, ultimate responsibility and accountability

Figure 10.1 Levels of parental involvement

PRACTICAL TASK PRACTICAL TASK **PRACTICAL TASK** PRACTICAL TASK **PRACTICAL TASK**

Consider an Early Years setting that you know, and think how each of the roles of non-participation, being there, co-operation, collaboration, partnership and control might exist there. What would the actions and activities of the parents look like in each of these areas? How could you help parents develop greater involvement?

Communicating with parents

In order to promote a partnership between Early Years settings and parents and carers there needs to be a process of communication and dialogue, which can be hard to establish if you rely solely on children being delivered and collected by their parent or carer. In many families, if both or the only parent is out at work, children may be brought to school by another carer, a friend's parent, a childminder or an out-of-school-club employee. Teachers and practitioners need to consider a variety of ways in which they can effectively communicate with parents, when they may see them only occasionally during the term. Creative ideas can work wonderfully well – but don't rely on your own creativity – often the best ideas come from parents themselves. Verbal and written forms of communication from the school to home may include:

- written reports summarising the child's strengths and developmental achievements and progress;
- end-of-year profiles;
- weekly bulletins describing the events that have taken place and those planned for the following week;
- daily record books which allow parents to comment and are used as a tool for daily communication;
- parents' evenings;
- daily verbal reports;
- individual meetings with the teacher;
- school open evenings.

However, settings need to consider alternative ways of communicating with parents who for other reasons they might not see on a regular basis, and those for whom written forms of communication are inaccessible. These might include parents who have literacy problems or who do not have English as their first language. Settings also need to allow parents to raise issues or address their concerns or questions back to the setting – and create a two-way dialogue. Ways in which this can occur might include the following.

- A termly visit by a staff member (key worker) to the child's home to understand more about their background and relationship with the wider community.
- Being available to parents on an informal basis at a regular time to discuss anything of importance to them.
- A parents' questionnaire that explores their perception of the school or focuses on a particular issue.
- Initiating a parents' group whose agenda is decided entirely by parents.
- Drawing up documentation of children's learning that is co-designed with parents.
- Parents adding to their child's profiles by including information on activities undertaken outside school.
- Encouraging 'parent buddies' – parents who agree to get the ideas of other parents and feed them back to the school, and who will act as a conduit of information for those parents who cannot easily participate in the setting, or perhaps have difficulties with written communication.
- A parents' noticeboard for advertisements, notices of events or messages from parents to other parents.
- A space within the school or setting where parents or carers can make a drink and chat if they arrive early to drop off or collect their child.

Using technology can improve interaction with parents, as there is a greater ability to respond, and allows more interaction with parents who cannot come into the setting. This might include using:

- email;
- a school website that includes a message board and the latest newsletter, and a space for comments and suggestions;
- a parents' blog;
- text messaging.

Wide and varied methods and means of communication are necessary not only to let parents know about the care and development of their child, and information about the school, but also to emphasise the importance of parents' own role in their child's learning.

PRACTICAL TASK PRACTICAL TASK **PRACTICAL TASK** PRACTICAL TASK **PRACTICAL TASK**

Make a list of the ways in which an Early Years setting currently communicates with parents. Consider undertaking a SWOT (strengths, weaknesses, opportunities and threats) analysis of these different forms. How might they be improved? How easy is it for parents actively to shape and to influence these forms of communication – or do they encourage passivity?

Barriers to parental involvement

As we have already demonstrated, parents may not realise the importance of their role in supporting their child's learning, and may lack confidence to become involved in any way within the setting, or indeed with tasks they consider to be 'educational' at home. Parents who themselves have had negative experiences at school or with learning may avoid activities with their child that spotlight their own difficulties, such as reading. Their own confidence and self-belief may limit their involvement. Parents who see themselves as consumers or customers of an Early Years service may prefer to 'leave it to the professionals – after all, that's why they're getting paid'. Parents who have limited support networks, are single parents or have demanding jobs might not consider that they have the energy or time to become involved at any level with the setting aside from attending parents' evenings, or reading school reports. As Early Years practitioners and teachers, the language that you use and the 'professionalism' that you embody can also stop parents from being confident to make a meaningful contribution, believing that their non-expert view is of no value.

CLASSROOM STORY

Michelle is 19 and has two children – a boy Sam, aged 4, and a girl, Taylor, aged 2. She lives alone with the children, although regularly sees her boyfriend, who is the father of her two children. He works shifts at the local car factory as a panel beater. Michelle is on income support and lives in a council house. She is also a diabetic and has to take regular injections of insulin to manage her condition. Sam attends the local Nursery five mornings a week where he receives his free 2.5 hour sessions. The Nursery is one and a half miles away from their home. There is no bus service to take them to the nursery so Michelle and the children walk there and back every day, as they do not own a car. One day, the Nursery teacher announces that the Nursery is organising a trip to a local museum and they are looking for parent volunteers to accompany the children. There will be an additional cost for the trip, and they will be leaving Nursery earlier than usual and arriving back half an hour later than usual. Michelle has begun to get to know some of the other mothers at Nursery and is beginning to feel more comfortable about getting involved. She would dearly like to go on the trip; however, a number of barriers stand in her way.

PRACTICAL TASK PRACTICAL TASK **PRACTICAL TASK** PRACTICAL TASK **PRACTICAL TASK**

List the barriers that could stop Michelle from attending the trip. How could these be avoided in the future? What could the Nursery do to support Michelle and to help her accompany her child?

Reasons for non-involvement

There may be many reasons why parents and carers do not or cannot get involved in the setting, although this does not mean that they are not involved in their child's learning in other ways. These might include the following.

- Living geographically remotely from the Early Years setting.
- Reliance on public transport to get to and from the school.
- Children spending only a short amount of time in the setting.
- Parents or carers in paid employment or with limited spare time.
- Parents or carers having other pressing family commitments.
- Parents' or carers' marital status.
- Parents or carers not wishing to get involved. They may wish to use their time in other ways yet feel guilty if they are not willing to become involved, which can then become an added pressure.
- Fathers (or male carers) feeling that the setting is not welcoming to dads – this can be exacerbated by teacher attitudes and expectations.
- Disability or illness that hinders parents' or carers' ability to participate consistently. These may be physical or mental health issues that cause distress and embarrassment.
- Language barriers – if a parent does not speak English as their first language, they may feel self-conscious and nervous about getting involved.
- Low parental self-belief and confidence that hinders the parent or carer by believing that they have nothing to offer.
- Cultural expectations that parents or carers have of school that the teachers or practitioners should do the job without any parental involvement.

Other issues that can also crop up are to do with the way teachers negotiate the partnership with parents. Creating a real relationship with parents may unmask social, economic and relationship problems that were not previously apparent in the family. Schools need to be aware of the implications of creating a partnership with parents and consider how they will signpost parents and carers to other services, or work with them to help support them. An important aspect of *Every Child Matters* (2003) is that schools are aware of additional services to support and strengthen family life, and may need to take a lead in providing additional services to support families.

It is important to guard against the possibility of cliques developing where parents or carers who become 'regulars' in the Early Years setting appear to have access, insight and information which other parents and carers do not have, creating resentment and barriers. Further, it has been found that barriers can be created if staff are seen to be over-friendly or intimate with certain parents or carers. See later in the chapter for more guidance on how to manage this important relationship.

Attitudes and skills you will need to develop a partnership with parents

One of the most difficult aspects to face in developing a partnership with parents and carers is that of your own attitudes and beliefs. It is all too easy to label parents as 'pushy', 'disinterested' or 'fretful' – when there may be perfectly justifiable reasons why they may come across in this way. If this is the case, it is a useful exercise to examine your own attitudes and feelings to consider why a parent or carer makes you feel this way. It may be that their cultural background, religious beliefs or family arrangements conflict with your own values. However, EYFS emphasises the importance of valuing diversity and embedding anti-discriminatory practice in your setting. Recognising the reasons for your own discomfort is the first step in being able to address the matter and make the necessary changes. (Of course, suspecting a safeguarding issue is a different matter and needs to be discussed with the safeguarding Co-ordinator at the school.)

What needs to be remembered is that all parents love their children and want what is best for them. Clark (in Tizard, 1974) believes that changes in parental attitudes towards school and changes in teacher attitudes towards parents are the major benefits of any programme of school-based parental involvement. But changes in attitude need to be shared by everyone involved. It is vital that all of the staff understand and share the rationale for developing a true partnership with parents and carers and that this is discussed, made explicit and owned by all of the staff. Otherwise parents and carers will soon learn which members of staff appreciate their input and which do not, and which accept and value them despite their apparent lack of involvement. As a new entrant to teaching, you may be tempted to accept the status quo of the school that you are working in with regard to its current level of involvement with parents. As you become more experienced and confident, it is important to question whether what is regarded as good practice is really working as well as it could, and whether it is reflecting the shared values of the Early Years Foundation Stage in terms of working with parents.

Managing the relationship

As an Early Years teacher, you will have many demands on your time, and managing your availability to meet with parents will be one aspect of your working week that might become problematic if you are committed to developing a real partnership with parents and carers. You will be required to work with many families of various backgrounds who will have differing expectations and assumptions about the school and its approach. It is important that you define your availability and work with other staff members within the setting to share the responsibility of involving parents. Planning ahead is vitally important if you are to balance the demands of your job and be proactive in working with parents. Working with other staff who may not have the same attitudes to involving parents can cause tensions and challenges too. The EYFS is a statutory framework that requires practitioners to develop an authentic relationship with parents and carers; one that is not simply tokenistic. This means that effective teamwork is vital to respond to the responsibilities and pressures that can be created by opening up issues of shared control with parents. Training may be needed for those practitioners in your setting who feel nervous of and resistant to working with parents.

Very often, those who show the most resistance are actually those who are the most fearful too. You will need to encourage and work alongside those members of staff who are unwilling to accept the importance of a shared relationship, and ensure that they understand the need to change.

Another consideration to take into account is that of space. You may need occasional use of an additional space within the school to meet with parents, or to hold meetings. This can be an issue if classrooms are already at full capacity, but is vital if parents are to feel welcomed and valued. A cordoned-off area of another room or the school hall could be used, and will enable parents to meet and discuss pertinent issues with each other or other staff members without interruption, and at times that are suitable to them. Confidentiality and respect are critical if relationships are to be maintained with sufficient levels of trust and co-operation. This is an aspect of practice that is often awkward for parents to understand, and is something that can be made explicit in a parental involvement policy (see below). You will need to be tactful and diplomatic with parents who may appear to disregard this aspect of practice. The ability to be both assertive and kind is not easy, particularly when dealing with a delicate situation, but this is a skill that you will need to learn to work effectively with parents and carers.

In terms of parents' involvement in the setting, some organisational criteria here too will be useful. For example, what is the optimal number of parents and carers that may wish to help in a session? Who decides this? How do you encourage parents who do not usually respond to get involved? How do you decide which parents might accompany the class if they are going on a visit? If the setting is offering training to parents, how will you ensure the spaces are filled fairly and equitably?

In order to develop a deeper dialogue and honest relationship with parents, your school might need to consider offering training or workshops on aspects of play, the EYFS, or other issues that are pertinent to a shared approach in learning. Training in which parents and teachers equally take part and which has a practice element to it are often very effective and can allow discussions and conversations to take place that are not possible on a day-to-day basis. Staff at Pen Green in Corby have demonstrated the effects of working closely with parents to deepen an understanding of their children's learning through play. Using schemas as a framework of observation and as a way of sharing information, they have attempted to overturn the usual power hierarchies by emphasising the role of parents as 'equal and active partners' (Whalley et al., 2001, p58) in the learning process. These sessions can also help parents to understand the importance of play in their children's learning and development and reduce anxieties about behaviour and homework.

Above all, developing a real partnership with parents takes determination, persistence and energy. With time it can be an extremely fruitful relationship that produces benefits for all involved. Use the EYFS as a basis for exploration and don't be afraid to take some risks. Your own openness and willingness to develop this vital relationship will hugely influence its effectiveness.

REFLECTIVE TASK

Consider the historical context of your setting in working with parents. What has worked well? What has not been so effective? What changes need to be made to reflect a true partnership with parents?

Consider your own attitudes and skills. What skills do you need to develop further to become more effective at working with parents?

Making the implicit explicit

One way in which you might make explicit the school's approach to working with parents is through the development of a parental involvement policy. As well as outlining the rationale, approach and importance of parental involvement in their child's learning, your school may want to ensure that the policy maintains respect and value for parents who do not actively engage with the setting. It needs to demonstrate that the partnership the school desires is not weighted towards itself, but that it recognises the significance of the parents' role and the influence of the home in children's outcomes. To be really effective, the policy needs to be drawn up with parents to ensure it reflects and engages their views and aspirations. You may need to be creative in how you encourage parental participation in the writing and definition of the document, and how it is disseminated – perhaps by holding open meetings that parents run themselves, or by designing it as a brochure to look attractive and colourful. It will also need to be updated on a regular basis (probably annually) to take account of the changing views of parents and the school. As well as being a useful document for parents which will help them understand the school's philosophy on parental partnership, this policy should also act as a set of guidelines for Early Years practitioners and parents to follow when working together. This also provides an opportunity to clarify the expectations of the school when parents are working alongside staff, and indeed many settings now offer induction training to parents who become regularly involved. Areas that you may wish to include the following.

- Confidentiality and safeguarding – what to do when presented with sensitive information, and how to maintain confidentiality when working with children and families.
- Code of conduct – how staff and parents are expected to behave when in the school and the standards that need to be upheld.
- Respecting diversity – how the school celebrates and engages with diverse families and ensures that participation of all parents is valued.
- Communication – the ways in which parents and carers can communicate with the school, and how parents can expect the school to operate in terms of developing a shared and open relationship.
- Philosophy of parental involvement – why the school places importance on parental participation and what its aims are in developing a partnership with parents.
- Training – what is on offer throughout the year for parents and staff to develop a stronger working relationship and to ensure both partners learn from each other.

Parents' first impressions

The initial meeting with parents and carers is important to all parties and really can set the scene for a rich and fruitful partnership. For many parents who may be looking around a Nursery for the first time, the initial impression you give will be highly significant and will shape their beliefs and understanding about the way the school operates. Therefore it is vital that this initial visit or meeting puts them at their ease, and immediately establishes the value that the school places upon their role. You may wish to give them a copy of the parental involvement policy (remembering that not all parents will be literate in English) and start to introduce them to the idea of sharing information about the home to enable staff to under-stand their child better. The school policy can provide a useful tool to introduce parents and carers to the setting and explain the philosophy behind the school's intended partnership with parents. If parents are interested you may even wish to raise their awareness of training and other events that will help them understand more about their child's play and learning.

Conclusion

The Early Years Foundation Stage gives stronger encouragement than ever before to developing an effective partnership with parents. One of the key benefits of this is to extend and enrich children's learning opportunities while in the setting. Whatever the type of setting, there is always some kind of working relationship between parents and carers and staff. The nature and depth of this relationship will vary depending on individuals and individual settings. From the moment that parents contact the setting, they will be gathering an impression about the way that parents are valued and conceptualised by the school. The trust that is created and the relationship that ensues develops from the first home visit that the key worker makes to the child's home, or the first meeting that the child's parents or carers have in school. Early Years staff need to be attentive, authentic and genuine when dealing with parents if they are to develop a real partnership that is meaningful. If parents are to work alongside staff, it is vital that there are shared understandings and aims, and that parents and carers are able to fully participate on an equal level. Developing a partnership with parents may occur on different levels and may evolve over time, and the skills and attitudes of the Early Years practitioner are as vital in shaping this relationship as are the parents themselves and the setting.

A SUMMARY OF **KEY POINTS**

This chapter has hopefully alerted you to the importance of not only establishing effective working relationships with parents and carers but also to have gone beyond superficial and uncritical understandings of what is commonly referred to as parental involvement.

> **Parents and carers are a critical influence in the well-being and emotional and cognitive development of their children.**

> **Teachers and schools have a responsibility to develop an authentic partnership with parents that respects and values their role.**

> **Participation in the setting is only one way in which parents can be involved in their children's learning.**

> **Early Years settings have a wonderful opportunity to create a meaningful partnership that can influence children's learning long after they have left the setting.**

> **Effective communication with parents and carers is imperative to ensure a shared dialogue.**

> **There needs to be an explicit philosophy to working with parents that is shared and disseminated throughout the setting.**

> **Managing the relationship with parents and carers is a skilled and important aspect of the role of the Early Years teacher.**

MOVING *ON* > > > > > > MOVING *ON* > > > > > > MOVING *ON*

In order to meet the standards for QTS you will need to demonstrate that you can communicate effectively with children, parents and carers and colleagues. Within your first few months of teaching you may want to evaluate your relationship with parents and carers as part of this process, and use this as a springboard for further personal development. You may wish to appraise your school's relationship with parents and carers, particularly with regard to shared learning opportunities and their involvement in shaping the curriculum and pedagogy of the setting.

If the school doesn't already have one, you could start to develop a parental involvement policy in collaboration with a few parents. Or you might wish to devise a way of documenting an aspect of children's learning that is firmly based within the home, but which can be shared in the setting.

REFERENCES REFERENCES **REFERENCES** REFERENCES **REFERENCES** REFERENCES

Belsky, J. (1984) The determinants of parenting: a process model. *Child Development,* 55, 83–96.

Bronfenbrenner, U. (1979) *The ecology of human development: experiments by nature and design*. Cambridge, MA: Harvard University Press.

Central Advisory Council for Education (1967) *Children and their primary schools* (the Plowden Report). London: HMSO.

Crozier, G. (2000) *Parents and schools: partners or protagonists?* Stoke-on-Trent: Trentham Books.

Crozier, G. and Reay, D. (eds) (2005). *Activating participation; parents and teachers working towards partnership.* Stoke-on-Trent: Trentham Books.

Desforges, C. (2003) *The impact of parental involvement, parental support and family education on pupil achievement and adjustment: A literature review.* London: DfES.

DfEE (2000) *Schools, 'Parents' and 'parental responsibility'.* London: DfEE.

DfES (2003) *Every Child Matters.* London: DfES.

DfES (2004) *Every Child Matters: change for children.* London: DfES.

Flouri, E. and Buchanan, A. (2001) *Father involvement and outcomes in adolescence and adulthood.* End of Award Report (Ref R000223309). Swindon: ESRC.

Griffiths, A. and Hamilton, D. (1984) *Parent, teacher, child.* London; Methuen.

Pugh, G. and De'ath, E. (1984) *Parents, professionals and partnership: rhetoric or reality.* London: Macmillan.

Reynolds, J. (2005) *Parents' involvement in their children's learning and schools: how should their responsibilities relate to the role of the state?* London: Family and Parenting Institute.

Siraj-Blatchford et al. (2002) *Researching Effective Pedagogy in the Early Years* (REPEY). London: DfES.

Sylva, K., Melhuish, E., Sammons, P., Siraj-Blatchford, I., Taggart, B. and Elliot, K. (2003) *The Effective Provision of Pre-School Education (EPPE) Project: findings from the pre-school period.* London: IOE.

Tizard, J., Schofield, W.N. and Hewison, J. (1982) Collaboration between teachers and parents in assisting children's reading. *British Journal of Educational Psychology,* 52, 1–15.

Vincent, C. (1996) *Parents and teachers. Power and participation.* London: Falmer Press.

Whalley, M. et al. (2001) *Involving parents in their children's learning*. London: Paul Chapman.

FURTHER READING FURTHER READING **FURTHER READING** FURTHER READING

Crozier, G. and Reay, D. (eds) (2005) *Activating participation; parents and teachers working towards partnership*. Stoke-on-Trent: Trentham Books.

Desforges, C. (2003) *The impact of parental involvement, parental support and family education on pupil achievement and adjustment: A literature review.* London: DfES.

Whalley, M. et al. (2001) *Involving parents in their children's learning*. London: Paul Chapman.

Useful websites

www.teachernet.gov.uk

www.standards.dcsf.gov.uk

www.standards.dcsf.gov.uk/eyfs

www.literacytrust.org.uk

www.workingwithfathers.com

11

Working with others to support children and families: the importance of multi-agency working
Teresa Curtis

Chapter objectives

By the end of this chapter you should have:

- **developed an understanding of what is meant by multi-agency working and the implications for practice;**
- **understood the policy framework that has led to the requirements for multi-agency working;**
- **become alert to some of the potential challenges of multi-agency working;**
- **appreciated the roles and responsibilities of others who work with children and their families.**

This chapter addresses the following Professional Standards for QTS:

Q21, Q32

Introduction

This chapter will elaborate on the meaning of multi-agency working and explore the implications for you working with young children and their families. The agenda established by *Every Child Matters* (2003) is now firmly located within the practice context and practitioners from every sector are required to operate within the framework of successful inter-agency working.

This chapter explicitly links with EYFS Practice Guidance, Commitment 3.4: 'The wider context', which requires you to work 'in partnership with other settings, other professionals and with individuals and groups in the community' in order to support children's development and progress towards the outcomes of *Every Child Matters.*

Every Child Matters: Children Act 2004

The drive towards multi-agency working began much earlier than 2003. Cases concerning the death of Dennis O'Neil in 1945; the 1973 inquiry into the death of Maria Colwell; and the 1988 Cleveland inquiry, all highlighted communication failures between agencies which had led to tragic consequences. As a result of these cases, the Children Act 1989 was established. This stipulated a duty of care for all professionals working with children, and a requirement that all agencies work together to support families and children.

Since the Children Act 1989, there have sadly been further tragic cases of neglect concerning young children. The death of Victoria Climbié in 2000 lead to the Laming report (DoH, 2003).

Lord Laming's inquiry raised searching questions about why organisations whose role it was to work together to protect vulnerable children such as Victoria, had failed in their duty. *Every Child Matters* is often seen as a direct response to this report. The implementation of *Every Child Matters: Change for Children*, which became law through the Children Act 2004, has had a far-reaching impact on the direction for children's services both at central and local level.

Every Child Matters is also a fundamental part of a social policy designed to extend and strengthen the services for children and families, reduce child poverty, increase educational attainment and improve the health and well-being of children. Hence, its five outcomes clearly emphasise the policy of inclusion as a means of achieving economic and social equilibrium.

As outlined in Chapter 1, the five outcomes of *Every Child Matters* are as follows.

- Being healthy: good physical and mental health; living a healthy lifestyle.
- Staying safe: protection from harm and neglect.
- Enjoying and achieving: enjoying life and developing skills for adulthood.
- Making a positive contribution: positive involvement with society and community.
- Economic well-being: able to achieve full potential and not being hampered by economic disadvantage.

All agencies involved with children and families must demonstrate that they are working towards these outcomes. When your school receives an Ofsted inspection, the team will be required to make judgements on how well your school is working to meet these outcomes.

Other extensive changes have been brought about by the introduction of this policy, notably the establishment of Children's Trusts, which contain multi-disciplinary teams led by a Director of Children's Services. Each children's trust must work to ensure the implementation and delivery of children and young people's plans. The development of extended schools will provide 'wrap around care' for children outside normal school hours; and there has been the establishment of the role of a Children's Commissioner. This role, which is currently occupied by the paediatrician Professor Al Aynsley-Green, has the remit to act as an advocate for children's rights.

A further significant development is the introduction of the Common Assessment Framework (CAF), as a tool for all practitioners to use to identify children and families who have additional needs and to ensure agencies work collaboratively to meet them. The Common Assessment Framework and extended schools will be discussed in more detail later in the chapter.

PRACTICAL TASK PRACTICAL TASK **PRACTICAL TASK** PRACTICAL TASK **PRACTICAL TASK**

Send for or download a copy of *Every Child Matters* from www.everychild matters.org and consider what key indicators and outcomes are most relevant to your role as an early years teacher.

Multi-agency working

The term 'multi- agency work' refers to the number of agencies from the statutory, voluntary and private sectors that are involved in the lives of young children and their families. Children in your care may have had some statutory involvement with agencies such as health and welfare as well as the education service. Healthcare professionals including

GPs, midwives and health visitors form a network of universal provision designed to provide all families with access to healthcare such as medical treatment, ante-natal care, childhood immunisations and developmental screening under the auspices of primary healthcare. These services are located in the communities in which your children and their families live and work. The social services system was established to provide help and support for families and children who may have particular needs, ranging from children with disabilities or welfare issues, to those requiring fostering and adoption services and to children in need of protection from abuse. Traditionally the education service has existed to provide education for all children of statutory school age. Increasingly, it has become involved in provision for much younger children, through the drive to provide free Nursery education for all children by the age of three years. This in turn has had an impact on the growth of provision. The private, voluntary and independent sectors have also expanded because of the demand for more daycare for the under-threes. The rationale for this is found in policy initiatives to enable more women to return to work and the belief that early intervention, through quality provision, is seen as a positive means of engaging young children and their families in attaining positive educational and social outcomes, which will lay the foundations for lifelong learning and attainment. As an Early Years teacher, it is important that you build positive relationships with other practitioners and Early Years settings who provide for children transferring to your school or class. (Please refer to Chapter 1, which discusses transitional stages in the lives of children.)

The terminology that is used to explain integrated working can be in itself complex and difficult to interpret.

PRACTICAL TASK PRACTICAL TASK PRACTICAL TASK PRACTICAL TASK PRACTICAL TASK

Consider the following terms and write a definition of their meaning:

- multi-agency;
- multi-professional;
- trans-professional;
- integrated working.

Multi-agency can be considered as the number of agencies that are working together. Therefore it includes the statutory, voluntary and private sectors. Multi-professional refers to the professionals within those agencies who are required to work together. However, the term 'multi-professional' can be criticised in that it is exclusive not only of parents and carers, but of those who work closely with and have considerable knowledge of children and families but are not defined as 'professionals' by the nature of their role. Examples of these might be found in the roles of classroom assistants, family support workers or voluntary workers.

Trans-professional refers to the work that takes place across the professional roles. It implies co-operation but retains a sense of separate identities and working practices.

Integration, however implies a unified, universal approach for a multitude of agencies and disciplines, the difficulties of which are highlighted by Campbell (2003).

PRACTICAL TASK **PRACTICAL TASK** PRACTICAL TASK **PRACTICAL TASK** PRACTICAL TASK **PRACTICAL TASK**

Consider how these terms might be applicable within your role in the Early Years Foundation Stage. Name as many instances as possible where a teacher in the EYFS will be required to:

- engage with other agencies;
- be part of a multi-professional team;
- share information trans-professionally;
- work in integrated settings.

Sure Start and children's centres

The drive towards inter-agency working has been gaining momentum since the early 1990s. This began with the establishment of a number of Early Excellence Centres designed to co-locate a range of services for children and families. This was seen as a mechanism for increasing accessibility for health, education and welfare in one location within the community (Bertram et al., 2002).

The introduction of the Sure Start programme by the Labour government in 1999, with its emphasis on the centralisation of children's services, has since radicalised the vision of centralised children's services. Sure Start was originally modelled on the US programme known as Head Start. The ethos of Sure Start is aimed at reducing social exclusion and improving significant aspects of social and cognitive development based on the premise that early interventions are effective in engaging children and families in education, health and welfare. Early engagement is considered significant in widening participation, thus reducing the prospects of future poverty cemented by poor education and health (Glass, 2006). The findings of the longitudinal EPPE (Effective Provision of Pre-school Practice) study which began in 1999, provided further affirmation of the need for quality pre-school provision as a means of enhancing future social and educational opportunities. The publication of the Acheson report (1998) highlighted extensive inequalities in health and educational opportunities in areas of low socio-economic status. A key focus for Sure Start has been the development of children's centres. The provision of a children's centre in every area by 2010 is a target of *Every Child Matters*, with the creation of 'one-stop shops' where families can access, health, welfare and education for their children alongside advice and support for issues such as parenting. There is an expectation that each children's centre provides a 'core offer' of services. These include:

- daycare provision;
- parenting classes;
- healthcare advice;
- welfare advice;
- opportunities for adult learning.

The co-location of services has highlighted the need for practitioners to create new frameworks for multi-agency working and to develop a more profound understanding of the roles of others in supporting children and families. You may find that your school is located near or alongside a children's centre. It is not unusual for Nursery education provision to be integrated with the daycare element of the core offer required for children's centres. Working in a multi-professional context will provide you with the ideal opportunity to work in a far more holistic way where the care and learning needs of your children become seamless. Imagine the benefits of working with children from a much younger age, and the opportunities to build authentic relationships not only with parents, but other professional staff within the centre.

Other colleagues you may find yourself working with in children's centres include the following.

Early Years Professionals

This is a new qualification introduced in 2007 which has been created to raise the standards of provision across Early Years settings by increasing the number of graduates in Early Years settings.

It is the intention to have Early Years Professionals (EYPs) in all children's centres offering Early Years provision by 2010 and in every full daycare setting by 2015. The EYPs will work in a range of settings in the private, voluntary, independent and maintained sectors and will be expected to lead and improve practice across the Early Years Foundation Stage (CWDC 2007). Currently, there are no guidelines for the salary structure of the EYP and it is likely that there will be considerable variations across sectors.

Nursery Nurses

Nursery nurses (or other Early Years specialist practitioners) are qualified to work with children up to 8 years old and will have completed a professional qualification over two or three years.

These qualifications are awarded by a range of professional bodies and may be gained through study at colleges of further education or through work-based assessment which results in the award of an NVQ. Conditions of service and salaries again vary across the sectors. Many experienced Nursery nurses are being encouraged to consider studying for a foundation degree in Early Years practice through which they can then access further study to become an Early Years Professional.

Placing services together in one building will make it easier for professionals to communicate with colleagues and ultimately to improve services for children and families. As a teacher, you will not work in isolation, as the education and well-being of children become increasingly the collective responsibility of a network of professionals and other staff who work together to ensure that needs are met. However, you may face many challenges as you work to develop extended professional working relationships, such as:

- communication between the workers involved who have a range of professional language and terminology;
- the number of agencies who become involved with children and families;
- the changing nature of the population through migration and mobility, which often means that some families require more support;
- the different values, belief systems and professional knowledge base that are held by different disciplines;
- the differences in status, income and career progression that may create rivalry and tensions;
- the challenges presented by working together as a team;
- the continuous nature of workforce reform with national standards for under-8s, daycare and childminding (DfES, 2003), the ten-year childcare strategy (HMT, 2004), and the Children's Plan (DCSF, 2007).

If you are based in or near a Children's Centre then clearly the opportunities to work with other professionals, and to begin to build systems and infrastructures, should be far easier than if your school has limited links with other professional services.

REFLECTIVE TASK

Consider under what circumstances you might be required to contact the following professionals:

- the school nurse;
- the health visitor;
- the social worker
- the speech and language therapist.

Where would they be based and how could they be contacted?

This task highlights the importance of finding out about the other services you will need to become aware of as a teacher new to the wider community. You will discover more about their roles later in the chapter.

Extended schools

The extended school initiative, which was first introduced through the Education Act 2002, is intended to replicate the philosophy and ways of working set out in the Children's Centre initiative. Extended schools are considered to be a key way of achieving the five outcomes of *Every Child Matters*. Through working with local authorities and other local providers, schools will provide access to a core of integrated services. These services, consist of:

- wraparound care, which means that children can access the school from 8am until 6pm;
- a varied menu of available activities for children in that period;
- parenting support and parenting programmes;
- swift access to specialist support services, for example, behaviour support;
- community access to ICT, sports and art activities.

It is expected that all schools will provide extended facilities by 2010 (Teachernet, 2008).

The roles of other professionals: the wider context

The role of the Early Years Foundation Stage teacher can no longer be considered in isolation for many of the reasons discussed previously. You will now be regarded as very much part of a multi-disciplinary team working in a range of settings other than traditional Nursery/Reception classes. The introduction of the Early Years Foundation Stage also presents new challenges in relation to developing an understanding of the birth-to-three age group, You are therefore required to demonstrate knowledge and understanding of the relationships between care, learning and development. In order to meet these requirements you should have an understanding of the roles of others; and know how to foster positive relationships, which in turn will enable you to create learning environments for young children.

There are an increasing number of people who are involved in the lives of young children and their families which might be seen as a consequence of the expanding range of services and provision. The following section looks at the roles of other professionals whom you may expect to work with.

Professionals who work to support children with learning and behavioural difficulties

You will encounter throughout your career children whom you feel may not be achieving at the level you would expect. A child may experience difficulties with reading or spelling and, despite the teaching and learning strategies you have employed, they make little progress. You may also come across a child who has great difficulty concentrating and completing tasks such as construction or jigsaws. There may also be other children who give cause for concern because they appear withdrawn or unhappy or who persistently seem to hurt other children. What do you do in cases such as these? Initially you will work with other staff to observe and collect data about the child's behaviour. This will help you understand more about the circumstances that may have led to a particular incident. After collecting this data you will then need to involve the Special Educational Needs Co-ordinator (SENCo). All schools must have a member of staff who is responsible for special educational needs in the school. You may also eventually need to consult with an educational psychologist who may visit the school to assess the child. This will be on the advice of the SENCo, who will be the person who normally arranges this visit. The educational psychologist will offer further help and advice and possibly suggest further strategies to support the child.

The Special Educational Needs Co-ordinator (SENCo)

The role of the SENCo is to:

- ensure implementation of the school's SEN policy;
- maintain an overview of provision for children with special educational needs;
- support and advise colleagues;
- disseminate good practice among learning support assistants;
- maintain records of children with special educational needs;
- liaise and work with parents of children with special educational needs;
- contribute to staff development training;
- liaise with external agencies, including LA's educational psychology services, health and social services and voluntary bodies.

The Educational Psychologist

The educational psychologist works with children and young people who experience emotional, behavioural and learning difficulties. The aim is to promote emotional and psychological development through strategies which help provide greater insight and under-standing of the child's difficulties. This will help you and the child's parents develop planned interventions to support the child. The educational psychologist advises on targets to work toward by implementing an Individual Education Plan (IEP) and will work to support you in becoming confident in developing your own strategies and solutions (Association of Educational Psychologists, 2006).

Educational psychologists are mainly employed by local authorities but are increasingly becoming members of multi-disciplinary teams as part of children's services. They are involved in assessing children in order to provide advice for writing a statement of special educational needs. This is a legal document which identifies the specific needs of a child and the precise ways in which these needs will be addressed. This is a process known as 'statementing', which is part of the Special Educational Needs Code of Practice (2001).

The code of practice defines learning difficulty in section 1:3 as;

a) *have a significantly greater difficulty than the majority of children of the same age; or*

b) *have a disability which prevents or hinders them from making use of educational facilities such as those generally provided for children of the same age in schools;*

c) *are under compulsory school age and fall within the definition at a) or b) above or would do so if special educational needs was not made for them.*

(DfES, 2001)

Learning difficulties can occur as a result of physical, emotional or developmental disorders. A child may have a diagnosed physical disability; a sensory disorder such as speech, hearing and vision; a physiological or neurological disorder which can cause mental disabilities; or an emotional disorder. A child's behaviour and disposition to learning are frequently affected by a diagnosed disorder or difficulty. Chapters 1 and 2 refer to the importance of being sensitive to the needs of individual children, and giving time to gain a greater understanding of how you can support individual needs.

Drawing on the expertise of the SENCO and/or educational psychologist will enable you to support a child with their individual learning needs. You will need to be aware of any child you are responsible for who has an IEP and will be expected to integrate their individual needs into your planning. You may also be involved at some stage in drawing up an Individual Education Plan in conjunction with the SENCO and the educational psychologist. It should provide achievable targets for the learning or the behaviour of the child. The SEN Code of Practice, implemented in January 2002, also emphasises parent partnership and the views of the child as well as highlighting the need for multi-agency working. At the end of this chapter, relevant sections of the Code of Practice are outlined to provide you with more in-depth guidance.

In order for you to provide the best possible care and education for children and to understand when you may need to consult other professionals, you need to know how to be a good observer of children in order to understand their development and their behaviour in a variety of situations.

PRACTICAL TASK PRACTICAL TASK **PRACTICAL TASK** PRACTICAL TASK **PRACTICAL TASK**

- List as many situations as possible where you may need to record an observation of a child or children.
- Identify the many methods that are used to observe children.
- What issues of confidentiality and ethics do you need to consider when observing children?

For further insight and guidance regarding effective observation, you may wish to refer the discussion in Chapter 9 and to Arnold (2003).

Behavioural support teams

Behavioural support teams provide support and training to settings on helping children with behavioural difficulties. They disseminate good practice through in-service training and can make suggestions for classroom practice, observe individual children and advise on appropriate referrals.

Support teachers for children for whom English is an additional language

Where you have children in your class for whom English is an additional language, you may have a support teacher who can work with the child in their home language. This service is important in helping you plan to overcome any difficulties the child may be experiencing. It is also helpful to understand the cultural experiences of the child to avoid misunderstandings and improve communication, and to provide relevant learning experiences.

Learning support advisory teachers

These are specialist teachers who advise schools planning and carrying out work programmes for children with learning difficulties. They will also provide training and support.

Special advisory teachers

The special advisory teachers have experience of working with children who have a range of learning difficulties; for example, hearing or visual impairment.

Special needs teachers

Special needs teachers have had additional training to work with children with special needs. They are often peripatetic and may specialise in working with particular disabilities.

Special needs support assistants

These may work with children who have an IEP on a one-to-one basis. They may have a Nursery Nursing or Teaching Assistant qualification. Increasingly adults who are seeking experience before applying to take a teaching qualification may apply for such positions.

Speech and language therapist

Speech and language therapists work with individual children to overcome speech, language and communication difficulties and disorders. They work as part of multi-disciplinary teams and may visit the child's setting or have their own community or hospital-based clinics. They are highly specialised and have studied at university for a minimum of four years.

Education services for visual- and hearing-impaired children

These specialised services provide advice and equipment for children with sensory impairments. They will assess the needs of the child and work closely with parents and the school to ensure that the child's requirements are met.

Parent support workers/advisers

Local authorities are obliged to employ specialist parent advisers/support workers who support families specifically who have a child with a special educational need. These professionals act as an advocate for the child and family to ensure that they are supported appropriately during the statementing process, and at any other time.

The health and well-being of children

Increasingly your role as a teacher requires that you have an understanding of how to help children learn to maintain a healthy lifestyle and to become aware of the way their body functions. Many schools are now working towards achieving 'healthy schools status', which is an initiative designed to encourage schools to work towards creating a healthy community for all children and staff (access www.wiredforhealth.co.uk for further information). There will be numerous occasions when you may wish to consult or work closely with other health professionals; for example, health visitors, school nurses, and community dentists.

The health visitor

Health visitors are qualified, experienced nurses who have undertaken further training in community and public health. The health visiting service can be accessed by every member of the community and is particularly relevant for families with young children. They can provide advice, support and information on a variety of topics such as child health, parenting and managing children's behaviour. Health visitors participate in running support groups for families as well as baby clinics and developmental screening clinics. They also have statutory responsibilities in safeguarding and protecting young children from abuse. Because they visit families in the local community, they have a great deal of knowledge and understanding about issues that may impact on the children in your class. This information is often important for you to know, as a child's learning or potential to achieve can be affected. For example, if a mother has severe post-natal depression she may not be able to support her child in ways that other parents might. The health visitor may be able to offer help and support to the family and the school in such a situation. Health visitors are generally based in local health clinics, GP surgeries and children's centres.

The school health service

The school health service is provided by local primary care trusts as a preventative health service for all school-aged children.

The school nurse

The school nursing service ensures that every school, primary and secondary, has a designated school nurse. The school nurse's role within that school will vary according to the nature and size of the school; for example, large secondary schools increasingly have a school nurse allocated solely to that school to meet the personal social and health education needs of that community. Many primary schools, on the other hand, will have less contact as the school nurse will visit many schools in the area.

The main responsibilities of a school nurse in primary education are concerned with:

- monitoring the growth and development of the children in the school;

- maintaining health records on individual children;
- providing immunisations within school to cohorts of children;
- conducting individual health assessments with children;
- referring children to appropriate medical services as required; for example, to enuresis clinics (bedwetting) or to CAMHS (child and adolescent mental health services);
- working collaboratively with others to safeguard children and adhering to child protection policy and procedures;
- supporting teachers in educating children and their parents about their health and well-being;
- liaising with parents, health visitors and other staff.

Because their role has an emphasis on prevention, they are not generally involved in providing treatments in school. They may monitor children with specific conditions such as asthma or diabetes but are not expected to deal with the day-to-day injuries that occur in schools. These are dealt with by trained first-aiders on the premises. School nurses will give advice on preventing conditions such as headlice but will not screen children for such conditions. That responsibility lies with parents as it is considered a public health issue best managed within the home.

The school health service also consists of medical staff and a community dental service.

Other health professionals in the community

General practitioner
General practitioners are doctors who are the first point of contact for primary care in the community.

Occupational therapist
Occupational therapists work in the community, schools or hospital. They can advise and provide resources and equipment to promote independence in children who may have specific difficulties.

Physiotherapist
Physiotherapists work with children who have mobility problems and also support children with respiratory disorders such as cystic fibrosis.

Play therapists
Play therapists use psychotherapeutic techniques to help children cope with difficult problems such as abuse and bereavement. This is a highly specialised service generally based in hospitals.

Portage
This is a service that supports pre-school children and their families whose development is delayed. Families are visited at home and are taught specific techniques to promote skills and development. The techniques used involve the breakdown of activities into small, achievable steps that are practised daily.

Child and adolescent mental health service (CAMHS)
This is a hospital- or community-based multi-disciplinary team consisting of paediatric mental health nurses, social workers, psychologists, psychiatrists, social workers, educational psychologists and occupational therapists. They work to help children and parents

through a range of emotional and mental health issues. The growing recognition of child mental health issues has brought a commitment from the government to increase the number of CAMHS teams nationally (The Children's Plan, 2007). Referrals are accepted for children as young as five and are generally made by education, social workers and health professionals.

The social worker

Social workers provide a range of statutory services for children and families. They must work to identify and support children who are considered 'in need' as well as work with children and families where abuse has occurred. They conduct in-depth assessments to assess risk for children in order to protect them from abuse. They are also involved in provision for 'looked after' children and for children who are being adopted. They have a close involvement with many families where there are children with disabilities and severe learning difficulties, offering financial advice and support, respite care as well as psychological support and counselling.

Other agencies who may be called on for a specific purpose include the following.

The police

The police have a major involvement in child protection and domestic violence, as well as providing road safety, advice to children and fostering community relations.

The fire service

Fire prevention officers are very familiar with and skilled at giving presentations to children to highlight issues of fire prevention and safety.

Transport services

Rail companies and road-safety officers will all provide children with specific safety advice.

Sports professionals

Local sports clubs often have a variety of community development programmes which they will provide in school. These may be experienced through coaching sessions and will hopefully engage children in participating and enjoying a range of sporting activities.

Voluntary agencies

There are numerous voluntary agencies who actively work as advocates for children and provide services and fund research to improve the lives of children. The most well known are the NSPCC, Childline, and Kidscape.

PRACTICAL TASK PRACTICAL TASK **PRACTICAL TASK** PRACTICAL TASK **PRACTICAL TASK**

Find out the names and roles of as many voluntary agencies and support groups working with and for children as you can.

Why is it important to be well informed about resources and organisations?

Figure 11.1 provides information on how to access other professionals and agencies.

Professional/agency	Contact details
SENCO	Directly in school
Educational psychologist	Via the SENCO
Health visitor and school nurse	Through the local primary care trust
Social worker	For any safeguarding issues, always inform the designated safeguarding/child protection officer in school
Support Services and other visitors	Via the headteacher/senior management in school

Figure 11.1 How to access other professionals and agencies

The Common Assessment Framework

The Common Assessment Framework (CAF) was a recommendation of the Laming report (DoH, 2003) as a means of improving information-sharing. It has been piloted and used in several areas of the country and is to be introduced nationally in 2008. The CAF is concerned with meeting the additional needs of children through information-sharing in a common format. The CAF is a generic form designed to be used by all practitioners using a common language through which all those involved with a child and family can understand what needs to be done and by whom. An action plan is then created, to be realised within a specified timeframe. Parents, carers and children are to be involved in the process of consultation and identification of need. Each practitioner can contribute to the assessment through sharing their specialised knowledge and understanding of the needs of the child and the family. Common assessments need not be carried out for every child or where a service exists within an agency that can already meet the needs of a child. For example, where a child is identified by a teacher as having behavioural difficulties and a behavioural support team can be accessed through the local authority, there would be no requirement to consider a CAF. However, where other agencies and professionals need to be involved then a CAF would be indicated. The parents or carers, and child if appropriate, would then complete the assessment in a shared way and appoint a lead professional to co-ordinate the process. The lead professional role is dependent on who is deemed the most appropriate person within their role.

It is important to understand that the CAF is not designed to replace current procedures for working with children who have either particular needs or are in need of safeguarding from abuse. Procedures for those situations will remain within the particular policy framework and protocols that currently exist within schools and Nurseries (see below).

It is not the intention of the CAF to make practitioners feel that they have additional burdens of work but rather to ensure that the needs of children remain paramount and information is shared appropriately. It is the intention that all information relating to children will be contained within a shared database through which appropriately-appointed professionals will be able to access information.

Samples of CAF forms and guidelines for completion can be downloaded from the ECM website, www.everychildmatters.org.uk.

CLASSROOM STORY

Consider how a CAF might be used in this instance.

Amy is a three-year-old child in the nursery. She is new to the setting, having recently moved from Scotland. You are aware that she has two older brothers in the nearby primary school. You have noticed that Amy appears rather small compared with the other children in the class and that she has a persistent rash around her wrists which appears to itch and is becoming worse. Other children are commenting on this. You discuss this with Amy's mother who becomes tearful and tells you that she has left an abusive relationship and is living in temporary accommodation. She does not know anyone in the area. She has registered with a local GP but is reluctant to ask for an appointment as she is worried about information about her current whereabouts becoming known. She is also worried about her boys in the school who, according to the teacher, appear to be having behavioural problems. She tells you that she is feeling very low and wonders how she will be able to cope.

REFLECTIVE TASK

How might a CAF be appropriate in these circumstances?

Which other agencies and professionals might you wish to become involved?

What would you see that needed to be included in the action plan?

Who would be the appropriate lead professional?

Safeguarding and child protection

Where there are concerns about the safety of children, the protocols and procedures to be followed for teachers lie within the framework of the amended *Working Together to Safeguard Children* (HM Government, 2006) which stipulates the following.

- As a trainee teacher, you should receive training about child protection during your course. Following your training you should receive updates on a three-yearly basis and on commencement of employment you should be given written information about the policy and procedures to be followed within the workplace. All teachers should be aware of and work towards the shared objectives of 'working together', which means that all teachers should provide a safe environment for children.
- You should be able to identify children who are at risk of or who are suffering from 'significant harm'.
- You should be able to identify where there are grounds for concern and contribute to an effective partnership with all those providing services.
- You will be involved in educating children about safety and managing risk through enabling them to recognise what is acceptable and unacceptable physical contact and to be able to recognise and resist pressure.
- You should provide opportunities to discuss domestic violence which is considered as abuse of children. It has been found that one in three cases of physical abuse of children involves domestic violence.
- Children should be listened to by teachers, and teachers should create an atmosphere where trust can flourish and positive reassurance given.
- Teachers should recognise that children with special educational needs are particularly vulnerable to abuse.

- Teachers should never, however, jump to conclusions about the circumstances of any child, but should share their concerns or anxieties with an appropriate designated person.
- It is also considered important that teachers recognise that children whose parents or carers abuse alcohol and/or drugs are at risk of violence, with the most vulnerable children being those whose parents or carers are violent, rejecting or neglectful.
- Teachers should also be mindful of children who sexually abuse and who may be party to sexual exploitation; for example, through the internet.
- Teachers must also be mindful of laws that prohibit female genital mutilation and forced marriages.

PRACTICAL TASK PRACTICAL TASK **PRACTICAL TASK** PRACTICAL TASK **PRACTICAL TASK**

Send for the free document *What to do if you are worried a child is being abused* from www.dfes.gov.uk. This is written for all those who work with children and will help you understand your role and what you need to do. All schools have a designated teacher who has received training in child protection. They are there to help and advise you.

Find out who is the designated person in your school.

Conclusion

In this chapter you have been introduced to the new ways of working with which teachers are now expected to engage. You should also be aware of some of the challenges that this presents.

The reasons for multi-agency working have been explained and you should now be familiar with the five outcomes of *Every Child Matters*, the role of Sure Start, extended schools and the introduction of children's centres as a way of providing services for children and families under one roof.

The role of the new Early Years professional has been discussed and in order to further your understanding of the vision that government has for children in the next decade, you should access and read the *Children's Plan Building a Brighter Future*, published in December 2007 by the newly created Department for Children, Schools and Families (DCSF). After reading this chapter you should have an awareness and understanding of the extensive range of professionals who work to support children and families and you should be mindful of the need for you as a teacher to work collaboratively with these colleagues. This requirement has been further emphasised by the introduction of the Common Assessment Framework and the role of teachers within that process.

Finally, you should be aware of the significance of your role in safeguarding children, protecting them from abuse, and the policy framework within which you must operate.

A SUMMARY OF **KEY POINTS**

> **Teachers are expected to work collaboratively with a variety of other agencies to meet the needs of children and families.**
> **There are a number of new initiatives that have been introduced to facilitate this, such as children's centres and extended schools.**
> **A new Early Years professional role has been introduced in order to raise the standards of care and education in the Foundation Stage.**

> There are an extensive number of people who work in the wider context to support children and their families.

> The introduction of the Common Assessment Framework means that teachers have a key role to play in identifying the needs of children and working closely with others to meet them.

> Teachers must be aware of their role and responsibilities in working to safeguard children and protect them from abuse.

MOVING *ON* > > > > > > MOVING *ON* > > > > > > MOVING *ON*

As a teacher in a school or children's centre, you will need to ensure that you keep yourself updated with new developments and initiatives that impact on your work with children and families. Teachers participate in professional updates as part of their employment conditions but you can supplement this by:

- creating and maintaining your own personal learning logs;
- compiling a glossary of information about the agencies and resources that are available in the local community;
- subscribing to professional journals and organisations;
- maintaining your own learning and development; for example, the Children's Plan (2007) aims to encourage new teachers to study at masters degree level.

REFERENCES REFERENCES **REFERENCES** REFERENCES **REFERENCES** REFERENCES

Acheson, D. (1998) *An independent inquiry into inequalities of health*. London: DoH.

Arnold, C. (2003) *Observing Harry: child development and learning, 0–5*. Maidenhead: Open University.

Association of Educational Psychologists (2006) *The role and function of educational psychologists – a position paper*. London: AEP.

Bertram T., Pascal, C., Bokhari, C., Gasper, M. and Holtermann, S. (2002), *Early Excellence Centre pilot programme second evaluation report* 2000–2001. DfES research report No. 361. London: HMSO.

Campbell A. (2003) Developing and evaluating early excellence centres in the UK: some issues in promoting integrated joined up services. *International Journal of Early Years Education*, 11(3).

Children's Workforce Development Council (CWDC) (2007) *Guidance to the standards for the award of Early Years Professional Status*. Leeds: CWDC.

DCSF (2007) *The Children's Plan, building a brighter future*. Norwich: TSO.

DfES (2001) *Special Educational Needs Code of Practice*. London: DfES.

DfES (2003) *Every Child Matters*. Green Paper. London: TSO.

DfES (2005) *What to do if you're worried a child is being abused*. London: TSO.

DfES (2002) *The Education Act.* London: HMSO.

DfES (2004) *The effective provision of pre-school education project: findings from pre-school to end of Key Stage 1. Final report*. London: DfES/Surestart.

DfES (2007) *Early Years Foundation Stage Framework*. London: DfES.

DoH (2003) *The Victoria Climbié inquiry. Report of an inquiry by Lord Laming.* London: HMSO.

French, J. (2007) Multi-agency working, the historical background, in I. Siraj Blatchford, K. Clarke and M. Needham (eds). *The team around the child.* Stoke-on-Trent: Trentham.

Glass, N. (2006) 'Sure Start, where did it come from, where is it going? *Journal of Children's Services*, 1(1), 51–7.

HM Government (2006) *Working together to safeguard children: a guide to interagency working to safeguard and protect the welfare of children*. London: TSO.

Her Majesty's Treasury (HMT) (2004) *Choice for parents, the best start for children: a ten year strategy for childcare*. London: HMSO.

Rodd, J. (2005) *Leadership in early childhood*. Maidenhead: Open University Press.

Wigfall, V. and Moss, P. (2001) *More than the sum of its parts?* London: National Children's Bureau.

FURTHER READING FURTHER READING **FURTHER READING** FURTHER READING

Arnold, C. (2003) *Observing Harry: child development and learning 0–5*. Maidenhead: Open University.

DCSF (2007) *The Children's Plan, building a brighter future.* Norwich: TSO.

DfES (2001) *Special Educational Needs Code of Practice*. London: DfES (Chapter 4 and Chapter 5).

DfES (2004) *Children Act*. London: DfES.

HM Government (2006) *Working together to safeguard children: a guide to interagency working to safeguard and protect the welfare of children*. London: TSO.

Useful websites

www.everychildmatters.org.uk
www.teachernet.co.uk
www.wiredforhealth.co.uk

Added to the page reference 'f' denotes a figure.